Discourse theory and political analysis

Discourse theory and political analysis

Identities, hegemonies and social change

edited by
David Howarth, Aletta J. Norval
and Yannis Stavrakakis

Manchester University Press
Manchester and New York

While copyright in the volume as a whole is vested in Manchester
University Press, copyright in individual chapters belongs to their
respective authors, and no chapter may be reproduced in whole or in part
without the express permission in writing of both author and publisher.

Published by Manchester University Press
Oxford Road, Manchester M13 9NR, UK
and Room 400, 175 Fifth Avenue, New York, NY 10010, USA
www.manchesteruniversitypress.co.uk

Distributed exclusively in the USA by
Palgrave, 175 Fifth Avenue, New York NY 10010, USA

Distributed exclusively in Canada by
UBC Press, University of British Columbia, 2029 West Mall,
Vancouver, BC, Canada V6T 1Z2

British Library Cataloguing-in-Publication Data
A catalogue record for this book is available from the British Library

Library of Congress Cataloging-in-Publication Data
A catalog record for this book is available from the Library of Congress

ISBN 13: 978 0 7190 5664 2

First published in 2000 by Manchester University Press
This paperback edition first published 2009

Printed by Lightning Source

Contents

List of contributors

Kevin Adamson is a doctoral student in the Ideology and Discourse Analysis Programme in the Department of Government at the University of Essex, and a teaching assistant in the Department of Government. He is currently doing research and has published on contemporary Romanian politics.

Sebastián Barros studied political science at the University of Buenos Aires, Argentina, and completed his MA in Political Theory and his Ph.D. in Government at the University of Essex. He has worked at the University of Buenos Aires, Argentina; University of Salamanca, Spain, and Essex, and is currently teaching political theory at the National University of Villa Maria, Argentina.

Steve Bastow is a Senior Lecturer in Politics at Kingston University, England. He has carried out extensive research on the French extreme right, in both the period before and after the Second World War. He has published articles on the French National Front and other aspects of French politics. He is currently working on third-way discourses in inter-war France and on the *Mouvement National* of Bruno Mégret.

Rosa Nidia Buenfil Burgos is Professor in the Department of Educational Research, Centre for Research and Advanced Studies, and also part-time Lecturer in the Faculty of Philosophy at the National University of Mexico. She completed her Ph.D. in the Department of Government, University of Essex, in 1990. She is author of three books about the educational discourse of the Mexican revolution and has published extensively on philosophical debates in education and educational policies in Mexico in the context of globalisation and postmodernity.

Gustavo Castagnola is a doctoral student in the Ideology and Discourse Analysis Programme in the Department of Government at the University of Essex. He is researcher in the National Research Council (CONICET) of Argentina and visiting lecturer at the City of London University (England) and the University of *Tres de Febrero* (Argentina). He is currently working on Latin American populist leadership and movements with special reference to Juan Perón, Eva Perón and Peronism.

Nur Betül Çelik is Assistant Professor in the Faculty of Communication at Ankara

University, Turkey, where she teaches social science methodology, theories of ideology and Turkish politics. She obtained her Ph.D. from the Department of Government, University of Essex, in 1996. She is the author of several articles on Kemalism and the theory of ideology.

Anthony Clohesy completed his Ph.D., 'Continuities and discontinuities in the discourse of Provisionalism', at the University of Essex, in 1997. He teaches in the Bridging Year Programme at the University of Essex where he lectures on British politics and political ideologies. His current research includes an examination of 'third way' politics from a discourse theory perspective.

Jason Glynos has completed his doctorate in the Ideology and Discourse Analysis Programme at the University of Essex, where he is a teaching assistant in the Departments of Government and Law. His published articles and research investigate the use of discourse theory and psychoanalytic ideas in political analysis and methodology, identity construction and ethical practice. He is currently co-editing a volume on *Lacan and Science* (Rebus Press, forthcoming).

Steven Griggs is Senior Lecturer in Public Policy at Staffordshire University, England. He has published articles on developments in French health policy and politics, and is currently studying the mobilisation and decision-making process surrounding the campaign of direct action against the construction of the second runway at Manchester Airport. His book, *French Politics Debates and Controversies*, co-authored with Robert Elgie, has recently been published by Routledge.

Chris Halverson is a graduate student in the Department of Government at New Mexico State University, USA, where he is completing a Master's degree in Government. His main research interests concern post-structuralism, discourse analysis and the formation of political identities.

Neil Harvey is Associate Professor in the Department of Government at New Mexico State University, USA. His main research interests concern indigenous peoples, land conflicts and development discourse in Chiapas and Mexico. He is author of several articles on this topic, as well as the book *The Chiapas Rebellion: The Struggle for Land and Democracy* (Duke University Press, 1998).

P. Sik Ying Ho is Assistant Professor in the Department of Social Work and Social Administration at the University of Hong Kong, China. She obtained her first degree in Social Sciences at the University of Hong Kong. Her Ph.D. thesis, following a discourse theory approach, examines gay politics in Hong Kong. Her current research focuses on issues of gender and sexuality in a post-colonial context.

David Howarth is Director of the Master's Degree Programme in Ideology and Discourse Analysis in the Department of Government at the University of Essex. He has published numerous essays, articles and books on discourse theory and its relationship to political theory and analysis. These include an edited collection entitled *South Africa in Transition. New Theoretical Perspectives* (Macmillan, 1988) and *Discourse* (Open University Press, 2000). He is currently conducting research on aspects of South African politics and new social movements.

Aletta J. Norval is senior lecturer in the Department of Government, University of Essex, where she is also Co-Director of the Doctoral Programme in Ideology and Discourse Analysis. Her publications include *Deconstructing Apartheid Discourse* (Verso, 1996) and *South Africa in Transition. New Theoretical Perspectives* (Macmillan, 1998), which she co-edited with David Howarth. She has also published widely on post-structuralist political theory. She is currently conducting research on issues in democratic theory.

Yannis Stavrakakis is a teaching fellow in the Department of Government at the University of Essex, where he is teaching on the Ideology and Discourse Analysis Programme. He is the author of *Lacan and the Political* (Routledge, 1999) and of numerous articles on psychoanalysis, discourse theory and politics.

A. Kat Tat Tsang is Assistant Professor in the Faculty of Social Work, University of Toronto, Canada, and Director of a research programme in psychotherapeutic processes. His research interests include mental health and sexuality, with a strong emphasis on cross cultural issues. He is active in research and human service development among the Asian gay, lesbian, bisexual and transgendered communities in Toronto.

Ernesto Laclau

Foreword

Most of the chapters included in this book originate in the graduate programme in Ideology and Discourse Analysis at the University of Essex. Since its establishment in 1982, this programme of research has rapidly expanded and been the source of a growing number of Ph.D. theses and research projects. In order to contexualise the essays included in this volume, it is pertinent to reactivate the theoretical premises upon which the programme is based and sketch out its overall aims in the field of social and political research.

The programme responded to the dissatisfaction with the dominant theoretical models of social explanation that existed at the time in the field of the social sciences (behaviouralism, structural functionalism, rational choice). What we set out to do was to elaborate an alternative approach to the understanding of the structuration of socio-political spaces by articulating a novel conception of *discourse*. This conception was constructed out of a plurality of theoretical matrices (post-Heideggerian phenomenology, Wittgenstein's conception of language games, post-structuralism), but it is undoubtedly the latter which has been the chief influence on the Essex approach to discourse analysis. However, 'post-structuralism' has always been conceived as a broad church, as a label covering a variety of intellectual trends, ranging from Foucault's analysis of discursive formations, to Lacanian psychoanalysis, Derrida's deconstruction and Barthes's semiology. The reader will find these various intellectual influences reflected in the different theoretical emphases of the essays presented here.

Moreover, this plurality does not amount to an 'acritical eclecticism', for the interrogation of the various theoretical approaches has been governed by a central substantive aim: the elaboration of a theory of *hegemony* as the main framework of political analysis. This centrality involves a series of displacements, both at the theoretical level and in terms of research strategies. From the first standpoint it required a thorough deconstruction of the Marxist tradition, which made it possible to understand the radically innovative potential of the Gramscian turn. This deconstruction was carried out in *Hegemony and Socialist Strategy*, a book that I wrote together with Chantal Mouffe, and which was published in 1985. The subsequent research that has been pursued in the Essex programme in Discourse Analysis makes it possible to articulate the original system of categories introduced in *Hegemony* in a more precise and detailed way. Several of the essays in this volume contribute to this increasing precision and sophistication in the theoretical apparatus. As far as the research strategies are concerned, I want to particularly mention the displacement of the research emphasis from mainly sociologistic categories, which address the group, its constitutive roles and its functional determinations, to the underlying logics that make these categories possible. It is in this sense that we have spoken of the logics of equivalence and difference, of empty and floating signifiers, and of myths and imaginaries. On the whole, the trend has been to move the centre of social and political research from 'ontically' given objects of investigation to their 'ontological' conditions of possibility.

Central, also, to most of the essays collected here – and also to the research strategy of the Essex programme in discourse analysis as a whole – has been the stress placed on the discursive construction of politico-ideological frontiers and the dichotomisation of social spaces. This emphasis is the result of the anti-objectivist trend of our research and of the consequent centrality of the concept of 'antagonism'. While most social approaches have seen antagonism as *objective* relations, fully graspable if one starts from the positive identities of the social agents, the discourse approach adopted by the contributors to this volume sees social antagonisms as the limit in the constitution of any objectivity. This has several consequences for sociopolitical analysis. To begin with, because antagonisms constitute the limits of objectivity, they also have a decisive role in shaping the latter. This presupposes that a dimension of negativity makes it impossible for identities to be reduced to any 'given' positivity. The second consequence is that no socio-political analysis is complete insofar as the constitutive exteriority of any 'positivity' has not been brought to light. This involves a relational dimension that is not fully captured by the classical notion of 'social relations'. Finally, processes of constructing social formations are redefined insofar as they are understood as governed by equivalential and differential logics. In other words, while sociologistic views of social reaggregation cannot go beyond the limits of mechanistic or functional models, a notion such as 'equivalence' presupposes forms of relations between entities which are only apprehensible through a linguistic/discursive approach.

Let us stress, to conclude, that the Essex discourse-theoretic approach is not a closed system which has already defined all its rules and categories, but an open-ended programme of research whose contours and aims are still very much in the making. A number of the discursive dimensions that have progressively emerged as important are still not sufficiently developed. For instance, the theory of rhetoric and speech act theory offer promising new avenues of research. However, what has been accomplished so far has laid the foundations for these future inquiries.

Acknowledgements

This book is very much the product of sustained collective endeavour. Most of the contributors have been associated with the Ideology and Discourse Analysis Programme in the Department of Government at the University of Essex over the last fifteen years. And although many are now dispersed to the four corners of the globe, the degree of co-operation and continued interaction amongst us is a tribute to the powerful intellectual, political and personal ties that link this research programme together. As always, the Department of Government at the University of Essex has provided an energetic and supportive context in which to discuss, criticise and develop current approaches to political science and political theory. In particular, the editors would like to thank Joe Foweraker, Jason Glynos, Steven Griggs, Alejandro Groppo and Todd Landman for their stimulating comments and criticisms, as well as the helpful remarks by the anonymous reviewer of the text. The editors are most grateful to Nicola Viinikka at Manchester University Press for the efficient and cheerful way she has dealt with our numerous queries and inevitable delays. Finally, we would like to thank Ernesto Laclau and Chantal Mouffe, whose intellectual work has inspired this project.

1 *David Howarth and Yannis Stavrakakis*

Introducing discourse theory and political analysis

This book responds to the explosion of interest in the concept of discourse and discourse analysis in the humanities and the social sciences.[1] However, it takes a different tack to the prevailing currents of research. To begin with, the emphasis of each chapter is on the application of discourse theory to empirical case studies, rather than the technical analysis of discourse viewed narrowly as speech or text. In so doing, each contribution works creatively within Ernesto Laclau and Chantal Mouffe's research programme in discourse theory as elaborated over the last fifteen years. This programme comprises a novel fusion of recent developments in Marxist, post-structuralist, post-analytical and psychoanalytic theory.[2] Moreover, while this theoretical approach fully endorses contemporary critiques of positivist, behaviouralist and essentialist paradigms, it is not content to remain at a purely theoretical level. Nor does it eschew important questions of method and epistemology neglected by over-hasty dismissals of science and rationality. Instead, it seeks, where possible, to find points of convergence with these approaches, and endeavours to put forward plausible and empirically justifiable explanations of the social and political world.[3]

More specifically, this newly emerging approach is directed at the analysis of key *political* issues. This is especially important because those contributing to 'the new discursivity' have, with some notable exceptions, neglected a range of traditional topics in political theory and political science.[4] For instance, while a recently published reader on discourse analysis includes contributions from leading sociologists, anthropologists and cultural theorists, noting approvingly the way in which discursive methods have been applied to broader social processes, there are no essays on political analysis.[5] Hence there is little or no examination of populist and nationalist ideologies; the discourses of new social movements; the political construction of social identities; the forms of hegemonic struggle; different logics of collective action; the formulation and implementation of public policy; and the making and unmaking of political institutions; not to mention the traditional topics of political science, such as voting behaviour and political decision-making.[6]

While it is impossible to do justice to the immense changes in our contemporary condition, it is possible to discern a number of paradigm cases of politics in our increasingly globalised world. Taken randomly, the signifiers 'Rwanda', 'Kosovo', 'the European Union', 'Tiananmen Square', 'Nelson Mandela', 'global warming', 'the Third Way' and the 'New World Order' bear witness to a rapid explosion of radical ethnic and national identities, the emergence of new social movements, and the appearance and dissolution of founding political myths and collective imaginaries. Issues of identity formation, the production of novel ideologies, the logics of social movements and the structuring of societies by a plurality of social imaginaries are central objects of investigation for discourse theory. Together they constitute the matrix of empirical and theoretical questions addressed by the various essays included in this volume. Each of the chapters presents original research on carefully delimited questions opened up by discourse theory. While they range considerably in their geographical and historical focus and scope, they are unified by their attempt to grapple with some of the central issues of our times. Moreover, they use a shared language of explanation and interpretation, and aim to develop the conceptual infrastructure in ways that will enable the examination of comparable cases. In so doing, each contribution locates the issue investigated within existing approaches to the topic, introduces and articulates new explanatory concepts within the overall parameters of discourse theory, and produces conclusions that advance our understanding of the contemporary world.

The aim of this introductory chapter is to outline the basic contours of the theoretical framework informing this book. It comprises four parts. We begin by setting out the key assumptions of discourse theory. We then trace the emergence and constitution of discourse theory by examining the way this research programme has distinguished itself from the dominant approaches in social science research. In the third part we present the basic concepts and logics of the approach, and how they have been applied in the different chapters of the book. Finally, we outline the conceptual and thematic organisation of the various contributions to the volume.

The underlying assumptions of discourse theory

Discourse theory assumes that all objects and actions are meaningful, and that their meaning is conferred by historically specific systems of rules. Consider, for instance, a forest standing in the path of a proposed motorway. It may simply represent an inconvenient obstacle impeding the rapid implementation of a new road system, or might be viewed as a site of special interest for scientists and naturalists, or a symbol of the nation's threatened natural heritage. Whatever the case, its meaning depends on the orders of discourse that constitute its identity and significance. In discourses of economic modernisation, trees may be understood as the disposable means for (or obstacles to) continued economic growth and prosperity, whereas in environmentalist discourses they might represent essential components of a viable eco-system or objects of intrinsic value and beauty. Each of these discourses is a social and political construction that establishes a system of relations between different objects and practices, while providing (subject) positions with which social agents can identify. In our example these subject positions might be those of 'developers', 'naturalists', 'environmentalists' or 'eco-warriors'. Moreover, a political project will attempt to weave together different strands of discourse in an effort to dominate or organise a field of meaning so as to fix the identities of objects and practices in a particular way.

As a first approximation, then, discourse theory investigates the way in which social practices articulate and contest the discourses that constitute social reality. These practices are possible because systems of meaning are contingent and can never completely exhaust a field of meaning. In order to unpack and elaborate upon this complex set of statements, we need working definitions of the categories of discursivity, discourse, and discourse analysis.[7] The *discursive* can be defined as a theoretical horizon within which the being of objects is constituted. In other words, *all* objects are objects of discourse, as their meaning depends upon a socially constructed system of rules and significant differences.[8] This idea of the discursive as a horizon of meaningful practices and significant differences does not reduce everything to discourse or entail scepticism about the existence of the world. On the contrary, it circumvents scepticism and idealism by arguing that we are always internal to a world of signifying practices and objects. It thus views as logically self-contradictory all attempts to escape and conceptualise this world from an extra-discursive perspective.[9] As Laclau and Mouffe put it in a frequently quoted passage:

> The fact that every object is constituted as an object of discourse has nothing to do with whether there is a world external to thought, or with the realism/idealism opposition. An earthquake or the falling of a brick is an event that certainly exists, in the sense that it occurs here and now, independently of my will. But whether their specificity as objects is constructed in terms of 'natural phenomena' or 'expressions of the wrath of God', depends upon the structuring of a discursive field. What is denied is not that such objects exist externally to thought, but the rather different assertion that they could constitute themselves as objects outside any discursive conditions of emergence.[10]

In other words, to use Heidegger's terminology, human beings are 'thrown into' and inhabit a world of meaningful discourses and practices, and cannot conceive or think about objects outside it.[11]

We take *discourse* or *discourses* to refer to systems of meaningful practices that form the identities of subjects and objects.[12] At this lower level of abstraction, discourses are concrete systems of social relations and practices that are intrinsically *political*, as their formation is an act of radical institution, which involves the construction of antagonisms and the drawing of political frontiers between 'insiders' and 'outsiders'. In addition, therefore, they always involve the exercise of *power*, as their constitution involves the exclusion of certain possibilities and a consequent structuring of the relations between different social agents.[13] Moreover, discourses are *contingent* and *historical* constructions, which are always vulnerable to those political forces excluded in their production, as well as the dislocatory effects of events beyond their control.[14]

'Thatcherism' as analysed by Stuart Hall and others is an example of what we mean by a political discourse.[15] Hall demonstrates how the construction of Thatcherist discourse involved the articulation of a number of disparate ideological elements. These included traditional Tory values about law and order, 'Englishness', the family, tradition and patriotism, on the one hand, and classical liberal ideas about the free market and *homo economicus* on the other. Moreover, he shows how these elements were linked together by establishing a clear set of political frontiers within the Conservative Party and its supporters (between the so-called 'Wets' and 'Drys'), and between those who supported the crisis-ridden discourse of social democracy and those who wanted its radical restructuring. Where Hall differs from our approach is in his retention of the ontological separation between different types of social practice, whether understood as ideological, sociological, economic or political. Discourse theorists, by contrast, affirm the discursive character of all social practices and objects, and reject the idea that ideological practices simply constitute one area or 'region' of social relations. Thus, for instance, the distinctions between political, economic and ideological practices are pragmatic and analytical, and strictly internal to the category of discourse. This is worth stressing because it distinguishes our approach from those approaches to political analysis that use the concept of discourse, but regard discourses as little more than sets of ideas or beliefs shared by policy communities, politicians or social movements.[16]

Discourse analysis refers to the practice of analysing empirical raw materials and information as discursive forms. This means that discourse analysts treat a wide range of linguistic and non-linguistic data – speeches, reports, manifestos, historical events, interviews, policies, ideas, even organisations and institutions – as 'texts' or 'writing' (in the Derridean sense that '*there is nothing outside the text*'[17]). In other words, empirical data are viewed as sets of signifying practices that constitute a '"discourse" and its "reality"',[18] thus providing the conditions which enable subjects to experience the world of objects, words and practices. This enables discourse theorists to draw upon and develop a number of techniques and methods in linguistic and literary theory commensurate with its ontological assumptions.[19] These include

Derrida's 'method' of deconstruction, Foucault's archaeological and genealogical approaches to discourse analysis, the theory of rhetoric and tropes,
Saussure's distinction between the paradigmatic and syntagmatic poles of
language, the Jakobsonian concepts of metaphor and metonymy especially as
reformulated by Lacan, and Laclau and Mouffe's logics of equivalence and
difference.[20]

One question that arises in this regard concerns the application of discourse theory to empirical cases. From a discourse theory perspective, this
problem is crystallised around the need to avoid the twin pitfalls of empiricism and theoreticism. Put briefly, while discourse theorists acknowledge the
central role of theoretical frameworks in delimiting their objects and methods of research, thus rejecting crude empiricist and positivist approaches,
they are concerned to prevent the *subsumption* of each empirical case under
its own abstract theoretical concepts and logics. In other words, instead of
applying a pre-existing theory on to a set of empirical objects, discourse theorists seek to *articulate* their concepts in each particular enactment of concrete research.[21] The condition for this conception of conducting research is
that the concepts and logics of the theoretical framework must be sufficiently
'open' and flexible enough to be adapted, deformed and transformed in the
process of application.[22] This conception excludes essentialist and reductionist theories of society, which tend to predetermine the outcome of
research and thus preclude the possibility of innovative accounts of phenomena. It also rules out the organic development of the research programme as it tries to understand and explain new empirical cases.

Discourse theory and mainstream approaches to political analysis

The emergence and development of discourse theory has been stimulated by
a number of perceived weaknesses in existing paradigms of social science
research. However, while it rejects simplistic behavioural, rationalist and
positivist approaches, it endeavours to draw critically upon Marxist, social
constructivist, and interpretative models of social science research, such as
those inspired by Max Weber and others. It thus offers novel ways to think
about the relationship between social structures and political agency, the role
of interests and identities in explaining social action, the interweaving of
meanings and practices, and the character of social and historical change. To
begin with, discourse theory challenges the class reductionism and economic
determinism of classical Marxism. By radicalising Gramsci's and Althusser's
reworking of Marxist conceptions of politics and ideology, and drawing
upon post-structuralist critiques of language, it deconstructs the Marxist
ontology in which all identity is reduced to a class essence, and introduces a
relational conception of discourse.[23] In so doing, discourse theory conceives
of society as a symbolic order in which social antagonisms and structural
crises can not be reduced to essential class cores determined by economic

processes and relations.[24] It also implies that all ideological elements in a discursive field are contingent, rather than fixed by a class essence, and that there is no fundamental social agency or political project that determines processes of historical change in an *a priori* fashion. Instead, discourse theory puts forward an alternative conceptual framework built around the primacy of political concepts and logics such as hegemony, antagonism and dislocation.

In addition, by drawing on hermeneutical critiques of behaviouralism, discourse theory opposes the crude separation of socially constructed meanings and interpretations, on the one hand, and objective political behaviour and action on the other. Following the writings of Weber, Taylor, Winch and Wittgenstein, discourse theory stresses that meanings, interpretations and practices are always inextricably linked.[25] However, discourse theorists are not just concerned with the way in which social actors understand their particular worlds, in which case the object of research would be to comprehend social actions by empathising with the agents who act. As discourses are relational systems of meaning and practice that constitute the identities of subjects and objects, attention is focused more on the creation, disruption and transformation of the structures that organise social life. A consequence of this hermeneutical orientation is that theory cannot be separated wholly and objectively from the reality it seeks to explain, as theoretical practices are themselves partly constitutive of (and shaped by) the social worlds in which the subjects and objects of research find themselves. At least in the social sciences, this means that there is a weakening of the once sacrosanct distinction between objective scientific explanations and subjective hermeneutical descriptions and understandings.[26]

Discourse theorists also reject rationalist approaches to political analysis, which presume that social actors have given interests and preferences, or which focus on the rational (or irrational) functioning of social systems. In these conceptions of politics, the actions of agents can both be explained and predicted by reference to individual calculations of economic self-interest,[27] or relations of power and domination can be inferred from the failure of social agents to recognise and act upon their 'real interests'.[28] Similarly, social systems are either assumed to consist of functionally interrelated elements, or are intrinsically contradictory entities that are constantly crisis-ridden and transformed in predetermined ways. As against these approaches, discourse theorists stress the historical contingency and 'structural impossibility' of social systems, and refuse to posit essentialist conceptions of social agency. Instead, agents and systems are social constructs that undergo constant historical and social change as a result of political practices. Indeed, a major task of the discourse theorist is to chart and explain such historical and social change by recourse to political factors and logics.

Finally, discourse theory stands firmly opposed to positivistic and naturalistic conceptions of knowledge and method. It firmly rejects the search for scientific laws of society and politics grounded on empirical generalisations, which can form the basis of testable empirical predictions.[29] Moreover, it opposes naïve conceptions of truth, in which the only test of theories and empirical accounts is against an unproblematical objective reality.[30] As we have already suggested, discourse theory takes its lead from interpretative methods of social inquiry in which emphasis is placed on understanding and explaining the emergence and logic of discourses, and the socially constructed identities they confer upon social agents. This does not, however, entail an 'anything goes'[31] approach to the generation and evaluation of empirical evidence made in its name. While the truth or falsity of its accounts are partly relative to the system of concepts and logics of discourse theory used (as in any other empirical inquiry), the ultimate tribunal of experience is the degree to which its accounts provide plausible and convincing explanations of carefully problematised phenomena for the community of social scientists. Lastly, as against the charges of relativism that are sometimes levelled at the programme,[32] it also rejects the rigid separation of facts and values, accepting that the discourse theorist and analyst is always located in a particular historical and political context with no neutral Archimedean point from which to describe, argue and evaluate.[33]

The basic concepts and logics of discourse theory

Articulation, discourse, nodal points and empty signifiers
As we have intimated, discourse theory investigates the way social practices systematically form the identities of subjects and objects by articulating together a series of contingent signifying elements available in a discursive field. Moreover, while discourse theory stresses the ultimate contingency of all social identity, it nonetheless acknowledges that partial fixations of meaning are both possible and necessary.[34] In this way, it provides an account of social change that neither reduces all discontinuity to an essential logic, nor denies any continuity and fixity of meaning whatsoever. Besides the concept of discourse itself, Laclau and Mouffe introduce four basic categories in order to account for this conception of identity. These are the categories of articulation, elements, moments and nodal points. To begin with, Laclau and Mouffe argue that all identity emerges through the articulation or rearticulation of signifying elements. Hence they define *articulation* as 'any practice establishing a relation among elements such that their identity is modified as a result of the articulatory practice'. *Discourse* is 'the structured totality resulting from this articulatory practice'. *Moments* are the 'differential positions' that 'appear articulated within a discourse', whereas *elements* are those differences that are 'not discursively articulated' because of the 'floating' character they acquire in periods of social crisis and dislocation.[35]

Nevertheless, Laclau and Mouffe's affirmation of both the ultimate contingency and the partial fixity of meaning leaves them with something of a paradox. If all social forms are contingent, if 'the transition from "elements" to "moments" is never complete',[36] how then is *any* identity or social formation possible? A first response to this problem involves the introduction of the concept of *nodal points* to account for the structuration of elements into a meaningful system of moments, into a discourse.[37] Nodal points are thus privileged signifiers or reference points ('points de capiton' in the Lacanian vocabulary[38]) in a discourse that bind together a particular system of meaning or 'chain of signification'. In communist ideology, to take an example used by Žižek, a number of pre-existing and available signifiers ('democracy', 'state', 'freedom', and so forth) acquire a new meaning by being articulated around the signifier 'communism', which occupies the structural position of the nodal point. Thus, due to the intervention of this nodal point, these elements are transformed into internal moments of communist discourse. Democracy acquires the meaning of 'real' democracy as opposed to 'bourgeois' democracy, freedom acquires an economic connotation and the role and function of the state is transformed. In other words, their meaning is partially fixed by reference to the nodal point 'communism'.[39]

Drawing on some of these insights, Steve Bastow's chapter on inter-war French fascism and the neo-socialism of Marcel Déat shows how essentialist and ideal-typical explanations fail to provide an adequate characterisation of Déat's neo-socialist discourse. They thus foreclose a clear understanding of how neo-socialists could end up collaborating with Nazi Germany during the Second World War. By contrast, he emphasises that the various mutations of Déat's neo-socialism in the 1930s comprised a contingent and unstable articulation of disparate elements, each organised around a different nodal point. He shows, moreover, how the tensions in these articulatory configurations help us to explain the crisis and changing nature of the discourse during the late 1930s and 1940s.

In his more recent work, Laclau has further developed the logic of discursive structuration by introducing the category of the 'empty signifier'. As we have already noted, in discourse theory the social field can never be closed, and political practices attempt to 'fill' this lack of closure. As Laclau puts it, 'although the fullness and universality of society is unachievable, its need does not disappear: it will always show itself through the presence of its absence'.[40] In other words, even if the full closure of the social is not realisable in any actual society, the idea of closure and fullness still functions as an (impossible) ideal. Societies are thus organised and centred on the basis of such (impossible) ideals. What is necessary for the emergence and function of these ideals is the production of empty signifiers. In order to illustrate this paradoxical statement Laclau uses the Hobbesian example of the state of nature as a condition of radical social disorder and disintegration:

> [I]n a situation of radical disorder 'order' is present as that which is absent;
> it becomes an empty signifier, as the signifier of this absence. In this sense,

various political forces can compete in their efforts to present their particular
objectives as those which carry out the filling of that lack. To hegemonize something is exactly to carry out this filling function.[41]

Thus, the articulation of a political discourse can only take place around an
empty signifier that functions as a nodal point. In other words, emptiness is
now revealed as an essential quality of the nodal point, as an important condition of possibility for its hegemonic success.

Although Laclau uses the example of order, other signifiers can function
in a similar way. Generalising the argument, he argues that 'any term which,
in a certain political context becomes the signifier of the lack, plays the same
role'. 'Politics', he continues, 'is possible because the constitutive impossibility of society can only represent itself through the production of empty signifiers.'[42] Numerous chapters in this volume deploy the category of an empty
signifier in their analyses. In Chapter 5, Anthony Clohesy shows how the
term 'justice' performs the role of an empty signifier in Irish Republicanist
discourse. He argues that it is precisely because of the emptiness of this vital
signifier in this discourse that different political strategies were able to confer different meanings and connotations on to the evolution of Republicanist discourse. This enables him to trace out the overall trajectory of
Republicanism, and show the remaining aporias within its evolving discourse
and strategy.

The primacy of politics[43]

However, this solution – the conceptualisation of nodal points and empty
signifiers – still begs the question as to the emergence and constitution of
these partial fixations. It is here that Laclau and Mouffe affirm the primacy
of the political dimension in their social ontology. Discourses and the identities produced through them are inherently political entities that involve the
construction of antagonisms and the exercise of power. Moreover, because
social systems have a fundamentally political character, they are always vulnerable to those forces that are excluded in the process of political formation. It is around this set of processes that Laclau and Mouffe seek to erect a
political theory of discourse. In so doing, they introduce the concepts of
social antagonism and hegemony, as well as the logics of equivalence and difference, each of which needs greater examination.

The construction and experience of social antagonisms are central for discourse theory. At the outset, social antagonisms introduce an irreconcilable
negativity into social relations. This is because they reveal the limit points in
society in which social meaning is contested and cannot be stabilised. Antagonisms are thus evidence of the frontiers of a social formation. As Aletta Norval discusses in the concluding chapter, they show the points where identity
is no longer fixed in a differential system, but is contested by forces which
stand outside – or at the very limit – of that order.[44] In so doing, their role is

formative of social objectivity itself.[45] As they cannot be reduced to the pre-constituted interests and identities of social agents, the construction of antag-onisms and the institution of political frontiers between agents are partly *constitutive* of identities and of social objectivity itself. In this way, the con-struction and contingent resolution of antagonistic relations precludes the possibility of necessary and determining logics operating in history and soci-ety. In Lacanian terms, antagonisms disclose the *lack* at the heart of all social identity and objectivity.[46] The space of the social is thus revealed as a field that can never be closed or constituted as an objective full presence: 'The limit of the social must be given within the social itself as something sub-verting it, destroying its ambition to constitute a full presence. Society never manages fully to be society, because everything in it is penetrated by its lim-its, which prevent it from constituting itself as an objective reality.'[47] It is this central impossibility which, as we have already pointed out, makes necessary the production of empty signifiers, a production which in turn makes possi-ble the articulation of political discourses, of partial fixations of meaning.

What are social antagonisms in Laclau and Mouffe's perspective? They insist that social antagonisms occur because social agents are *unable* to attain fully their identity. Thus, an antagonism is seen to occur when 'the presence of [an] "Other" prevents me from being totally myself. The relation arises not from full totalities, but from the impossibility of their constitution.'[48] This 'blockage' of identity is a mutual experience for both the antagonising force and the force that is being antagonised: 'Insofar as there is antagonism, I can-not be a full presence for myself. But nor is the force that antagonises me such a presence: its objective being is a symbol of my non-being and, in this way, it is overflowed by a plurality of meanings which prevent it being fixed as full positivity.'[49] Given this, the task of the discourse analyst is to explore the dif-ferent forms of this impossibility, and the mechanisms by which the blockage of identity is constructed in antagonistic terms by social agents.

To illustrate this conception, let us consider the clash between local resi-dents and the Manchester Airport authority over the building of a new run-way, as presented by Steven Griggs and David Howarth in this book.[50] In this micro-political analysis of popular protest, they argue that it was the failure of the local residents' normal means of influencing public policy via lobbying and the Public Inquiry – consonant with their 'Middle-England', middle-class identities – that galvanised their opposition to the runway project and led them to form unusual alliances with militant environmentalists and 'eco-war-riors'. Similarly, those who favoured the building of the runway accused their opponents of preventing the economic regeneration of Manchester and of jeopardising 50,000 jobs in the North-West region. Both sets of opponents perceived each other as 'blocking' their respective identities and interests, and drew upon divergent ideological resources to construct this mutual hos-tility. In this highly simplified and condensed illustration, we see that social antagonism arises because of the inability of differently located social agents to achieve their respective identities – 'residents and homeowners', 'Airport managers and business entrepreneurs' – rather than a clash of pre-existing forms of positive identification. The protest action, and its possibility of being extended into other spheres of society, results in the establishment of a political frontier separating the two sides, while simultaneously constituting different modes of identification.

Logics of equivalence and difference

In order to account for the construction of social antagonisms, Laclau and Mouffe must provide an understanding of the ways in which antagonistic relations threaten discursive systems. If this is to be shown, then a place must be found for the existence of a purely negative identity. In other words, they must theorise an identity that cannot be integrated into an existing system of differences. To do so, Laclau and Mouffe introduce the *logic of equivalence*. This logic functions by creating equivalential identities that express a pure negation of a discursive system. For instance, in her account of the Mexican revolutionary mystique Rosa Buenfil argues that the Mexican revolution can be understood as an overdetermination of different social movements organised around a mystical discourse. She argues that this was made possible because 'the people' were able to weaken their internal differences and organise themselves as 'the oppressed', by opposing themselves to a series of others. In this way, the government, the incumbent President, the Church, landlords and entrepreneurs were made equivalent to one another by being presented as 'the oppressors' of the people.

If the logic of equivalence functions by splitting a system of differences and instituting a political frontier between two opposed camps, the *logic of difference* does exactly the opposite. It consists in the expansion of a given system of differences by dissolving existing chains of equivalence and incorporating those disarticulated elements into an expanding order. Whereas a project employing the logic of equivalence seeks to divide social space by condensing meanings around two antagonistic poles, a project employing a logic of difference attempts to weaken and displace a sharp antagonistic polarity, endeavouring to relegate that division to the margins of society.[51] Kevin Adamson's careful examination of Romanian politics after the revolutionary events of 1989 shows how the mutation of revisionist socialism into a distinctive social democratic ideology involved the transformation of signifiers associated with neoliberal transition discourse. Thus elements such as the 'market' and 'privatisation' were gradually incorporated into a fledgling social democratic discourse, and were organised around the powerful metaphor of 'the transition'. This fundamentally challenged the dominant neoliberal interpretation of transition from socialism to democracy. Similarly, David Howarth's examination of the transformation of Black Consciousness discourse into the non-racial democratic discourse of the UDF and the ANC in South Africa during the late 1970s and early 1980s shows how this process occurred against the backdrop of the ruling National Party's strategy of transformism.[52] In this quintessential logic of difference, the National Party sought to expand its bases of consent by differentially incorporating 'Indians', so-called 'Coloureds' and certain categories of 'urban blacks' into the dominant order by offering them certain political, social and economic concessions. In so doing, the South African state endeavoured to disarticulate the growing political alliances between these groups, thus weakening the anti-apartheid opposition.

These examples should not lead to the conclusion that the logics of equivalence and difference are mutually exclusive. There is always a complex interaction between the two, just as there is a play between identity and difference, and universality and particularity.[53] This is demonstrated in Neil Harvey's and Chris Halverson's chapter on the singular experience of women's struggles in the Zapatista movement. They show that the Zapatista movement not only poses a challenge to the Mexican state by articulating a radical anti-government identity, but it also enables marginalised groups within the indigenous communities to contest exclusionary practices and open up spaces of differences within the collective identity. As they argue, 'the significance of Zapatista discourse is given not only by its radical anti-government position, but rather by the numerous ways in which indigenous men, women and children are able to appropriate it for their particular and shared struggles against injustice'. While their chapter can be understood in terms of logics of equivalence and difference, it also points toward the possibility of a different conception of politics. This conception would not be reducible to questions of hegemony, power and violence, but asserts instead the irreducible nature of singular experience, the limitations of any totalising discourse and, consequently, the possibility of disarmament and coexistence, or what Derrida has called a 'politics of friendship'.

Subject positions, dislocation and political subjectivity
In discourse theory, questions surrounding the way social agents 'live out' their identities and act – questions that pertain to the concept of subjectivity – are of central importance. In this regard, discourse theorists distinguish between *subject positions* and *political subjectivity* in order to capture the positioning of subjects within a discursive structure, on the one hand, and to account for the agency of subjects on the other. In order to locate the emergence of this conception in Laclau and Mouffe's writings, it is useful to consider their views in relation to Althusser's influential theory of the subject. Drawing on Freud and Lacan, and opposing perspectives such as phenomenology, empiricism or rational choice theory, which view the subject as an originator of its own ideas and values, or endowed with essential properties such as rationality, Althusser insists that subjects are constructed – 'interpellated' or 'hailed', as he puts it – by ideological practices. In other words, individuals acquire an identity of who they are and their role in society by being

positioned in certain ways by a whole series of unconscious practices, rituals, customs and beliefs, with which they come to identify.[54] According to Laclau and Mouffe, however, Althusser's account is inadequate in two respects. First, ideological practices are regarded as a 'relatively autonomous' region of a social formation, a proposition that runs counter to the idea of discourses including all types of social practice. Secondly, subjects are constituted by ideological practices, which are in turn determined by underlying social structures. This strongly reduces the autonomy of social agents to the mere effects of pre-existing social structures.

In other words, while Laclau and Mouffe accept Althusser's critique of a unified and self-transparent subject – a subject which is the source of its own ideas and actions – and thus accept that the identities of subjects are discursively constructed, they do not affirm the deterministic connotations of Althusser's theory. By contrast, they distinguish between *subject positions* and *political subjectivity*.[55] Drawing on Foucauldian themes, the former category designates the positioning of subjects within a discursive structure.[56] Rather than a homogenous subject with particular interests, this means that any 'concrete individual' can have a number of different subject positions. A particular empirical agent at any given point in time might identify herself, or be simultaneously positioned, as 'black', 'middle class', 'Christian', and a 'woman'.[57] If the concept of subject position accounts for the multiple forms by which agents are produced as social actors, the concept of political subjectivity concerns the way in which social actors *act*. In other words, in order to go beyond the privileging of the structure over the agent in structuralism without recourse to a voluntaristic privileging of the agent, as is evident in different currents of methodological individualism, Laclau argues that the actions of subjects emerge because of the contingency of those discursive structures through which a subject obtains its identity.

This presupposes the category of *dislocation*, which refers to the process by which the contingency of discursive structures is made visible.[58] This 'decentring' of the structure through social processes such as the extension of capitalist relations to new spheres of social life[59] shatters already existing identities and literally induces an identity crisis for the subject. However, dislocations are not solely traumatic occurrences. They also have a productive side. 'If', as Laclau puts it, 'on the one hand they threaten identities, on the other, they are the foundation on which new identities are constituted.'[60] In other words, if dislocations disrupt identities and discourses, they also create a lack at the level of meaning that stimulates new discursive constructions, which attempt to suture the dislocated structure. In short, it is the 'failure' of the structure, and as we have seen of those subject positions which are part of such a structure, that 'compels' the subject to act, to assert anew its subjectivity. As Yannis Stavrakakis argues in his account of the emergence of Green ideology, this ideological form emerges as a response to the dislocation of radical discourses during the late 1960s. The crisis of the left creates a lack of meaning and a need for rearticulation of the radical tradition. One of the dominant versions of this rearticulation took place around the nodal point 'nature' which during the same period – and due to the severity of the environmental crisis – emerged as the *point de capiton* of a newly emerging paradigm regulating the relation between humans and their environment.

Returning to our discussion of agency, the political subject is neither simply *determined* by the structure, nor does it *constitute* the structure. Rather, the political subject is forced to take decisions – or identify with certain political projects and the discourses they articulate – when social identities are in crisis and structures need to be recreated. In Lacanian terms, the emergence of political subjectivity is the result of a lack in the structure. It is this lack in the structure that 'causes' subjects to identify with those social constructions that seem capable of suturing the rift in a symbolic order. In short, it is in the process of this *identification* that political subjectivities are created and formed. Once formed and stabilised they become those subject positions which 'produce' individuals with certain characteristics and attributes.

The two chapters by P. Sik Ying Ho and A. Kat Tat Tsang, and Jason Glynos provide an overview of the play between lack and identification by focusing on one of the areas in which the politics of subjectivity seems of the utmost importance, namely, that of sexual identity. By examining the emergence of lesbigay identities in Hong Kong, Ho and Tsang show how identifying with particular names, with new subject positions, constitutes the first step in asserting a new sexual identity. In his chapter, Jason Glynos suggests how Lacan breaks with a biological versus social constructivist dichotomy in conceptualising sexual difference. Methodologically, he takes contemporary theoretical discussions on sexual identity as themselves the empirical base upon which he sets Lacanian categories to work. Lacan's categories of the imaginary, real and symbolic are deployed in a way that allows him to, first, reframe standard theoretical debates on sexual identity and, secondly, to suggest an alternative way of formulating sexual difference.

Hegemony, myths and imaginaries

Thus far we have outlined the basic ontological assumptions and conceptual innovations underpinning discourse theory, and have stressed the centrality of dislocations and social antagonisms in forming the political identities of social subjects. We now need to consider the concept of hegemony, which is also central to discourse theory. For discourse theory, hegemonic *practices* are an exemplary form of political activity that involves the articulation of different identities and subjectivities into a common project, while hegemonic *formations* are the outcomes of these projects' endeavours to create new forms of social order from a variety of dispersed or dislocated elements. As we have noted, this conception radicalises Gramsci's concept of hegemony. As against Lenin's conception of hegemony, in which a vanguard party has the historically determined role of engineering temporary class alliances in order to conduct revolutionary struggle, Gramsci understands hegemony to be the articulation of different forces by the working class, in which the proletariat transcends its corporate interests and represents the universal interests of 'the people' or 'nation'. In short, for Gramsci hegemony is not simply an instrumental political strategy, but a general political logic involving the construction of a new 'common sense' – what Gramsci calls 'intellectual, cultural and moral leadership' – that can structure an emergent 'historical bloc'.[61]

In developing their conception, Laclau and Mouffe deconstruct the remaining essentialist assumptions in Gramsci's texts. These are his insistence on the role of a 'fundamental social class' in bringing about social change, and his commitment to 'a decisive nucleus of economic activity' structuring all societies, both of which imply that society is a self-enclosed totality whose character is determined and comprehended by objective laws of history.[62] As we have already noted, Laclau and Mouffe's theory of discourse is predicated on the ultimate impossibility of societal closure, a condition that makes articulatory practices and political agency possible. In order for there to be hegemonic practices, Laclau and Mouffe stipulate two further conditions. These are the existence of antagonistic forces, and the instability of the political frontiers that divide them.[63] Thus, hegemonic practices presuppose a social field criss-crossed by antagonisms, and the presence of elements that can be articulated by opposed political projects. The major aim of hegemonic projects is to construct and stabilise the *nodal points* that form the basis of concrete social orders by articulating as many available elements – floating signifiers – as possible.[64]

No discourse then is capable of completely hegemonising a field of discursivity, thus eliminating the experience of dislocation and the construction of antagonisms. However, it would be incorrect to conclude at this high level of abstraction that all discourses are equally successful or unsuccessful in their attempts to achieve hegemony. In this respect, Laclau introduces the conceptual distinction between *myths* and social *imaginaries*. In both cases the background against which these formations emerge is that of structural dislocation. Let us first examine the case of myth. At the outset, Laclau points out that the 'condition for the emergence of myth … is a structural dislocation'.[65] Myths construct new spaces of representation that attempt to suture the dislocated space in question. Their effectiveness is essentially hegemonic, as they involve the formation of 'a new objectivity by means of the rearticulation of the dislocated elements'.[66] From their emergence until their dissolution, myths can function as a surface of inscription for a variety of social demands and dislocations. However, when a myth has proved to be successful in neutralising social dislocations and incorporating a great number of social demands, then we can say that the myth has been transformed to an imaginary.[67] A collective social imaginary is defined by Laclau as 'a horizon' or 'absolute limit which structures a field of intelligibility', and he gives examples such as the Christian Millennium, the Enlightenment and positivism's conception of progress as evidence of these social phenomena.[68]

Many chapters in this collection utilise these ideas about hegemony in producing their accounts. In the second chapter of the book, Sebastián Barros and Gustavo Castagnola analyse the long-term effects of the crisis of Peronist hegemony between 1955 and 1973. They show how the initial framing of political identities in Peronist discourse, in which popular sectors were incorporated into the dominant order, turned the political arena into a battlefield of competing political forces each attempting to impose their own particular and irreconcilable demands. The presence of these particularistic identities precluded the formation of a common social imaginary and obstructed the emergence of a stable hegemonic formation in Argentinian politics during the period. Using a similar logic, Nur Betül Çelik shows how new antagonisms and dislocations have eroded the hegemony of Kemalist discourse in Turkey during the 1980s and 1990s. She examines the emergence and changing nature of Kemalist hegemony since the 1940s, showing how its ambiguous character has both restricted the rules of the political game, while making possible the construction of alternative political identities. As she shows, the dissolution of this hegemonic formation carries both the possibility of greater democratisation and the emergence of more authoritarian and anti-democratic political forces. For his part, in Chapter 11 of the book, Howarth examines the crucial discursive shift in oppositional discourse to the apartheid regime in South Africa during the 1970s and 1980s. He argues that the change from Black Consciousness ideology to democratic non-racialism can at an archaeological level be explained by the failure of the Black Consciousness Movement to transform its myth of 'Black Solidarity' and 'Black Communalism' into a viable collective social imaginary that could structure the emergence and consolidation of a post-apartheid order. Instead, he shows how the dislocatory experience of the Soweto uprisings in 1976, and the 'post-Soweto' realignment of political forces from 1977 until mid-1986, resulted in the emergence and consolidation of a proto-democratic imaginary under the auspices of the United Democratic Front and its allies.

Organisation of the chapters

To conclude this introduction we need to say a few words on the nature of the individual chapters, their particular ordering and the way they function within the overall logic of the book. They can be classified in a variety of ways depending on the concepts and theorists to which they refer, their specific objects of study, and the particular style of their exposition. While the different chapters all use discourse theory as a common language of interpretation, each concentrating on a limited number of concepts and logics, this perspective is often combined with a particular stress on Lacanian theory, Derridean deconstruction, Foucauldian archaeology/genealogy, or some other theoretical tradition. The Lacanian influence is evident in the chapters by Glynos and Stavrakakis, while the Derridean influence is easy to discern in the contributions of Harvey and Halverson, Clohesy and Norval. A more Foucauldian emphasis is visible in the chapters by Ho and Tsang, and Howarth. Other chapters have attempted to articulate discourse theory with more mainstream theories of politics. Thus Howarth and Griggs draw upon different theories of collective action in the rational choice and social movement fields, while Bastow challenges and incorporates certain conceptions of the history of ideas to analyse his particular object.

While we have already indicated the way in which particular concepts are variously deployed in the different chapters, the chapters are also focused around their specific objects of investigation. One group of chapters concentrates on the emergence and formation of new discursive structures. Thus Bastow's account of Marcel Déat's 'third way' concentrates on the specificity of this new discursive articulation, whereas Stavrakakis explores the dislocatory conditions of possibility for the constitution of Green ideology. Clohesy provides a careful analysis of the changing contours of Republicanist discourse in Northern Ireland, while Adamson examines the forging of social democracy in Romania. A further grouping is organised around the themes of identities and subjectivities. Griggs and Howarth focus on the central role of group identities in enabling residents and eco-warriors to overcome their collective action problems, while Glynos shows the impossibility of constructing gendered sexual identities because of the inherent lack in any symbolic order. Ho and Tsang examine the construction of new forms of sexual identification and subjectivity in Hong Kong. A third series of chapters are focused around the role of social movements and political agencies. Buenfil Burgos examines the logic of the Mexican revolution focussing on the formation of a revolutionary subjectivity, whereas Harvey and Halverson examine the logic and effects of the Zapatista movement on the Mexican collective imaginary. A final set of chapters is concerned specifically with questions of hegemony, especially the emergence, formation and dissolution of collective imaginaries. The chapters by Çelik, Barros and Castagnola belong to this group.

Although not present in all the chapters, another organising logic is the particular spatial and regional context in which the chapters are located. Some chapters concentrate on a set of issues specific to Latin American politics. Hence Barros and Castagnola reconstruct the impact of Peronist populism in Argentine politics, Buenfil Burgos traces the contours of the Mexican revolutionary mystique, and Harvey and Halverson examine the impact of the Zapatista movement on Mexican politics. Other contributions situate their analyses in a context of peripherality. For instance, Çelik examines the failure of Kemalist hegemony at the margins of the European Union, whereas Adamson explores the question of transition in Eastern Europe by considering the case of Romania. Ho and Tsang, and Clohesy are concerned with the formation of discourses and identities in Hong Kong and Northern Ireland respectively, both areas that occupy a liminal position to their respective metropoles.

A final principle of organisation concerns the different levels of analysis of the different chapters. Here the division is largely binary, as most chapters consist either of macro-level investigations of discourses at the national and regional levels, or are concerned with the micro-level analysis of particular identities and events. The chapters examining the long-term emergence and formation of discourses and collective imaginaries operate at the macro-level of investigation, whereas chapters that explore the actions and effects of new social movements, or the production of new forms of subjectivity in restricted geographical and historical contexts clearly fall into the micro-level category. It is clear then that this collection is open to multiple readings, something which shows the ability of discourse theory to articulate itself with a multitude of analytical dimensions and to provide a challenging recasting of political analysis as it is traditionally known.

Notes

1 A cursory glance at current debates in academic disciplines as diverse as social psychology, history, anthropology, linguistics, sociology, international relations, cultural studies and literary criticism shows a proliferation of studies that deploy the concept of discourse and the methods of discourse analysis. Moreover, there has been a spate of new journals, handbooks and textbooks devoted entirely to the development and application of discourse theory and analysis in the social sciences. See, *inter alia*, E. Burman and I. Parker (eds), *Discourse Analytic Research* (London, Routledge, 1993); D. Campbell, *Writing Security* (Manchester, Manchester University Press, 1992); T. van Dijk (ed.), *Handbook of Discourse Analysis* (London, Academic Press, 1985), 4 vols; T. van Dijk (ed.), *Discourse Studies* (London, Sage, 1997), 2 Volumes; J. George, *Discourses of Global Politics* (Boulder, Lynne Rienner, 1994); P. Hall, *Cultures of Inquiry* (Berkeley, University of California Press, 1998); S. Hall (ed.), *Representation* (London, Sage, 1997); J. Milliken, 'The study of discourse in International Relations', *European Journal of International Relations*, 5:2 (1999), 257–86; A. Munslow, *Discourse and Culture* (London, Routledge, 1992); J. Potter and M. Wetherell, *Discourse and Social Psychology* (London, Sage, 1987); H. White, *Tropics of Discourse* (Baltimore, Johns Hopkins University Press, 1978). Journals devoted solely to the analysis of discourse include *Discourse and Society*, *Discourse Studies* and *Discourse Processes*. Among the new textbooks, see D. Macdonnell, *Theories of Discourse* (Oxford, Basil Blackwell, 1986); S. Mills, *Discourse* (London, Routledge, 1997); G. Williams, *French Discourse Analysis* (London, Routledge, 1999)

2 For broad overviews of this research programme, see D. Howarth, 'Discourse theory and political analysis', in E. Scarborough and E. Tanenbaum (eds),

Research Methods in Social Science (Oxford, Oxford University Press, 1998), pp. 268–93; J. Torfing, *New Theories of Discourse* (Oxford, Basil Blackwell, 1999); A. M. Smith, *Laclau and Mouffe* (London, Routledge, 1998).

3 For an interesting discussion of the convergences and divergences of different theoretical paradigms, see M. Lichbach, 'Social theory and comparative politics', in M. Lichbach and A. Zuckerman (eds), *Comparative Politics: Rationality, Culture, and Structure* (Cambridge, Cambridge University Press, 1997), pp. 239–76.

4 N. Fairclough, *Discourse and Social Change* (Cambridge, Polity, 1992).

5 A. Jaworski and N. Coupland (eds), *The Discourse Reader* (London, Routledge, 1999). See also C. Willing (ed.), *Applied Discourse Analysis* (Buckingham, Open University Press, 1999).

6 While political analysts using the concept of discourse address these issues, they do not do so from what we call a discourse-theory perspective.

7 A further elaboration of these distinctions and definitions can be found in D. Howarth, *Discourse* (Buckingham, Open University Press, forthcoming).

8 E. Laclau and C. Mouffe, *Hegemony and Socialist Strategy: Towards a Radical Democratic Politics* (London, Verso, 1985), p. 107.

9 This reasoning takes its lead from Heidegger's concept of 'the world', as developed in *Being and Time*, and the later Wittgenstein's ideas of 'forms of life', which he elaborates in *The Philosophical Investigations*. See M. Heidegger, *Being and Time* (Oxford, Basil Blackwell, 1973); L. Wittgenstein, *Philosophical Investigations* (Oxford, Basil Blackwell, 1953). See also M. Barrett, *The Politics of Truth* (Cambridge, Polity, 1991), pp. 76–7.

10 Laclau and Mouffe, *Hegemony and Socialist Strategy*, p. 108.

11 See S. Mulhall, *Heidegger and Being and Time* (London, Routledge, 1996).

12 This builds, of course, on Michel Foucault's definition of discourses as those 'practices that systematically form the objects of which they speak'. See M. Foucault, *The Archaeology of Knowledge* (London, Tavistock, 1972), p. 49.

13 See T. B. Dyrberg, *The Circular Structure of Power* (London, Verso, 1997).

14 E. Laclau, *New Reflections on the Revolution of Our Time* (London, Verso, 1990), pp. 31–6.

15 See S. Hall, *The Hard Road to Renewal* (London, Verso, 1988). See also A. M. Smith, *New Right Discourse on Race and Sexuality* (Cambridge, Cambridge University Press, 1994).

16 See, *inter alia*, P. Hall (ed.), *The Political Power of Economic Ideas* (Princeton, Princeton University Press, 1980); P. John, *Analysing Public Policy* (London, Pinter, 1999), pp. 144–66; G. Majone, *Evidence, Argument, and Persuasion in the Policy Process* (New Haven, Yale University Press, 1989); A. Weale, *The New Politics of Pollution* (Manchester, Manchester University Press, 1992), pp. 57–60. G. Majone, 'Public policy and administration: ideas, interests and institutions', in R. Goodin and H. D. Klingermann, *A New Handbook of Political Science* (Oxford, Oxford University Press, 1996), pp. 610–27.

17 J. Derrida, *Of Grammatology* (Baltimore, Johns Hopkins University Press, 1974), p. 158.

18 J. Derrida, 'But, beyond ... (Open letter to Anne McClintock and Rob Nixon)', *Critical Inquiry*, 13 (1986), 165.

19 The fact that these methods and techniques are relative to the underlying

assumptions of discourse theory is true of all social science research, no matter how supposedly neutral and objective.

20 See Howarth, 'Discourse theory and political analysis', pp. 284–8; Y. Stavrakakis, *Lacan and the Political* (London, Routledge, 1999), pp. 57–9, 76–8.

21 In this respect, discourse theorists meet up with other methods of reading and research. Derrida, for instance, speaks of the 'singularity' of each deconstructive reading, which cannot be reduced to any general theory and 'method' of deconstruction. See M. B. Naas, 'Introduction: for example', in J. Derrida, *The Other Heading. Reflections on Today's Europe* (Bloomington, Indiana University Press, 1992), pp. vii–lix. The enactment of each deconstructive reading is also evident in Foucault's 'genealogies' of punishment, subjectivity and sexuality. Each genealogy is seen as a specific 'history of the present' designed and executed around a present set of concerns that provoke an inquiry into *how* these issues became problematic, and *how* their particular form can be dissolved and transfigured. See M. Foucault, *Discipline and Punish* (London, Allen Lane, 1977), pp. 30–1.

22 This condition is directly analogous to the later Wittgenstein's critique of a mechanical application of rules. See H. Staten, *Wittgenstein and Derrida* (Lincoln, University of Nebraska Press, 1984).

23 This movement is evident in the overall trajectory of Laclau and Mouffe's writings. Thus, in *Politics and Ideology and Marxist Theory* (London, New Left Books, 1977) Laclau develops an internal critique of Marxist theory, by sketching out an area of social relations not subject to the all-encompassing laws of Marxism. However, their later writings represent a far more radical critique of Marxist theory. In *Hegemony and Socialist Strategy*, they position themselves explicitly on a post-Marxist terrain and abandon the underlying ontological and epistemological foundations of classical Marxism. These arguments are then elaborated in Laclau's *New Reflections on the Revolution of Our Time* and deployed in Mouffe's *The Return of the Political*. They are also evident in the two authors' more recent collections of essays, which include *The Making of Political Identities, Deconstruction and Pragmatism, Emancipation(s)* and *The Challenge of Carl Schmitt*. See E. Laclau (ed.), *The Making of Political Identities* (London, Verso, 1994); E. Laclau, *Emancipation(s)* (London, Verso, 1996); C. Mouffe, *The Return of the Political* (London, Verso, 1993); C. Mouffe (ed.), *Deconstruction and Pragmatism* (London, Routledge, 1996); C. Mouffe (ed.), *The Challenge of Carl Schmitt* (London, Verso, 1999).

24 This is in keeping with the post-structuralist claim that the connection between the signifier (the sound-image) and the signified (concept) is internal to language and can never be fixed in an ultimate fashion. Because of this, social identities can never be fully determined, but are organised around the 'play' of different signifiers.

25 See C. Taylor, 'Interpretation and the sciences of man', in Taylor, *Philosophy and the Human Sciences*, Vol. 1 (Cambridge, Cambridge University Press, 1985); P. Winch, *The Idea of a Social Science*, 2nd edn (London, Routledge, 1990); L. Wittgenstein, *Philosophical Investigations*. While post-behaviouralists are now inclined to reject a complete separation of fact and theory, they remain committed to the view that theories can be tested by an independent empirical reality, and that there is a fundamental division between 'facts', theories and values. See

D. Sanders, 'Behavioural analysis', in D. Marsh and G. Stoker (eds), *Theory and Method in Political Science* (Basingstoke, Macmillan, 1995).

26 There have been numerous attempts in the philosophy of science to separate objective explanations from subjective interpretations. These range from naive verificationism to Popper's more sophisticated falsificationism. However, as Thomas Kuhn, Richard Bernstein and Fred Dallmayr demonstrate, these attempts to draw boundaries on the supposed objectivity of science flounder because they misunderstand the nature of scientific practice, and because they misrepresent the human and social sciences. See R. Bernstein, *Beyond Objectivism and Relativism: Science, Hermeneutics and Praxis* (Oxford, Basil Blackwell, 1983); F. Dallmayr and T. McCarthy (eds), *Understanding and Social Inquiry* (Notre Dame, University of Notre Dame Press, 1977); T. Kuhn, 'Natural and human sciences', in D. Hiley, J. Bohman and R. Shusterman (eds), *The Interpretative Turn* (Ithaca, Cornell University Press, 1991).

27 For a classic statement of this model of politics, see M. Olson, *The Logic of Collective Action* (Cambridge, Mass., Harvard University Press, 1965).

28 S. Lukes, *Power* (London, Macmillan, 1974).

29 For a classic statement of this conception of science, see C. Hempel, *Aspects of Scientific Explanation* (New York, Free Press, 1965).

30 For a clear critique of the correspondence theory of truth, see A. F. Chalmers, *What Is This Thing Called Science?* 2nd edn, (Buckingham, Open University Press, 1982).

31 The phrase is, of course, Paul Feyerabend's, and appears in his *Against Method* (London, Verso, 1975), p. 296.

32 See N. Geras, *Discourses of Extremity* (London, Verso, 1990).

33 See Bernstein, *Beyond Objectivism and Relativism*, Part 2; Mouffe, *The Return of the Political*, pp. 14–18.

34 As Laclau and Mouffe insist: 'The impossibility of an ultimate fixity of meaning implies that there have to be partial fixations – otherwise, the very flow of differences would be impossible. Even in order to differ, to subvert meaning, there has to be a meaning. If the social does not manage to fix itself in the intelligible and instituted forms of society, the social only exists, however, as an effort to construct that impossible object. Any discourse is constituted as an attempt to dominate the field of discursivity, to arrest the flow of differences, to construct a centre.' See Laclau and Mouffe, *Hegemony and Socialist Strategy*, p. 112.

35 *Ibid.*, p. 105. Thus, for example, the constitution of Green ideology can be understood as the *articulation* of a number of pre-existing elements ('direct democracy', 'decentralisation', and so on) into a new configuration that transforms their meaning ('direct democracy', for example, previously articulated in anarchist or other radical discourses, now becomes 'Green democracy'), simultaneously producing the moments of a new discursive ensemble (Green ideology). This hypothesis is further explored in Y. Stavrakakis, 'Green ideology: a discursive reading', *Journal of Political Ideologies,* 2:3 (1997). No such discursive articulation is final. The new meaning that elements acquire by being articulated in a discourse is contingent, and not the revelation of their previously hidden or essential meaning. There is no transcendental signified limiting the field of signification, as discursive articulation is only limited by the *availability* of signifiers (elements) and the *creativity* of the political forces involved in the

articulatory practice. However, the fact that there can be no definitive fixation of meaning does not mean that the social is reduced to a chaotic post-modern universe. Partial and temporary fixation is the condition of possibility for the constitution of social reality.

36 Laclau and Mouffe, *Hegemony and Socialist Strategy*, p. 113.

37 *'The practice of articulation ... consists in the construction of nodal points which partially fix meaning'*, as Laclau and Mouffe argue (Laclau and Mouffe, *Hegemony and Socialist Strategy*, p. 113). In this respect Laclau and Mouffe's analysis of discourse is compatible with that of Claude Lefort when he describes the function of ideological discourse as an attempt to organise social life around the metaphor of a centre (C. Lefort, *The Political Forms of Modern Society*, Cambridge, Polity, 1986, pp. 218–19). There are also certain affinities with the morphological analysis of ideology introduced by Michael Freeden in 'Political concepts and ideological morphology' (*Journal of Political Ideologies*, 2:2 (1994); see also his *Ideologies and Political Theory*, Oxford, Oxford University Press, 1996) as well as with the articulation of a psychoanalytic (Lacanian) theory of ideology by Slavoj Žižek. For an introduction to Žižek's analysis of ideology, see *The Sublime Object of Ideology* (London, Verso, 1989); 'Between symbolic fiction and fantasmatic spectre: towards a Lacanian theory of ideology', *Analysis*, 5 (1994); 'Introduction: the spectre of ideology', in S. Žižek (ed.), *Mapping Ideology* (London, Verso, 1994); 'Invisible ideology: political violence between fiction and fantasy', *Journal of Political Ideologies*, 1:1 (1996). See also A. J. Norval's 'The things we do with words: contemporary approaches to the analysis of ideology', *British Journal of Political Science* (1999).

38 See J. Lacan, *The Seminar. Book III. The Psychoses 1955–6*, ed. J.-A. Miller (London, Routledge, 1993).

39 Zizek, *Sublime Object of Ideology*, p. 102.

40 Laclau, *Emancipation(s)*, p. 53.

41 *Ibid.*, p. 44.

42 *Ibid.*, p. 44.

43 In Laclau and Mouffe's more recent work there is sometimes a tendency to differentiate between politics and the political. For a brief account on the nature of this distinction, which falls outside the scope of this introductory chapter, see Stavrakakis, *Lacan and the Political*, pp. 71–5.

44 See Howarth, 'Discourse theory and political analysis', pp. 274–8. For a further example of this logic, see D. E. Apter and N. Sawa, *Against the State* (Cambridge, Harvard University Press, 1984).

45 See A. J. Norval, 'Frontiers in question', *Acta Philosophica*, 2 (1997), 51–76.

46 This dual constituting and destabilising role means that the concept of antagonism has strong resonances with Derrida's notion of a 'constitutive outside'. In his deconstructive readings of metaphysical texts, Derrida shows how the privileging of certain poles of key binary oppositions – essence/accident, mind/body, speech/writing – are predicated on a simultaneous relation of exclusion and dependence. That is to say, efforts by writers and philosophers in the Western tradition to prioritise one pole of the dialectic is shown to fail in that the dominant term *requires* that which is excluded for its identity, thus problematising a clear hierarchical relation between the two.

47 Laclau and Mouffe, *Hegemony and Socialist Strategy*, p. 127.

48 *Ibid.*, p. 125.
49 *Ibid.*
50 See also S. Griggs, D. Howarth and B. Jacobs, 'Second runway at Manchester', *Parliamentary Affairs*, 51:3 (1998), 358–69.
51 The different modalities of political frontiers involving the logics of equivalence and difference are discussed in Aletta Norval's concluding chapter of this volume.
52 In this respect also see A. J. Norval, *Deconstructing Apartheid Discourse* (London, Verso, 1996), especially Ch. 4.
53 See W. E. Connolly, *Identity\Difference* (Ithaca, Cornell University Press, 1991). See also D. Howarth, 'Complexities of identity/difference', *Journal of Political Ideologies*, 2:1 (1996), 51–78.
54 L. Althusser, 'Ideology and ideological state apparatuses', in Althusser, *Lenin and Philosophy and Other Essays* (New York, Monthly Review Press, 1971), pp. 127–86.
55 Compare Laclau, *New Reflections on the Revolution of our Time*, pp. 60–1; Laclau and Mouffe, Hegemony and Socialist Strategy, pp. 114–22; E. Laclau and L. Zac (1984), 'Minding the gap: the subject of politics', in Laclau, *The Making of Political Identities* (London, Verso, 1994).
56 Laclau and Mouffe, *Hegemony and Socialist Strategy*, p. 115.
57 This notion of a dispersion of subject positions does not mean a complete separation of positions in that various subjectivities can, and are, articulated together into discourses which hold different positions together in a contingent unity. A socialist, populist or nationalist discourse may try, for example, to weld various subjectivities together into an overdetermined subject position, thus modifying the meaning of its component parts.
58 Laclau, *New Reflections on the Revolution of our Time*, pp. 39–41.
59 This is the example used by Laclau throughout *New Reflections on the Revolution of our Time*.
60 Laclau, *New Reflections on the Revolution of our Time*, p. 39.
61 A. Gramsci, *Selections from the Prison Notebooks*. ed. Q. Hoare and G. Nowell-Smith (London: Lawrence & Wishart, 1971), pp. 181–2.
62 *Ibid.*, p. 161.
63 Laclau and Mouffe, *Hegemony and Socialist Strategy*, p. 136.
64 *Ibid.*, p. 112. According to Laclau and Mouffe, 'a social and political space relatively unified by the institution of nodal points and the constitution of tendentially relational identities' is called a 'hegemonic formation', a concept which shares strong affinities with Gramsci's idea of a historical bloc. See ibid., p. 136; Gramsci, Selections; A. Showstack Sassoon, *Gramsci's Politics*, 2nd edn (London, Hutchinson, 1985), pp. 119–25.
65 Laclau, *New Reflections on the Revolution of our Time*, p. 61.
66 *Ibid.*, p. 61.
67 *Ibid.*, p. 64.
68 *Ibid.*

The political frontiers of the social: Argentine politics after Peronist populism (1955–1973)

On 17 October 1945 a crowd converged in the main square in Buenos Aires, in front of the House of Government, asking for the liberation of a man who had been incarcerated days before. Most of the women and men who voiced this demand were workers. The man whose freedom was demanded was Juan Perón. On that day, a populist political movement was born: it would be called Peronism. Even though the political core of Peronism was located in its popular support, Perón managed to transform this particular movement into a nationwide, hegemonic one. Peronist hegemony allowed Perón to be elected president of the country in 1946 and 1951. However, 1954 marked the beginning of a long hegemonic crisis. This chapter will focus on the period that runs from the first stage of this crisis, Perón's overthrow and political exile in 1955, to his return to Argentina in 1973. In analysing this period, we will show that a proper approach to Peronist populism requires a rigorous account of the way in which Peronism framed the political identities and frontiers of the country. And this task presupposes placing at the very centre of analysis the particular historical context in which Peronism emerged and developed.

Although the breakdown of the Peronist regime signalled the end of Perón's political hegemony at a national level, this development did not entail the ending of the centrality of Peronist discourse in Argentine politics. Between 1955 and 1973, several attempts were made to solve the so-called 'Peronist question': how to eliminate, assimilate or control the Peronist movement. All these attempts failed. These failures not only provoked a political crisis characterised by a permanent stalemate but also showed the vitality of the Peronist political heritage even after Perón's overthrow. The way in which Peronism framed political identities, and therefore the political frontiers of the Argentine political system, survived Perón's fall and 'guided' the political behaviour of both Peronist *and* non-Peronist political actors. In other words, the populist rupture[1] introduced by Peronism in Argentine politics dominated political developments in Argentina well after the populist movement lost its hegemonic grip at a national scale.

Despite its absolute historical centrality, the populist experience was almost ignored or misapprehended in the 'traditional' accounts of the political process of the period.[2] The brief bibliographical survey that follows attempts to articulate the need to problematise these readings. After critically assessing the arguments and conclusions of the two main approaches, we will examine the way in which a discourse theory perspective can go beyond the limits marking the literature in question.

Economic and institutional rationalities: the dominant approaches to Argentine politics

Surveys of Argentine political history between 1955 and 1973 have followed two main trends. While some studies focus on the economic interests of groups, others concentrate on an analysis of the way in which the supposedly inherent institutional rationality of political actors shapes the political processes. Even though focusing solely on the Argentine case, the analytical corollaries of these approaches embraced a large range of historical and political topics. In the brief exposition which follows, we are only interested in stressing that these perspectives provide inadequate and/or unsatisfactory accounts of the political processes that took place in Argentina during the second half of the twentieth century and, in particular, *vis-à-vis* the role of Peronism.

From the first point of view, the political developments in Argentina after Perón's overthrow in 1955 were but the expression of tensions existing within the economic structure of the country.[3] The authors who follow this viewpoint stress that analysing the Argentine economic structure reveals the coexistence of 'objectively' opposite interests. They point out that the particular political interests of the various economic groups were objectively antagonistic: therefore, and quoting the title of a work written by one of the defenders of this perspective, the articulation of a viable hegemonic formula for Argentina after 1955 was 'impossible'.[4] This created a persisting political instability. According to this approach, the difficult task of integrating Peronism into the political system after Perón's fall could be understood as the Argentine version of a typical Latin American phenomenon: the incapacity of the economies of the region to satisfy the material aspirations of the popular sectors. Nevertheless, as the Argentine experience during the 1990s shows, the political support of these sectors is neither necessarily nor directly linked to the satisfaction of their supposedly 'objective' economic interests. The unemployment and poverty provoked by the economic policies introduced by the Peronist government between 1989 and 1999 did not erode the political support of the sectors that have been most seriously affected by those policies: the popular sectors still provide the main electoral support to Peronism.[5]

The second approach in question focused its attention on the institutional behaviour of actors within the political system. From this perspective, the impossibility to articulate a stable political order after 1955 was due to the weakness of the Argentine party system. This weakness was attributed to the inability of both non-Peronist political leaders and certain 'corporations'[6] to engage in any kind of political negotiation in order to stabilise the political arena. As in the case of the former approach, the Peronist question was not ignored. Nevertheless, as we will immediately show, the institutionalist idiom of these surveys could not provide a satisfactory account of the role of the Peronist movement in the shaping of the political coalitions and conflicts marking the period after 1955.

Those who focused on disputes within non-Peronist political groups concluded that the stabilisation of the Argentine political order required a political agreement amongst the non-Peronist political elite. Thus, from this point of view, it was possible to achieve some kind of stable political solution – even though the problem of the complete incorporation of Peronism to the legal political system was postponed.[7] Undoubtedly, the scant disposition of the non-Peronist political elite to negotiate permanent political agreements contributed to the breakdown of the party system. Nevertheless, it is questionable whether an agreement generated within a system where Peronism was foreclosed could have been the solution for Argentine politics. On the one hand, during this period, corporations outside the party system (institutions that at the time were called 'factors of power' such as the military, the Catholic Church, business organisations, and trade unions) were politically strong. Thus, it is difficult to accept that a political agreement built in the context of a political system with these characteristics would have been enough to guarantee the stability of the whole political order. On the other hand, one of the most important 'factors of power' was the strong Peronist unionism itself. Therefore, it is even more difficult to accept the fundamental assumption of this approach: that Peronism could be left out of any possible stabilisation of the political order. On the contrary, the political agreement of Peronist union leaders was indispensable to construct a stable political regime in Argentina.

The perspective that stressed the political importance of corporations in the political system did take into account these considerations. It emphasised the fact that the political behaviour of the corporations shaped decisively the political fluctuations that took place after 1955. Nevertheless, regarding the political behaviour of the Peronist movement, these approaches have misunderstood not only its specific role but also its very political logic. On the one hand, this approach reduced the political performance of Peronism to the strategies of its unionist sector. On the other hand, it presented these strategies as inherently opposed to the consolidation of a stable party system.[8] But recent studies have shown the shallowness of these conclusions. The political behaviour of Peronism cannot be reduced to the tactics of Peronist trade unionism, and – more importantly – the political logic of this sector was not inherently predisposed to disturb the functioning of the party system.[9]

To sum up our argument in this section, if the first perspective overstressed the economic 'structural' limits of politics, the second viewpoint exaggerated the importance of the institutional strategies of formal political actors.[10] Both approaches misunderstood the historical significance of Peronism by reducing its political significance to some kind of economic logic or institutional rationality. The capacity for political survival of this movement in Argentina shows that its vitality is not ultimately linked either to the satisfaction of the material demands of the popular sectors or to the predominance of a supposedly intrinsic political logic of trade unionism. The different approaches to Argentine politics we have summarised converge however on one point: they describe a situation of 'social draw', an 'impossible' or 'zero-sum game' in which reciprocal vetoes and general paralysis were the main characteristics. The reasons for this stalemate vary from account to account; some analysts focus their attention on the different economic interests of the subjects involved, while others stress the important role played by institutional rationality. We do not dispute the descriptive part of this analysis: the political scene in Argentina at the time seemed to be paralysed by the capacity of the different actors to veto each other's demands. However, from the point of view put forward here, the origin of the political stagnation in Argentina is to be found in the impossibility of constituting a stable overall hegemonic articulation, and not in the intrinsic rationality, be it economic or institutional, of the actors involved; it is the political dimension which is of crucial importance to us.

The limits of the economistic account of Argentina's stalemate are well illustrated in the case of Guillermo O'Donnell's influential article, 'State and alliances in Argentina, 1956–1976'.[11] In O'Donnell's view, the possibility of a stable hegemonic political order was potentially present because the 'objective conditions' could sustain a long-term alliance between agrarian and industrial urban economic interests. This potential alliance would have provoked a modernisation of the capitalist structure of Argentina, and would have thus extended the legitimacy of the political system. Nevertheless, for O'Donnell, the instability of the political formation was caused by the strong opposition that this potential coalition encountered in the presence of another 'defensive alliance' formed by popular sectors and weak industrial urban groups. Consequently, the causes of the political instability are to be located in the conflicting economic interests of the sectors involved. The 'defensive alliance' was *economically subordinated* but *politically capable* of impeding the construction of an alliance that would have provided a stable political formation. Thus, although O'Donnell's analysis is based on highlighting the economic interests of the conflicting alliances, the reason for the stalemate and the lack of an 'overall domination' was the *political* power of the defensive alliance he describes. Furthermore, this political power is not

related to the economic weight of the groups: despite its economic subordination the 'defensive alliance' was politically capable of blocking the initiatives of the economically dominant sectors. This means that the hypothesis
stating that the political stalemate was provoked by the presence of different
economic interests is inconsistent. Even when the political stalemate is
described in terms of the economic interests of the groups, as in O'Donnell's
case, the reasons for the stalemate cannot be explained in the same terms.
Thus, the lack of a stable hegemony is rather to be found in the way in which
the groups *politically* obstructed each other than in their 'objectively' antagonistic economic interests.

A similar objection can be directed against those analyses that centre their
attention on the institutional rationality of the actors involved in the political process. As we have pointed out, within this perspective the difficulties in
building a stable political system after 1955 are attributed to the weakness of
the Argentine party system. Let us examine the work of Marcelo Cavarozzi
as an example of this school of thought. His main assumption is that institutions can be understood as having 'their own laws, which are not the simple
result of the interrelationship among the different forces that participate in
them'.[12] From this standpoint, Cavarozzi provides a rather narrow definition
of what counts as a democratic institution: democratic institutions are
restricted to the party system and parliament. In Cavarozzi's account, it is not
until the 1966 military coup that we can find attempts to overcome social
and political conflict through some kind of institutional agreements. In 1966
the armed forces took office through a military coup and established a dictatorship that lasted until 1973. The military government introduced a variety
of different political formulae in order to overcome the duality, the paratactical division of the political system and aimed to channel the extra-institutional conflict to the interior of the institutional setting. However, these
projects failed. Extra-institutional politics was once more the norm, the only
difference being an increase in its violent characteristics. Again, as in the case
of economistic accounts, the institutional strategy that is assumed to guide
the behaviour of the different groups fails to explain the instability of the
Argentine political formation after 1955. In the end, Cavarozzi's taxonomy
of the ways in which the rationality of different institutions works itself out
in the political arena proves to be of little use. As he points out himself, the
rationality that he attributes to the institutions involved in this political
process does not match the actual historical behaviour of the actors in the
Argentine experience. Although he *describes* how institutions failed to contain conflict and introduce some kind of political articulation, he does not
explain why groups did not behave according to their supposedly inherent
institutional rationality. This means that we must search for an explanation
in a realm different from the institutional one.

Peronism and anti-Peronism: an impossible articulation

It is our hypothesis that the reason for the political stagnation of Argentina after 1955 should be traced back to the particular way in which the formation of political identities shaped the political frontiers in the wake of the irruption of Peronist populism. It is this political dimension which can shed some light on the Argentine political experience beyond the dominant economistic and institutionalist approaches. To support this thesis we have to focus our attention on the analysis of Peronist discourse itself. Peronism introduced a new articulation of the political order based on the incorporation of the, until then, excluded popular sectors. Nevertheless, this incorporation was not merely the recognition of the political rights of these sectors. From its inception, Peronism proclaimed the inclusion of the popular sectors – and in particular of the working class – by proposing a radical redefinition of the idea of citizenship. Before the emergence of Juan Perón as a political leader, citizenship was reduced to a set of political rights. Peronism reshaped the idea of citizenship by incorporating into it, and actually putting at its very core, a social identity content. Under the perspective introduced by Peronism, the set of rights associated with citizenship were primarily identified with social issues. As Daniel James has pointed out:

> Perón's political success with workers laid ... in his capacity to recast the whole issue of citizenship within a new social context. Peronist discourse denied the validity of liberalism's separation of the state and politics from civil society. Citizenship was not defined simply in terms of individual rights and relations within political society any longer, but was now redefined in terms of the economic and social realms of civil society.[13]

The incorporation of the popular sectors by Peronism also reshaped the political frontiers that would divide the political life of the country during the rest of the twentieth century. Two features of this framing are absolutely crucial. On the one hand, by defining 'the Argentine drama' as a struggle between 'social justice' and 'social injustice', Perón enlarged the scope of political identities by linking them to the field of the social. Politics was pictured as an activity mainly concerned with social issues and disputes. On the other hand, and this is of the utmost importance, Peronism presented these social issues and disputes within a polarised antagonistic schema. Social differences were portrayed as warlike divisions. In this way, the irruption of the popular sectors in Argentine politics through Peronist populism transformed the political arena into a battlefield in which different social groups tried to impose their particular and irreconcilable goals. In that sense Peronism constitutes a paradigmatic case of populist discourse insofar as one of the defining characteristics of populism is the tendency 'to divide society between dominant and dominated ... the totality of society [is conceived] around a fundamental antagonism'.[14] Perón always insisted upon this idea of defining political citizenship starting from its social features and always presented politics as a struggle between antagonistic social groups.

Even though crucial in order to understand the fixity of the political identities that would dominate Argentine politics from 1945, the Peronist reshaping of the features of the Argentine political frontiers does not present us with the whole picture. It is very important to stress that this way of representing the political arena – as dominated by dividing social disputes and antagonistic political forces – was assimilated by the non-Peronist groups as well. In fact, from 1945 onwards Argentine politics was dominated by the division between Peronist and non-Peronist political sectors. Although not in a totally exclusive way, the political alignments had mainly to do with the attitude towards Peronism: the central problem in Argentine politics was whether to be in favour or against Peronism. This shows the centrality that Peronist discourse had acquired. Regardless of whether one was for or against Peronism, the political arena could only be represented among sharply antagonistic lines, that is to say using the imaginary and representational resources provided by the Peronist populist rupture. This centrality would remain dominant even after Perón's fall in September 1955.

The 1955 revolution that overthrew and sent Perón into exile was an attempt to systematically destroy Peronism. In so doing, however, non-Peronist groups showed to what extent they were also involved in the same logic of establishing political frontiers upon strong dividing lines, in fact lines of exclusion. The military regime that started the 'Liberating Revolution' decreed the non-existence of Perón, Evita and Peronism. It was illegal to display photographs, paintings or sculptures of the former president or his wife, to use the words 'Peronism', 'Peronist', 'Justicialismo', or the abbreviation 'PP' (Peronist Party), to celebrate the dates commemorated by the 'tyranny', to fly the Peronist flag or to sing the Peronist hymn, and so on.[15] This attempt to eradicate every trace of Peronism from Argentine social and political life was explicitly justified in terms that neglected its social foundations. The necessity to eliminate all the institutions and organisations created under Perón's regime, was presented as an effort to show the popular sectors that the Peronist government had built its legitimacy using a very sophisticated demagogic system of propaganda. However, as an Argentine politician (who was involved in the conspiracy that resulted in Perón's overthrow) put it, the 1955 revolution marked 'the victory of one class over another class'.[16] This fact could be easily recognised through some of the ideological features that accompanied the political measures introduced by the military government in order to abolish all the institutions and organisations created during the previous ten years. These measures were usually presented as embodying 'civilisation' in contrast to the Peronist 'barbarism'; they were meant to represent European libertarian values against the cultural resentment of 'deep Argentina'. Therefore, it is not surprising that the efforts made by the 'Liberating Revolution' to eradicate Peronism ended in failure. In fact, the rampant repression suffered by the popular sectors reinforced their Peronist identity; more so since this repression reproduced the antagonistic representation of the political field introduced by Peronism. The explicit ideological justification that accompanied this attempt to eliminate Peronism did not work; in any case, the demagogic propaganda of Peronism was preferable to the military repression. In the end, the so-called Peronist Resistance to the military regime called their opponents 'gorillas' at the same time that the coalition in power called the followers of Perón 'little black heads' (*cabecitas negras*). Less than a year after seizing power, the failure of the 'Liberating Revolution' showed the dramatic collapse of the public space: 'Animals up in power and a crowd of inferior beings below: there was not a common imaginary of Argentine citizenship.'[17] *Or maybe there was: the imaginary horizon of an exclusionary division of the social imposed by the Peronist political logic.*

Thus, even after 1955, when the 'Liberating Revolution' overthrew Perón, the political space remained divided into two antagonistic fields built around social differences. On the one hand, certain particular positions (trade unions, youth organisations, right- and left-wing groups, some nationalist groups, and so on) entered into a system of equivalences that made up the Peronist pole of the antagonism. On the other hand, the liberal oligarchy, the middle classes, traditional political parties, the Catholic Church and the armed forces formed the anti-Peronist pole. This strict split of the political space into two fields overdetermined by an equivalencial division prevented the constitution of the two conditions for a stable hegemonic practice: the presence of a plurality of antagonistic forces and the instability of the frontiers separating them.[18] Far from this, the Argentine socio-political scene after Peronism could be described as a situation of strict antagonism in which the frontiers separating the two positions were rigidly sedimented. Therefore, the political space was structured around weak and precarious hegemonic links, excluding the possibility of an enduring hegemonic articulation.

The fact that political frontiers were identified with sharp social divisions also explains the failure of the most ambitious attempt to co-opt Peronism after 1955. Between 1958 and 1962, president Arturo Frondizi tried to integrate Peronism. Even though his economic policies were marked by the use of repressive means, Frondizi vigorously promoted the institutional reconstruction of Peronist trade unions. Hoping to receive votes in exchange for his government's positive attitude towards the workers, Frondizi encouraged the rebuilding of trade unions along the institutional lines followed by the Peronist regime. However, it was precisely the renewed power of Peronist trade unions that inaugurated the political crisis that resulted in Frondizi's overthrow in 1962. By transforming themselves into an electoral machinery, Peronist trade unions defeated Frondizi's party in the national election held in March of that year. Frondizi's bet had failed. This failure showed not only the strong identification of the popular sectors with Peronism, but also the extent to which this identification was, at the same time, socially based and politically shaped. Contrary to Frondizi's prediction, the reinforcement of the institutions of the working sectors did not stop but promoted the political vitality of Peronism. Far from being a way of obtaining the political support of workers, Frondizi's rebuilding of the Peronist trade unions allowed the workers to employ their social institutions as a political tool. On the non-Peronist side, the Frondizi experience showed that any effort to negotiate with the Peronist movement generated an implacable hostility from the anti-Peronist political groups. Since Perón's fall in 1955, the political legitimacy of the Argentine governments rested mainly upon the support granted by the non-Peronist groups. Thus, Frondizi's overthrow was provoked less by the Peronist electoral victory than by the attitude assumed by non-Peronist political groups. On March 1962, during the political crisis opened by the Peronist victory at the polls, these groups condemned Frondizi's government to a complete isolation. Frondizi's final political isolation was the merciless price that the non-Peronist political groups had reserved for the President's willingness to negotiate with the Peronist movement.

After 1962 the strength and fixity of the political frontiers grounded on the contours introduced by Peronist populism shaped Argentine politics in an even more crucial way. The vitality of these political frontiers not only perpetuated the political stalemate, but also showed the extent to which this stalemate was beyond any intrinsic institutional rationality, and exacerbated the political violence that would gradually dominate Argentine politics. During Arturo Illia's presidency (1963–66) the political struggle between Peronist trade unions and the party in office was frontal. The clashes between government and trade unions were grounded neither in ideological nor in economic considerations. Especially in relation to foreign capital and investment, Illia's government applied a set of policies that were similar to those applied during most of Perón's administration. Furthermore, during Illia's presidency, Argentina enjoyed a period of relative economic growth that allowed his government to avoid the implementation of the repressive measures towards the workers that had been a common feature of the previous governments. Despite this, neither the non-Peronist party in office nor the Peronist trade unions showed any disposition to negotiate. The former tried to disturb and/or dismantle the power of the trade unions by using institutional tools and by promoting divisions inside the Peronist movement. The latter rejected all the political and economic measures carried out by the government regardless of the benefits that these measures could entail for the popular sectors. Finally, President Illia was overthrown. As in the case of the former civil administration, the political vitality of Peronist trade unionism contributed to seal the fate of the government; the hostility of Peronist unions created the impression that Illia's administration was incapable of establishing a minimum political order. Nevertheless, unlike Frondizi's, Illia's policies were not criticised because of their sympathy towards

Peronism. This time the problem was not tolerating Peronism, but being unable to control it. Eventually, the military decided to take this task upon themselves. In June 1966, the armed forces took control of the government and proclaimed the beginning of the 'Argentine Revolution'.

At the time, the political conflict between government and trade unions during Illia's presidency was frequently seen as an expression of a confrontation grounded in inherently different institutional rationalities of the two political actors involved – political parties and trade unions. This kind of interpretation could provide an explanation that the economic accounts could not offer. As we have pointed out, the clash between Illia's party and the Peronist trade unions could not be explained by appealing either to the economic conditions prevailing in the country at that moment or to the economic policies adopted by the government. Thus, the military's seizure of power was seen as an opportunity to provide some stability to the political arena. Since the military and the trade unions as *corporations* shared a similar institutional rationality – both supposedly only interested in representing their particular demands – some kind of political agreement between them capable to stop the permanent instability of Argentine politics was expected. Many of the most prominent Peronist trade union leaders believed that the military would be better partners. Nonetheless, the military had other ideas. The first president of the military government, General Onganía, responded to the first demands voiced by Peronist trade unions with fierce repression. The political behaviour of the military government towards the trade unions showed, once again, that the political frontiers that divided Argentine society had more to do with the vitality of the articulation between social and political identities created by Peronism than with any kind of inherent institutional rationality. At stake were the political identities that prevailed in the armed forces and in the trade unions. Being anti-Peronist the former and Peronist the latter, there was no possibility of any negotiation between them.

However, the set of policies applied by the military regime in order to re-establish order in Argentina provoked exactly the opposite result. From 1969 onwards, Argentine society responded to the military repression with civil riots and the emergence of guerrilla groups. The search for a formula to restore order began to be attached to Perón's return to Argentina. The popular symbols of Peronism and the figure of Perón in exile started to gain a new centrality. Popular demands albeit particularised and originating from different groups, were analogous or equivalent in their rejection of the military government. The figure of Perón thus started to incarnate the representation of all these demands. The renewed centrality of Peronism at the beginning of the 1970s showed again the validity of the political frontiers shaped by the populist movement in the mid-1940s. Perón's political leadership within Peronism only became an alternative at a national level when most Argentine citizens thought that only the old leader was capable of controlling the violent social and political crisis that was shocking Argentina.

Behind the 62 per cent of votes obtained by Perón in the national elections of September 1973 converged a huge range of antinomic positions. Despite their diversity, all the expectations generated around the figure of Perón were based upon a common consensus: that politics has to do primarily with social issues and disputes. Perón regained the centre of the political arena representing, at the same time, the possibility of a revolutionary transformation of Argentina, and the only way of putting an end to the deep social and political crisis of the country.

   To conclude this section, Argentina's political history during the second half of the twentieth century was dominated by the antagonistic relationship between Peronist and non-Peronist groups. As we have pointed out, the fixity of these political frontiers was framed by the particular features of the political identities created by Peronism. By introducing a social dimension to the field of political identities, and by portraying social issues as permanent disputes, the Peronist populist rupture invested the political frontiers with a strong antagonistic fixity. Social differences did not merely assume a political dimension but were also pictured as the field of a permanent and irreconcilable struggle. This was the basic populist move of Peronist discourse: 'the same equivalents which in ... [another less antagonistic discourse] present themselves as a system of differences [unified within a stable political order] are reorganised as a system of equivalences by the discourse of [populist] antagonism. It is only thanks to this mutation that the discourse of antagonism can become a discourse of rupture.'[19] Inasmuch as this antagonistic relation implied the exclusion of the other, no articulation between the two poles of the antagonism was possible. The 'other' was merely rejected, externalised, excluded. Identities were constituted in such a way that articulatory practices between the elements of either of the two poles were impossible. The relation between groups could only be one of potential war.[20] The extreme particularism of Peronist and anti-Peronist positions meant that their demands could not be articulated into a wider hegemonic operation that would stabilise the political formation. In such a situation, only the disappearance of the other would have provided the possibility of a stable resolution of the socio-political division. Even Perón's return to Argentina after his long exile showed the dramatic contours of Argentine politics of that time. While Peronists hoped to celebrate a victory dreamt of during eighteen years of political exclusion, non-Peronist groups trusted that the prudence, wisdom, and mercy of the old leader would prevent the materialisation of this dream from being transformed into the beginning of a terrible nightmare. Finally, soon after Perón's death on July 1974, the nightmare could not be avoided: but this time its merciless shadows would cover the whole of the Argentine society in the guise of a new dictatorship.

Conclusion

As we have tried to show in this chapter, a discursive approach provides the means for an alternative understanding of the political stalemate of the Argentine political formation after 1955. The situation of 'social draw' or 'zero-sum game' was neither the result of an essential economic rationality cunningly operating during the consecutive economic crises, nor the result of the dominance of the intrinsic rationality of particular institutions. The political stalemate that affected Argentine political history during the second half of the twentieth century cannot be accounted for through any kind of logic beyond politics itself. As Laclau and Mouffe have pointed out:

> It is not the case that the field of the economy [or of any institutional rationality] is a self-regulated space subject to endogenous laws; nor does there exist a constitutive principle for social agents who can be fixed in an ultimate class [or rational] core; nor are class positions the necessary location of historical interests.[21]

A perspective centred on discourse theory can account for the stalemate of Argentine politics without introducing any essentialist assumption – be it the endogenous rationality of the economy or of institutions. By emphasising the central role of the constitution of political identities, a discursive approach provides a way of rethinking Argentine political history during the second half of the twentieth century. This approach has led us to focus attention on the formation of political identities since the emergence of Peronism. As we have shown, the incorporation of the popular sectors in Argentina made possible by Peronist populism transformed the political arena into a battlefield in which different social groups tried to impose their particular and irreconcilable goals. The overdetermination between the social and the political introduced by Perón prevented the formation of a common imaginary sustaining a stable political order. Social differences were immediately read in terms of political exclusion. The political frontiers thus framed by the constitution of political identities, prevented the emergence of a stable hegemonic articulation. Regardless of the economic situation or the institutional actors involved, the Argentine division was based on the politically determined non-recognition of the social other. In that sense Peronist populism introduced the representational resources which functioned as a 'negative' imaginary precluding the stability of Argentine politics.

Notes

1 For a detailed definition of the concept of populist rupture see E. Laclau, 'Populist rupture and discourse', *Screen Education*, Spring (1980), 87–93.
2 If, as we will show immediately, studies on the Argentine case either ignore or misunderstand the role of Peronism, the literature concerned with populist phenomena in general detached the Peronist rupture from its actual historical

context. In the analyses articulated by political scientists Peronism has been studied as a peculiar political penomenon analytically related more to experiences
like Italian fascism or American populism than to the Argentine historical situation itself. For this reason, this literature falls largely outside the scope of this
chapter.

3 See G. O'Donnell, *Modernización y Autoritarismo* (Buenos Aires, Paidos, 1972);
   J. C. Portantiero, 'Clases dominantes y crisis política en la Argentina actual', in
   O. Braun (ed.), *El capitalismo argentino en crisis* (Buenos Aires, Siglo XXI,
   1973); G. O'Donnell, 'Estado y alianzas en la Argentina, 1956–1976', *Desarrollo
   Económico*, 64 (Manuary–March 1977); J. C. Portantiero, 'Economía y política
   en la crisis argentina: 1958–1973', *Revista Mexicana de Sociología*, 2 (1977); A.
   Rouquié, 'Hegemonía militar, estado y dominación social', in A. Rouquié (ed.),
   Argentina Hoy (Buenos Aires, Siglo XXI, 1982); J. Sábato and J. Schvarzer, 'Fun-
   cionamiento de la economía y poder político en la Argentina: trabas para la
   democracia', in A. Rouquié (ed.), *¿Cómo renacen las democracias?* (Buenos
   Aires, Emecé, 1985); J. Corradi, *The Fitful Republic: Economy, Society and Politics in Argentina* (Boulder, Westview Press, 1985); T. Halperin Donghi, *La larga
   agonía de la Argentina peronista* (Buenos Aires, Ariel, 1995).
4 See G. O'Donnell, 'Un juego imposible: competiciones y coaliciones entre partidos políticos en la Argentina, 1955–1966', in O'Donnell, *Modernización y
   Autoritarismo*.
5 For an insightful comparative analysis of the economic conditions and political
   development in Latin America during the 1960s and the 1990s, see J. C. Torre,
   'America Latina, el gobierno de la democracia en tiempos difíciles' (Buenos Aires,
   Instituto Torcuato Di Tella, 1994).
6 It is important to stress that, according to this approach, corporations are pictured as institutions – such as the military, trade unions, the Catholic Church and
   business organisations – merely interested in defending their particular social
   interests and therefore incapable of articulating different social demands.
7 See E. Kvaternik, 'Sobre partidos y democracia en la Argentina entre 1955 y
   1966', *Desarrollo Económico*, 71 (October–December 1978); C. Smulovitz,
   Oposición y gobierno. Los años de Frondizi (Buenos Aires, CEAL, 1988); 'En
   búsqueda de la fórmula perdida: Argentina, 1955–1966', *Desarrollo Económico*,
   121 (April–June 1991).
8 See M. Cavarozzi, *Autoritarismo y democracia, 1955–1983* (Buenos Aires,
   CEAL, 1983), and 'Los ciclos políticos en la Argentina desde 1955', in G.
   O'Donnell, P. Schmitter and L. Whitehead (eds), *Transitions from Authoritarian
   Rule. Latin America* (Baltimore, Johns Hopkins University Press, 1986).
9 See S. Amaral and M. Ben Plotkin (eds), *Perón del exilio al poder* (San Martín,
   Cántaro, 1993); Halperín Donghi, *La larga agonía*; D. James, *Resistance and
   Integration. Peronism and the Argentine Working Class 1946–1976* (Cambridge,
   Cambridge University Press, 1988); C. Smulovitz, 'La eficacia como crítica y
   utopía. Notas sobre la caída de Illia', *Desarrollo Económico*, 131 (October–
   December 1993).
10 Although some debate has taken place between the authors representing the two
   main approaches we are discussing here, the debate did not variegate the fundamental position of each party but reinforced it. See, for example, O'Donnell, 'Un
   juego imposible'; Kvaternik, 'Sobre partidos y democracia'; C. Smulovitz, 'El

sistema de partidos en la Argentina: modelo para armar', *Desarrollo Económico*, 101 (April–June 1986).

11 O'Donnell, 'Estado y alianzas'.

12 Cavarozzi, *Autoritarismo y democracia*, p. 8.

13 James, *Resistance and Integration*, p. 16.

14 Laclau, 'Populist rupture', p. 91.

15 For example, Perón was referred to as the 'fugitive tyrant' or the 'deposed dictator' by the press and there was an opposition magazine called Pero.... For a good account of Perón's and Peronism's political tribulations after 1955 see C. Uriarte, *Almirante Cero. Biografía no autorizada de Emilio Eduardo Massera* (Buenos Aires, Planeta, 1992).

16 Mario Amadeo, quoted in R. Guardo, *Horas difíciles* (Buenos Aires, Editorial Del Autor, 1963), p. 50.

17 Uriarte, *Almirante Cero*, p. 13.

18 E. Laclau and C. Mouffe, *Hegemony and Socialist Strategy* (London, Verso, 1985), p. 136.

19 Laclau, 'Populist rupture', p. 91.

20 E. Laclau, *Emancipation(s)* (London, Verso, 1996), p. 32.

21 Laclau and Mouffe, *Hegemony and Socialist Strategy*, p. 85.

3 *Steve Bastow*

Inter-war French fascism and the neo-socialism of Marcel Déat: the emergence of a 'third way'

The focus of this chapter is the neo-socialism of Marcel Déat, a revised version of socialism which he developed from the mid-1920s as a reaction to the dislocatory effects of the increasing disjuncture between Marxist theory and the trends of capitalist society,[1] expanding the contingent pole of the dualism between the logic of necessity and the logic of contingency which Laclau and Mouffe have shown to underpin Marxist theory.[2] Fusing Durkheimian sociology with Marxism, Déat viewed the social domain as an ensemble of institutions embodying both spiritual and material elements,[3] of which economic institutions played only one, albeit a temporarily leading, role.[4] He called on socialists to gather together, not only working-class forces, but also republican and democratic ones, around a 'plan of action' (nationalisation, financial measures, the reorganisation of education, and so on), showing the threat of finance capitalism to the middle classes and that no true democracy could exist as long as such forces were not disciplined.[5] This break with economism led to a reconceptualisation of the state, no longer perceived as necessarily an instrument of class domination, but as the site of a political contestation with a right-wing authoritarianism promoting an economic nationalism on behalf of finance capitalism.[6] In turn, this suggested the possibility of a transformation to socialism via the state in a capitalist regime, gradually relieving capital from the reins of power.[7] The state could use its resources to 'give direction to the economy instead of submitting to it'.[8] A first step was the occupation of governmental power by socialist parties across Europe, enabling them to impose a socialist rationality upon the production process, and to break the links which capitalism had forged with the state.[9] This 'socialisation of power' would be followed by the socialisation of profit, through the regularisation of the market,[10] then that of property, at which point the state would be replaced by the democratic anti-capitalist institutions of the co-operatives and trade unions whose development the state was to encourage in the first two stages.[11]

In 1933, Déat and two fellow neo-socialists, Barthélemy Montagnon and Adrien Marquet, argued at the French Socialist Party (the *Section Française de l'Internationale Ouvrière*, the French Section of the Workers International, henceforth SFIO) congress that national action was a first priority.[12] Capitalism, because of the economic crisis, was no longer capable of establishing an international economic order.[13] Internationalism was not abandoned,[14] but the establishment of any international socialist framework was deemed dependent upon the establishment of a nationally managed economy.[15] This would then enable the construction of an economically organised Europe, which, should they abandon dictatorship, could incorporate Italy, Germany and possibly even the USSR.

Mobilisation around this programme would eventually lead to the expulsion of Déat and a number of fellow-travellers from the party in November 1933, Déat and other neo-socialists then forming the *Parti Socialiste de France* (the Socialist Party of France, henceforth PSdF). In the light of a perceived worsening of the domestic crisis, evidenced by riots on 6 February 1934, when a number of political movements tried to storm parliament, the PSdF called for mobilisation around a national 'Plan'. This necessitated: the supplementation of parliamentary democracy by corporate assemblies, enabling business to 'be submitted to the control of the nation',[16] and regional assemblies; the replacement of 'old' political parties, which mobilised only at the parliamentary level, by 'new' ones mobilising at both the latter level and that of civil society;[17] and the strengthening of state management of the economy.[18] Corporatism was claimed to not entail fascism, as it was not necessarily the threat to individual liberty it had been in Italy, Germany and Austria.[19]

During the German Occupation of the Second World War, however, Déat would become an advocate of collaboration,[20] and of a one-party state.[21] How are we to understand this development? I shall argue that approaches to neo-socialism have been unable to explain this because they are trapped in essentialist modes of conceptualisation which attempt to read neo-socialism from the perspective of an ideal-type fascism, giving it a meaning which is unalterably fixed from the moment of its development. After showing why such approaches are unable to explain how neo-socialists could end up as collaborators, I will then show how an approach rooted in the discourse theory of Laclau and Mouffe both helps to resolve this problem and offers a way forward to explaining the political careers of other proponents of 'third way' politics.

Approaches to neo-socialism

Analyses of neo-socialism reflect two divergent approaches to fascism in inter-war France. One strand of analysis minimises the existence of fascism in inter-war France. René Rémond suggests that although between the wars and during the Second World War there was a French fascism, incarnated in a small number of organisations, only one of these, Doriot's *Parti Populaire*

Français (French Popular Party, henceforth PPF), had a mass character of the fascist type.[22] Even then, Rémond does not see the PPF as 'fascist' in the period before the collaboration, a 'fascism' which is similarly denied to the neo-socialism of Marcel Déat.[23] Inter-war French nationalist groupings, principally incarnated in the monarchist *Action Française* (French Action, henceforth AF) and the leagues, had nothing specifically fascist about them. The most important of the leagues, the *Croix-de-Feu* (Cross of Fire, henceforth CF) could be assimilated neither to the Nazi party nor to Italian fascism.[24] The doctrinal content of the leagues derived from French nationalism at the turn of the century. Consequently, he argues, the 'fascist danger' claimed by the left in the 1930s must be seen as an exaggeration.[25] Where one can talk of a fascist influence, it is a question of the impregnation of a fascist 'spirit'. Girardet makes a similar argument.[26] What emerges is a picture of a France in the 1930s minimally touched by fascism. For such an approach, the neo-socialism of Déat in the 1930s is not explicable from the fascist 'paradigm'. Towards the end of the 1960s, the work of Soucy, Allardyce, Weber and Nolte challenged this orthodoxy,[27] suggesting that fascism provided a direct link between the French nationalism of the turn of the century and the intellectual and political behaviour of inter-war France. Soucy argued that the orthodoxy in France masked essential similarities between conservatives and fascists, developing the thesis that fascism was a radicalised form of conservatism, so that a number of significant 'fascist' movements could be found in inter-war France, including the AF, Valois's Faisceau, and the CF/ *Parti Social Français* (French Social Party, henceforth PSF).[28] Thus, it was false to see the French 'fascism' of the 1920s and 1930s as an implantation from abroad, and French fascism was much more extensive than had previously been supposed. Into this category Soucy would place the neo-socialism of Déat, although it is not seen as one of the more important of such movements.[29]

Similarly, though for different reasons, Sternhell makes a link between turn-of-the-century nationalism and fascism. This nationalism was claimed to announce a new discourse of the right, founding its 'organic' society on the mobilisation of the masses and on the integration of the proletariat with the nationalist community, implying a minimum of social justice,[30] prefiguring the rise of fascism. This pre-fascist nationalism takes the form of the discourse of the 'revolutionary right',[31] whose exponents have in common a revolt against liberal democracy and bourgeois society in general. For Sternhell, it is in France that a fusion is operated for the first time between nationalism and revolutionary syndicalism, resulting in his conclusion that French fascism was not imported.

These discourses of the 'revolutionary right' merge into a 'national socialism' of which France is the country of origin. Sternhell's later work follows this anti-Marxist current through to the period of the 1930s and 1940s.[32] He argues that the 1914–18 war acted as a catalyst for the fascistic tendencies already present in the 'revolutionary right', leading to the creation of an 'ideal-type' fascist ideology, no less coherent than any other modern ideology.[33] Unlike Soucy, however, who tends to highlight the social conservative elements of fascism, Sternhell argues that this fascism, a synthesis of nationalism and socialism enabled by a mutual adherence to an 'anti-materialism',[34] owes more to its left-wing component than to that of the ultra-right.[35] Nevertheless, Sternhell considers as fascist every individual attached to this antimaterialist current, those coming from both nationalism and from socialism. He thus traces a path from the break with traditional conservatism effected by Barrès through to the 'fascists' of inter-war-period France. Already in Barrès, argues Sternhell, can be found the ingredients which later form the ideology of the Faisceau in the 1920s, and that of such as Déat in the 1930s and 1940s, at the intersection of nationalism and revolutionary syndicalism: 'In Déat's writings, one does not find a single idea that had not, in one way or another, been expressed by Barrès fifty years before.'[36]

'Fascism' and neo-socialism

Both of these approaches' explanations of neo-socialism essentialise the meaning of neo-socialist discourse because their analyses are overdetermined by reference to the phenomenon of fascism. The bottom line of the 'spiritualist' thesis is that fascism is external to French political practice of the inter-war period. The 'fascist' thesis is that fascism must be seen as having a lineage internal to France itself. The first thesis tries to completely break the links between fascism and the discourses of the French radical right and left of the 1930s, while the latter tries to fix some necessary logic between these same discourses and the phenomenon of fascism, to the point of arguing that fascism is a phenomenon whose point of origin is France. Both of these 'schools' operate in a field whose 'nodal point' is fascism; that is, the elements to be analysed are viewed with reference to a core of values associated with fascism, although what constitutes this core varies in the analyses.

Analysts such as Sternhell produce a teleological reading that claims that the position outlined by Déat in 1933 is already "fascist". Neo-socialism forms 'not in 1942, but from 1933, an ideological ensemble whose nature is difficult to mistake',[37] and of necessity leads to the stance taken by Déat during the war. This is a gross misreading of the initial stages of neo-socialist discourse. A number of points should make this clear. First, in 1933, Déat has no clearly outlined notion of a totalitarian state. There is a certain tension between the state and the wishes of the individual, but this is a tension that has not yet been resolved in a totalitarian direction. Déat, on Durkheimian lines, envisages in *Perspectives socialistes* the formation of a dual collectivity, of a balance between State and the intermediary organisation of unions and co-operatives. By 1934, the intermediary organisations proclaimed by Déat are corporative, but at no time in this period does he reject the need for parliamentary institutions, even if he does suggest that they need reforming in order to conform to the demands of a new stage in societal evolution.

Secondly, Sternhell claims that neo-socialism's falling back on the nation 'obliges whomsoever desires to influence history' to accept 'the primacy of the nation'.[38] It is true that the logic of establishing cross-class alliances led Déat to privilege national solidarity rather than class as the only way to gather together such fragmented social agents. Thus, 'the revolution to be made is no longer a class revolution but a national revolution'.[39] However, Déat defined the nation in the 1930s in non-racial terms,[40] and explicitly rejected the racially based nationalism associated with fascism.[41] Moreover, the primacy of the national framework was purely contingent, and was not presented as an absolute primordiality. International action by the left was not denied. Indeed, the coexistence of a tension between nationalism and internationalism is not unique to neo-socialism, but can be traced back through the lineage of French socialism.[42]

Thirdly, there is no leadership principle at work in the PSdF. This is clearly missing from the institutional structure of the PSdF, in terms both of the party's constitution and of its day-to-day practice.[43] Further, in the pre-war Déat we find no articulation of the virtues of war. Indeed, Déat is a highly partisan pacifist with no desire to form the nation through the 'virile heroism' characteristic of war.

It seems clear, then, that neo-socialism was not fascist from its inception, unless one is willing to accept extremely broad definitions of fascism, such as Sternhell's equation, following Valois, that 'nationalism + socialism = fascism', or Griffin's definition of fascism as 'a palingenetic form of populist ultra-nationalism',[44] which suggests that fascism is not necessarily totalitarian, racially based, or imperialist. Not only does this inscribe movements like Déat's in a chain of equivalences which dissolves key differences with other movements, but it is ahistorical, and thus fails to explain how neo-socialism could move from a clearly anti-fascist position to one of collaboration. However, the 'Rémond school', in simply breaking all links between the positions of such groupings as neo-socialism and their subsequent wartime collaboration, offers no grounds for understanding why such a transformation in the discourse of neo-socialism took place.

What is needed, then, is an approach which does not take for granted the fascist character of neo-socialism, but seeks to show how it was transformed in ways which enabled that transformation. Philippe Burrin has attempted this.[45] However, its relation to an 'ideal-type' model of fascism weakens his explanation. Defining fascism as one of a 'family of ideologies of national gathering' characterised by the formula 'neither right nor left' and based in an antiliberalism which unites society around 'new structures of solidarity' and rejects 'conflict and division as fundamental aspects of all societies',[46] Burrin argues that neo-socialism, because it was based on an 'intense vision of popular movement', sweeping the people into a struggle against the crisis and for national renovation, lent itself to seduction by fascism. This was reinforced prior to the war by continuing frustration brought about by lack of domestic political success and the disaffection toward the regime which this caused.

Consequently, Déat was 'dazzled' by fascism, fascist regimes becoming 'the guarantee of viability' of the neo-socialist project, and 'the assured source' of its stimulation.[47] The support for both collaboration and the formation of a single-party state sees the final triumph of this process of Nazi seduction.[48] Thus, the move towards totalitarianism for Déat, and socialist planists in general, was a question of 'a conjunction between the search for a national socialism resolving the French crisis and certain aspects of fascism' which 'was brought about by the proximity of certain ideological plans, and above all by the subterranean effect of irrational values of dynamism and activism.'[49] However, even then it is a question of a very fragile commitment to fascist ideology.[50]

However, this formulation never really shows how the transition from one configuration of neo-socialism to the other is effected, lapsing into vague suggestions of a Déat 'dazzled' and seduced by Nazism, crystallising proto-fascist elements held to be contained in neo-socialism. But what is the evidence for this seduction? Simply the fact that the nationalism of neo-socialism is seen as the first stage of a process which could lead to fascism. We are faced here with the reintroduction of a surreptitious teleologism. The only other factor mentioned is the inexplicable category of 'the subterranean effect of irrational values of dynamism and activism'.

The discursive configuration of neo-socialism

I would argue that the transition from the revision of socialism in the 1920s to the collaboration of the war period can best be explained by a discursive analysis of neo-socialism. This reveals tensions within the discursive configuration of neo-socialism whose contingent resolution were resolved in ways which enabled support, if not for fascism, then for a form of totalitarian rule.

Let us begin by asking who the 'friends' and 'enemies' of the first formulation of neo-socialism are. Initially neo-socialism articulates the following *elements* which become *moments* of the neo-socialist discourse: the anti-capitalist alliance; the changed perception of the state; the need for the occupation of governmental power; the gradual syndicalisation of production utilising the process of rationalisation currently being undergone by capitalism; concerted international action between countries led by socialist governments to bring about a European order of rational distribution; pacifism. This discursive configuration was organised around the nodal point of the need to occupy governmental power.

The elements intended to be mobilised by such a programme, the 'friends', include those elements of the cross-class alliance, the producers, incorporating the working class, the peasantry, artisans, businessmen, small and medium industrialists, the liberal professions, especially civil servants, together with a heterogeneous category of 'consumers'.[51] These are to be mobilised by parliamentary activity, as well as by the trade unions, who were much more open to the idea of state intervention in the economy. Elements within the domestic and foreign political parties of the left, both the Socialist Party and other left and centre-left parties, were all seen as potential allies. Excluded from such a configuration are both finance capitalism and the political forms supportive of it, fascism and the reactionary right, and communism. Indeed, as we noted earlier, the programme explicitly aims to enter governmental power in order to prevent reactionary and authoritarian forces from controlling the institutions of state.

From the start, however, there are three main tensions within this discursive formulation which enable reformulations of the discursive configuration of neo-socialism. First, neo-socialism reproduces a clear tension between order and democracy which is inscribed within socialist discourse as a whole,[52] with a strong state being necessary for the transition to a syndicalist democracy. The impact of the Depression on France, and the emergence of a Nazi government in January 1933, led to a stronger emphasis on the need for 'order' and 'authority', Déat talking of the need for 'syndicalist or corporative discipline' to be imposed on French society. A second tension was that between nationalism and internationalism. The balance within this duality swung away from international towards national action as the Depression hit France, leading to the privileging of national solidarity, the nation replacing class as the motor for revolution. The initial configuration of neo-socialism did not necessitate the move towards privileging national solidarity, but the dual imperatives of national and international action did open it up as a possibility. A third tension, whose importance would become apparent only towards the end of the 1930s, was that between the socialist end and the means for achieving it, which was produced by the blurring of the divide introduced by Déat's expansion of the contingent pole of Marxist discourse.

In the period 1933–34 the discursive configuration of neo-socialism is reformulated, along the axes of the first two tensions noted above, around: the prioritisation of political action within the framework of the nation and the call for a nationally managed economy (planning), on which any international order is now predicated; national solidarity rather than class as the mode of political mobilisation; the need to supplement parliament with functional and regional forms of democracy (corporatism and decentralisation), though this is seen as voluntaristic not compulsory, as a stage on the road to the syndicalisation of production; pacifism. This reconfiguration is organised around the nodal point of planism, the idea that state planning will both enable the technocratic organisation and disciplining of capital, whilst at the same time acting as a voluntaristic myth uniting disparate social forces.

When one looks at the social elements which such a reconfiguration attempts to interpellate, however, one finds little difference. The political frontier established by the second phase of neo-socialism is more or less the same, although Déat does lay more emphasis on the non-class character of the political alliance to be constructed as a result of the prioritisation of action within the national arena. Greater emphasis is given to extraparliamentary mobilisation, but parliamentary mobilisation is not rejected, and the elements to be mobilised are on the left. Neo-socialism still establishes a political frontier placing Nazism and fascism, the agents of plutocracy, as the 'enemy'.[53] This is revealed both by Déat's rejection of the equation made by Nazism between race and nation, and his denial that corporatism need be the threat to individual liberty it had been in Italy and Germany.

Only towards the end of the 1930s does one begin to see a reconfiguration of the political frontier of neo-socialism in such a way that Nazism could become a partner in the task of the transition to socialism. This involves a number of factors.

First, the failure of neo-socialism to hegemonise the mainstream left in 1934–35 around the doctrine of planism, due to the success of the Popular Front strategy. Although as a member of the Popular Front, Déat continued to lobby for his ideas, he was a marginal figure. Déat's increasing isolation from the forces of the mainstream left estranged him to some extent from sympathisers who might well have encouraged the development of the democratic aspects of neo-socialism.

Secondly, the extent to which the Popular Front was a vehicle for the production of an anti-Nazi foreign policy on behalf of Soviet needs, seen as promoting an anti-fascist crusade mirroring the anti-bolshevism of the right,[54] led to an increasing antagonism towards communism. As a result Déat began to argue that pacifism was the only way to avoid a domestic civil war between anti-communists and anti-fascists, and the nodal point of neo-socialist discourse became that of pacifism versus bellicism. This introduced an element of ambiguity into the frontier between neo-socialism and reactionary forces. The split which pacifism suggests between socialists and communists led Déat to argue that the left majority must open itself to a large section of the right, enlarging the national gathering from a *Front populaire* to a *Front national*,[55] although he claimed this did not imply an adoption of right-wing attitudes and policies,[56] and denied holding any blanket anti-communism.[57] This enlargement was possible because the anti-Germanism, anti-communism and anti-Semitism of many elements of the right made them open to mobilisation around this theme.

This blurring of the 'friend/ enemy' status of the authoritarian right was furthered by Déat's decision that the nature of the German system was changing. As noted earlier, Déat was not against German or Italian entry into the new European economic order provided that they abandoned dictatorship. Indeed, he saw dictatorship as synonymous with autarkic national economies.[58] Thus, any perceived move away from autarky would be interpreted as a move away both from dictatorship and from the war mentality. As Germany moved eastward, he incorporated Germany into a proposed system of international co-operation.[59] Moreover, he argued that the 1939 signing of the pact of non-aggression and friendship between Germany and the USSR confirmed that they possessed the same structure and methods of regime; that Germany and Italy had moved in the direction of socialism.[60] By the time of the collapse of France, Déat was convinced that such a transformation had indeed occurred.[61]

By now, therefore, it is no longer clear who exactly the 'enemy' is for neo-socialism. This is rendered even more obscure by the fact that Déat, who has consistently positioned big capital as the 'enemy', is already opposed to the form of 'plutocratic' regime found in the West, only supporting the Western alliance as a strategy against any German expansion westward.[62]

Between 1936 and 1939, neo-socialist discourse was reconfigured again, incorporating Germany and Italy into the international economic order as they are moving in the direction of socialism, expanding the national gathering to include right-wing elements, forming a *Front national* based around pacifism, and increasingly viewing communism as antagonistic to his proposals. This new configuration is organised around the 'nodal point' of pacifism versus bellicism.

As the war becomes increasingly likely, a further shift in the duality between order and democracy takes place. Partly conditioned by an awareness of authoritarian exigencies of a wartime situation, Déat suggests that, temporarily at least, there is a need for discipline, for order. Detecting an increasing sense of disorder amongst the masses,[63] he suggests that totalitarianism is inevitable if war breaks out.[64] The only concession to democratic control is the statement that the system will be one which is not 'created according to the fantasy of the governors'.[65] If the governed do not know what to do, however, the governors must be allowed to put the general will into practice.[66] Such a situation was deemed by Déat to have arisen in the period following the collapse of France, although he emphasised that the totalitarian regime represented a 'stage' which would be transcended.[67]

The introduction of a 'totalitarian stage' was enabled precisely by neo-socialism's expansion of the contingent pole of the dualism between the logic of necessity and the logic of contingency which blurred the distinction between the socialist end and the means of achieving it. Support for some form of totalitarianism does not necessarily follow the adoption of such a view of the historical process. However, the blurring of the boundary between capitalism and socialism enables its incorporation into the framework of transition. Hence Déat's suggestion in 1940 that war 'statism' was the first stage in the erection of a 'new' Europe without calling his political vision into question.[68]

By the time of the period of collaboration, neo-socialism was further reconfigured, expanding the stages prior to the achievement of socialism to include a totalitarian stage, the need for a one-party state, and support for war on the side of Germany. The 'nodal point' was transformed once again, the discourse of neo-socialism now being 'sutured' around the vision of a European 'new order'. It is this reconfiguration which breaks down the positioning of Nazism as the enemy, enabling Déat to envisage the wartime collaboration and stimulating him to advocate a one-party state.

Four distinct configurations of neo-socialism, then, can be identified in the period before the advocation of collaboration in 1940, organised around four different nodal points: the need to occupy governmental power, planism, pacifism, then finally, the new European order. If the first configuration of neo-socialist discourse opened up a number of possibilities for development they did not entail either the wartime collaboration or Déat's adoption of relatively unreconstructed Nazi elements. Such developments represent the strategic adoption of a number of possibilities which it opened up. The relation between the neo-socialist Déat who breaks with the SFIO in 1933 and that of 1941 who argues for a single-party state and collaboration with the Nazis is not one of logical necessity, but of a process of argumentation through which a series of possible avenues was followed up, leaving other possible avenues ignored.

Conclusion

The political career of Marcel Déat, and the ideas of neo-socialism, clearly underwent a high degree of (non-teleological) evolution. Approaches to the analysis of Déat and neo-socialism have consistently failed to explain this because their analyses were overdetermined by a focus on fascism. Minimising the role played by fascism in 1930s France simply makes Déat's collaboration inexplicable. Teleologising Déat's political career, as Soucy and Sternhell do, systematically misinterprets neo-socialism in its earlier phase.

Déat's is not the only case in point. One might likewise analyse the political development of the so-called 'nonconformists' of the 1930s,[69] including figures such as Jean-Pierre Maxence, Robert Brasillach and Thierry Maulnier, where one finds a similar debate. Sternhell claims these 'nonconformists' to have been inherently fascist,[70] while other analyses deny this.[71]

Similar problems emerge regarding a figure like Bertrand de Jouvenel – also linked with the *Librairie Valois*, which published a number of his books[72] who was also concerned to develop an *économie dirigée*, contributed to many of the same journals and newspapers – *La Voix, L'Europe nouvelle, L'OEuvre, La République* – manifested a certain degree of fascination with Hitler, and came to mobilise for a period in the PPF. Like Déat, de Jouvenel was accused of fascism by Sternhell. Not only did de Jouvenel take Sternhell to court over this, but many analysts defended him against the charge of being a fascist, notably Raymond Aron.[73]

It seems to me that the question, however, is wrongly posed. One should

not ask whether such figures were fascist or not in the 1930s, but what political possibilities were opened up by the ideas which they developed, and how,
in a given context, some avenues were pursued whilst others were closed,
such that, at a certain point some of the figures attracted to a 'third way' politics developed a certain attachment to a fascist vision of the third way.

Analysis of the conceptual tensions within the discourse of neo-socialism
in its initial development, together with an awareness of the political terrain
within which it was operating, enables us to see how the process which led
neo-socialists to their eventual collaboration with Nazi Germany was one of
contingent transitions, that is, of successive re-articulations which took
place within an horizon of open possibilities. A similar approach would also
throw more light on the political development of other 'nonconformists' of
the 1930s.

Notes

1 On which see E. Laclau and C. Mouffe, *Hegemony and Socialist Strategy* (London, Verso, 1985), Ch. 1. See also H. Stuart Hughes, *Consciousness and Society*
   (London, Paladin, 1974), Ch. 3.
2 Laclau and Mouffe, *Hegemony and Socialist Strategy*.
3 See especially M. Déat, 'La définition du socialisme d'après E. Durkheim', *La Vie
   Socialiste* (henceforth LVS), 14 January 1922; 'Matérialisme historique et science sociale', *LVS*, 30 September 1922, 1–2; 'Marxisme et science des moeurs',
   LVS, 7 October 1922; 'Morale de classe et culture humaine', *Le Populaire*, 10
   June 1929, 1–2.
4 M. Déat, 'Religion et Régime social', *LVS*, 12 January 1929, p. 7.
5 M. Déat, 'Bolchevisme et socialisme', *LVS*, 15 January 1927, 8–10; 'Notes pour
   l'action', *LVS*, 21 July 1928, 8–12, 28 July 1928, 3–10.
6 See M. Déat, 'Puissance de la logique', *Le Populaire*, 26 June 1929, 1–2.
7 M. Déat, 'Socialistes et Jacobins', *LVS*, 8 June 1929, 8–10.
8 M. Déat, 'Pouvoir politique et puissance économique', *LVS*, 7 December 1929,
   9–10.
9 M. Déat, 'La séparation du capitalisme et de l'Etat', *Le Populaire*, 31 August
   1929, 2.
10 M. Déat, *Perspectives socialistes* (Paris, Librairie Valois, 1930), pp. 211–12.
11 *Ibid.*, pp. 224–6.
12 Se B. Montagnon *et al.*, *Ordre, Autorité, Nation* (Paris, Grasset, 1933).
13 M. Déat, 'Les chances de l'unité', *Le Populaire*, 19 July 1933, 6.
14 This domestic political strategy was linked to a broader international one of
   concerted action by socialist parties in their national struggles with capital,
   pushing countries towards agreements, ententes and international cartels, initiating a European order of rational distribution of resources and work. See, M.
   Déat, 'Le paix par le pain', *Le Populaire*, 16 August 1930, 6, and 'SOS à l'IOS',
   Le Populaire, 14 October 1930, 6. Such international economic reorganisation
   is necessary to prevent a return to the nationalistic imperialism of the pre-war
   period. Concomitantly, therefore, economic reorganisation is impossible with

nationalist, authoritarian dictatorships, but can only result from the prior creation of economic agreements by democratic (i.e. socialist) governments. See M. Déat, 'L'Europe ou la Guerre', *Le Populaire*, 13 November 1930, 6; 'La crise Allemande: I – le problème des crédits et la politique extérieure', *LVS*, 24 October 1931, 11; report of Déat's speech to the SFIO Congress, *Le Populaire*, 31 May 1932, 2.

15 M. Déat, 'Notre "Nationalisme"', *L'OEuvre*, 26 July 1933, 1, 4. Déat explicitly argues that his ideas do not represent an embracing of aggressive nationalism.

16 M. Déat, 'Le Plan de Man et les perspectives socialistes', *L'Europe Nouvelle*, 17 March 1934, 284–6.

17 See M. Déat, 'Concept nouveau de l'action politique', *Notre Temps*, 24 December 1933, 1–2; 'Fin des vieux partis', *Notre Temps*, 14 February 1934, 1–2; 'Nous resterons indépendants', *Paris–Demain*, 24 February 1934, 2.

18 For full details of the PsdF's 'planisme' see Comité du Plan, *Le Plan Français, doctrine et plan d'action* (Paris, Fasquelle, 1935); Comité du Plan, *Une nouvelle France, ses principes et ses institutions* (Paris, Fasquelle, 1936).

19 M. Déat, 'Syndicalisme et Corporation', *LVS*, 17 March 1934, 2–3.

20 M. Déat, 'Au pied du mur', *L'OEuvre*, 5 July 1940, 1.

21 On this see J-P. Cointet, 'Marcel Déat et le Parti Unique (été 1940)', *Revue d'Histoire de la Deuxième Guerre Mondiale*, 91 (July 1973), 1–23; A. Prost, 'Le rapport de Déat en faveur d'un parti national unique, essai d'analyse lexicale', *Revue française de science politique*, 23:5 (October 1973), 933–72.

22 R. Rémond, *Les Droites en France* (Paris, Aubier-Montaigne, 1982), p. 207.

23 *Ibid.*, p. 217.

24 *Ibid.*, pp. 213–14.

25 *Ibid.*, p. 217.

26 R. Girardet, 'Note sur l'esprit d'un fascisme français (1934–1939)', *Revue française de science politique*, 5:3 (July–September 1955), 529–30.

27 R. Soucy, 'The Nature of Fascism in France', *Journal of Contemporary History*, 1:1 (1966), 27–55; R. Soucy, *Fascism in France: the Case of Maurice Barrès* (Berkeley, University of California Press, 1972); E. Weber, *L'Action française* (Paris, Stock, 1964); G. Allardyce, *The Place of Fascism in European History* (Englewood Cliffs, Prentice Hall, 1971); E. Nolte, *Three Faces of Fascism: Action Francaise, Italian Fascism, National Socialism* (London, Weidenfeld & Nicolson, 1965).

28 See R. Soucy, *French Fascism: The First Wave* (London, Yale University Press, 1976) and *French Fascism: The Second Wave* (London, Yale University Press, 1995).

29 As the small amount of space devoted to Déat in his *French Fascism: The Second Wave* indicates.

30 See Z. Sternhell, *Neither Right Nor Left: Fascist Ideology in France* (Berkeley, University of California Press, 1986), pp. 25–6.

31 Z. Sternhell, *La Droite révolutionnaire, 1885–1914* (Paris, Seuil, 1978).

32 Z. Sternhell, *Ni droite, ni gauche* (Paris, Seuil, 1983).

33 *Ibid.*, pp. 297–8.

34 *Ibid.*, p. 291.

35 See Z. Sternhell, 'Sur le fascisme et sa variante française', *Le Débat*, 32 (November 1984), 34–5.

36 Sternhell, *Neither Right Nor Left*, p. 25. To see the continuing influence of this kind of approach note R. Eatwell, *Fascism: A History* (London, Chatto & Windus, 1995), p. 170.
37 Sternhell, 'Sur le fascisme', p. 39.
38 *Ibid.*, p. 38, n. 17.
39 M. Déat, 'Où en sommes-nous?' *Paris-Demain*, 17 March 1934, 1–2. See also M. Déat 'Catalogue des difficutés', *Paris-Demain*, 9 June 1934, 1; 'Epreuve de la démocratie', *LVS*, 10 March 1934, 1–3.
40 See M. Déat, Le droit à le réparation, *Le Populaire*, 28 March 1930, 2.
41 M. Déat, 'Notre "Nationalisme"', *L'OEuvre*, 26 July 1933, 1, 4.
42 See R. Girardet, *Le Nationalisme Français, 1871–1914* (Paris, Seuil, 1983), pp. 11–16.
43 For the constitution of the party see *La Vie Socialiste*, 2 December 1933, 3–5.
44 R. Griffin, *The Nature of Fascism* (London, Pinter, 1991), p. 26.
45 P. Burrin, *La Dérive Fasciste. Doriot, Déat, Bergery, 1933–1945* (Paris, Seuil, 1986), p. 157.
46 P. Burrin, 'La France dans le champ magnétique des fascismes', *Le Débat*, 32 (November 1984), 53.
47 Burrin, *La Dérive*, p. 276.
48 *Ibid.*, p. 338.
49 *Ibid.*, pp. 450–1.
50 *Ibid.*, p. 453.
51 See Déat, 'Notes pour l'action'.
52 See G. Lichtheim, *Marxism in Modern France* (London, Columbia University Press, 1966), pp. 14–15.
53 See Déat, 'Nous resterons indépendants'.
54 See M. Déat, 'Où en est le Front populaire?', *Le Front*, 15 August 1936, 2.
55 M. Déat, 'Conditions de la sécurité française. II. Recherche des forces', *L'Europe nouvelle*, 18 July 1936, 729–31.
56 M. Déat, 'Les tâches de l'USR', *Le Front*, 22 October 1936, 1, 3.
57 'Les débats du Congrès National', *Le Front*, 29 October 1936, 2.
58 Déat, 'Puissance de la logique'.
59 See M. Déat, 'Il n'y a plus qu'une politique de paix', *Le Front*, 6 May 1938, 1, 3; 'Quand le problème des colonies sera posé par l'Allemagne', *L'OEuvre*, 10 October 1938, 4; 'Veillons au salut de l'Empire', *L'OEuvre*, 21 November 1938, 1, 7.
60 M. Déat, 'Qui contaminera l'autre?', *L'OEuvre*, 31 August 1939, 4. Déat qualifies this by suggesting that the Nazis are split between elements attracted by communism and traditional conservatives. If this latter force can be contained, Déat foresees good prospects for peace.
61 See M. Déat, 'Ce sont aussi des révolutionnaires', *L'OEuvre*, 28 August 1940, 1.
62 See M. Déat, special supplement, *Tribune de France*, 2 June 1939, 15.
63 *Ibid.*, pp. 11–12.
64 M. Déat, 'Régime de guerre, régime totalitaire', *L'OEuvre*, 21 May 1939, 1, 4.
65 *Ibid.*, p. 4. Rather contradictorily, however, as late as June 1939 Déat would describe the totalitarian system as profoundly un-French. See M. Déat, 'Individus et Troupeaux', *La République*, 2 June 1939, 1, 4.
66 The analogies with Rousseau's call for a legislator would be mobilised during the

war by Déat. See M. Déat, 'Jean-Jacques Rousseau, totalitaire', *L'OEuvre*, 21 January 1943, 1–2; 'Critique du suffrage universel', *L'OEuvre*, 23–24 January 1943, 1–2.

67 M. Déat, 'Vocation de la France', *L'OEuvre*, 23 August 1940, 1.
68 M. Déat, 'L'Europe vue de l'Amérique', *L'OEuvre*, 11 March 1940, 1, 4.
69 J-L. Loubet del Bayle, *Les non-conformistes des années 30* (Paris, Seuil, 1969).
70 Sternhell, *Neither Right Nor Left*, Ch. 7.
71 See P. Milza, *Fascisme français. Passé et présent* (Paris, Flammarion, 1987), pp. 201–8.
72 B. de Jouvenel, *L'Economie Dirigée* (Paris, Librairie Valois, 1928), *Vers Les Etats Unis d'Europe* (Paris, Librairie Valois, 1930), *Un plan de valorisation colonial et de collaboration économique* (Paris, Librarie Valois, 1931).
73 See Eric Roussel's introduction to de Jouvenel, *Itinéraire, 1928–1976* (Paris, Plon, 1993), pp. 12–13.

New environmental movements and direct action protest: the campaign against Manchester Airport's second runway

This chapter examines the campaign against the building of Manchester Airport's second runway.[1] The campaign forms an important component of a continuing cycle of new environmental protest that emerged in the UK during the late 1980s and early 1990s.[2] Indeed, while citizen protests and popular mobilisations over the proposed construction and extension of airports are not new,[3] the campaign against the second runway was the first airport protest in Britain in which local residents and a committed group of direct action protesters were linked together. These environmental protesters, who rapidly acquired a folk-hero status, capturing the popular imagination with names such as 'Swampy', 'Animal', 'the Worm' and 'Muppet Dave', were prepared to use sophisticated techniques of bodily risk to obstruct the construction of the proposed runway. This peculiar alliance of traditional middle-class protesters and self-named eco-warriors, 'Vegans and Volvos', as a *Times* leader article put it,[4] with their marked differences of identity, social characteristics, political strategies and tactics, grabbed the attention of the local and national media, and altered popular perceptions about environmental issues.

This chapter describes and evaluates key aspects of the campaign against the building of the second runway. It provides a 'thick description' of the events and logics of this singular case by examining the ways in which residents and eco-warriors were able to overcome their respective collective action problems, and forge a tactical working alliance. However, these descriptions are informed by a series of theoretical concepts that have been carefully constructed using discourse theory and other related theoretical perspectives. The chapter begins by deconstructing the dominant theoretical idioms that have been developed to explain the formation and activities of groups and movements, and then elaborates an integrated theoretical framework with which to attend to the empirical questions we delimit.

Converging paradigms? Developments within rational choice and new social movement approaches

Notwithstanding the substantive and methodological differences amongst pluralist, corporatist, Marxist and New Right theories of groups, the classical rational choice critique of standard group theory focuses on the givenness of groups involved in the policy process. Thus none of the viewpoints tackle what Mancur Olson names the collective action problem, which centres on the existence of 'free-riders' who question the rationality of joining groups because the costs of membership are likely to exceed the benefits they obtain regardless of their involvement.[5] This arises because groups form and mobilise to achieve 'public goods' such as a better environment, which are indivisible and, once attained, not excludable. As Olson puts it succinctly, 'rational self-interested individuals will not act to achieve their common or group interests'.[6] Unless, therefore, the potential size of a group is small, thus facilitating the monitoring of potential free-riders, or unless the group can employ negative and/or positive sanctions against potential free-riders, no groups are likely to emerge in pursuit of their common interests.[7]

This key insight provides one of the important starting points for our rethinking of group formation and mobilisation. Not only does it raise key questions concerning the relationship between individuals and groups, as well as the internal dynamics of groups, it problematises the crucial concept of interests, and how they may be conceived. It argues that latent groups may be undermobilised or not formed at all, and suggests a number of 'supply-side' solutions to these structural impediments. These include the centrality of selective material incentives, the role of political entrepreneurs,[8] the possibility of groups 'piggybacking' on existing organisations, or making use of state resources, all of which reduce or offset the costs of collective action.[9] Nevertheless, there are a number of shortcomings with the classical model of rational choice. One primary difficulty is that it assumes that social agents are self-interested utility maximisers. This assumption suggests that the subjects of their analyses 'are without a history',[10] which means that key questions pertaining to the identities of agents, as well as their agency in relation to social structures, are not addressed and analysed.[11]

One response to this lacuna has been to stress the idea of group identities as one of the means to overcome collective action problems. Dunleavy has introduced the concept of a group identity to capture the potential membership of a prospective group.[12] He also distinguishes between exogenous and endogenous group identity sets, in which the former are defined by external factors independent of any group of people, whereas the latter are the self-willed products of 'like-minded people'. As a rule of thumb, groups with exogenous group identity sets are easier to form and mobilise because they have a more clearly defined membership, thus enabling political entrepreneurs to circumvent more easily the problem of free-riders associated in 'large-n' contexts. Nevertheless, even though Dunleavy introduces the concept of identity sets and group identities to supplement classical arguments, he does not provide a convincing conception of identity. On the contrary, he defines identity in terms of self-interest, and thus does not challenge the instrumental conception of social action and agency associated with rational choice models.

A more radical response to the aporia of classical rational actor approaches has been to problematise their exclusively instrumental conception of action. In his study of the American Civil Rights Movement, Dennis Chong[13] has developed a more fully-fledged heterodox rational choice model of collective action by stressing the social networks within which decisions to join movements and engage in sustained mobilisation are taken. Building upon Hirschman's critique of rational actor models,[14] Chong stresses the importance of the benefits accrued from participating in collective action, as well as the importance of positive and negative sanctions that are predicated on the involvement of actors in particular communities and social networks. This enables him to introduce a broader set of 'non-rational' motivations, such as the importance of status and prestige, to explain why social agents join groups, as well as to account for the rapid demobilisation and collapse of movements – so-called 'bandwagon effects' – that occur in certain social conditions.

Chong and Hirschman push us toward the more sociologically oriented social movement literature. Classical theories of social movements explain movements by reference to general theoretical laws of society and history.[15] This subsumptive method neglects the historically specific meanings and practices generated by movements, and fails to account for the diversity of identities and agencies associated with contemporary movements.[16] By contrast, Alain Touraine's 'sociology of action' approach draws attention to 'the behaviour of an actor guided by cultural orientations and set within social relations defined by an unequal connection with the social control of orientations'.[17] According to Touraine, social movements are 'the organised collective behaviour of a class actor struggling against his class adversary for the social control of historicity in a concrete community'.[18] Social movements thus contain three important elements: the identity of the actor, the definition of an opponent, and the 'stakes' of the conflict, which are equivalent to the 'cultural totality'. These three elements express, according to Touraine, the central conflict of any given societal type.[19]

While Touraine and other new social movement theorists transcend the subsumptive and narrow positions of the classical tradition,[20] their reformulations are not without difficulty. Beginning on a conceptual level, although Touraine and others stress the concepts of identity and ideology in their analyses, the concepts themselves are not properly clarified. Furthermore, Touraine does not abandon the idea of a macro-theoretical sociological synthesis with which to understand and evaluate contemporary social movements. His concept of a programmed society functions as a grand synthetical backdrop by which to judge whether or not social movements are successful or not. Thirdly, Touraine stresses the cultural and ideological dimensions of social movements, both for his evaluation of their success in achieving 'progressive' effects, and by stressing the importance of their own self-understandings as the key to explaining their emergence and formation. However, as Scott argues, this precludes the analysis of the different strategies movements may articulate in pursuing their goals, as well as the political context – what resource mobilisation theorists call the political opportunity structure[21] – which mediate and channel their demands.[22] Finally, while Touraine is at pains to develop a sociology of action, the multidimensional character of action is not explored, especially the role of instrumental action, which is of particular importance for resource mobilisation theorists.

A discursive approach

The above observations require us to develop a clearer conceptualisation of interests and identity, and to articulate them in a way that does not reduce one to the other. To begin with, as against those views that present interests and identities as fixed, essential or primordial, a discursive perspective insists that both interests and identities are contingent and political constructs with precise discursive conditions of existence.[23] Moreover, we see interests as relative to the identities of socially positioned agents. Thus to define and constitute interests is a political project in two senses. On the one hand, interests cannot be assumed to pre-exist agents (whether as subjective preferences, or real entities imputed on agents by external observers), as they are constructed politically and discursively via hegemonic projects. On the other hand, agents themselves are historical and political products whose identities are contingent upon their relation to other identities. It may seem obvious, but interests are always the interests of particular agents – and both the identities, and the interests which are relative to them, can never be assumed, but are strategic outcomes.[24]

  Such a view presupposes a particular conception of identity. Identities can be viewed as those 'points of temporary attachment to the subject positions which discursive practices construct for us. They are the result of a successful articulation or "chaining" of the subject into the flow of discourse.'[25] From this perspective, identities are relational entities whose meanings depend on a system of elements, against which any identity is differentiated. Moreover, they are always doubly differentiated, being both internally dispersed – comprising a number of different subject positions within and between social agents – and constructed by being defined against other identities. Social identities thus involve the drawing of boundaries between 'insiders' and 'outsiders', and require the constitution of 'others' or 'scapegoats' that are presented as blocking the full constitution of an agent's self-identity.[26] The political construction of identity via the creation of boundaries involves the production of empty signifiers, which represent the 'absent fullness' of a group – their lack of unity and community.[27] Empty signifiers are thus means of representation that enable the welding together of internal differences, while simultaneously showing the limits of the group identity, and its dependence on the opposition to other groups.[28]

As a consequence of this reformulation, the calculations and strategising of individual agents in resource mobilisation theory are always relative to a particular kind of subjectivity, namely, the self-interested maximisers which are produced by and functional to existing capitalist market orders.[29] This schema also enables Dunleavy's idea of group identity to assume its full significance. The distinction between endogenous and exogenous group identities is useful as long as both are predicated on the ontological primacy of identity formation. Thus, even exogenous identity sets require the construction of a group identity, with all the theoretical conditions that we have stipulated. Finally, in this view, real interests form part of the rhetoric of political persuasion by which actual, that is to say, historical and discursively specific interests are politically constructed. Having set out the parameters of our theoretical framework, we now return to the Manchester case.

The campaign against the second runway revisited

The campaign against the expansion of Manchester Airport came to prominence in the national press and in the popular imagination during the early part of 1997, when direct action campaigners resisted eviction from their protest camps on the construction site in the Bollin Valley. However, direct action was only the third and final phase of the campaign that began on 29 July 1991, when Manchester Airport announced its plans to build a second runway.[30] The 1991 proposal triggered the mobilisation of local residents in Knutsford, Mobberley and Styal, the villages and towns south of the Airport populated largely by middle-class professionals. In this initial phase of the campaign, the Knutsford and Mobberley Joint Action Group (KAMJAG) and the umbrella organisation, the Manchester Airport Joint Action Group (MAJAG), took the lead in the public consultation with the Airport and the preparation of the submission of local residents to the Public Inquiry.

The start of the Public Inquiry in June 1994 signalled the opening of the second phase of the campaign and ended on 15 January 1997, when the Inspector decided in favour of the new runway. Throughout this second phase, the nature of the campaign shifted away from the traditional lobbying politics of the local residents to the language of technical expertise and knowledge required by the Public Inquiry. It was the failure of the Inquiry to endorse the claims of local residents that finally dislocated the group identity of local residents and initiated the final campaign of direct action. Green activists established camps on the proposed construction site less than ten days after the pro-runway decision. Throughout this final phase of the campaign, direct action protesters used sophisticated techniques of bodily risk[31] to prevent the clearing of the proposed construction site, and skilfully exploited the local and national media to gain political influence. Although direct action tactics shifted attention away from the traditional NIMBY politics of the middle-class protesters, the campaigns of local residents and green activists came together as eco-warriors forged a temporary and precarious alliance with traditional middle-class protesters.

These different phases of the campaign raise three main sets of empirical questions. How did local residents' groups and direct action protesters overcome their collective action problems, and how successful were they in doing so? How is it possible to characterise the alliance that was established between local residents and direct action protesters, and how can we explain its emergence and formation? How can we account for the failure of the campaign and the overall effects of the protest action on the participants? It is to these questions that we now turn.

Overcoming the difficulties of collective action

Let us assume, following Olson, that local residents and direct action protesters each faced their own distinct collective action difficulties when launching their campaigns. How were these problems overcome? Indeed, to what extent were they overcome? In answering these questions, we draw upon our radicalised interpretation of Dunleavy's concept of group identities, Chong's account of social networks, and the role of political entrepreneurs, who were able to get collective action going by bearing some of its initial costs. We start with the residents' groups.

At the outset, the local residents surrounding the Airport were part of an exogenously defined identity set in that they were all affected by the disruption, pollution, concerns about the community's quality of life, and lack of consultation engendered by the new construction project. The existence of this exogenous group identity set facilitated the initial tasks facing group leaders as they sought to mobilise local support. From the beginning, there was a readily available group identity to overcome collective action difficulties, such that organisers and political entrepreneurs of the potential groups could target their campaign on those most directly affected by the Airport's decision. In addition, leaders of the residents' groups could exploit an overt collective good in opposing the proposed runway, which not only threatened the quality of residents' lives, but also local property prices. Unlike road-building projects, the additional noise and air pollution resulting from the new runway affected indiscriminately a wide swathe of local residents, a consideration that was reinforced by the inability of certain local residents to 'exit' from the area once Manchester Airport announced its plans.[32]

Moreover, the large-scale building plans threatened the identities and interests of local residents. The powerful regional and local 'growth coalition' assembled by Manchester Airport drew on its privileged relations with successive national governments, as well as the support of local business and political elites intent on making Manchester a 'headquarter city', to push through its expansionist plans.[33] The modernising vision of this increasingly confident and urban Manchester business elite, with its promises of regional development and 50,000 new jobs,[34] clashed directly with local residents in an area that is one of the wealthiest and environmentally most pleasant commuter belts outside the South-East of England. For residents, the decision to expand the Airport was not a technical necessity, but a deliberately motivated 'land-grab' deep into the heart of the Cheshire Green Belt. As one leading local campaigner put it, 'Manchester's King Kong was about to disrupt Cheshire's rural calm', avariciously devouring its green and pleasant land.[35]

In contrast, the direct action campaigners had an endogenous group identity set. Thus it could be anticipated that their collective action problems had to be overcome by soft incentives, such as expressive and participatory benefits.[36] And indeed, unlike the local residents, the reproduction of an eco-warrior identity required constant campaigning and the production of 'enemies' to reinforce their militant values and lifestyles. In short, although their identity can be understood against the backdrop of a wider series of dislocations in society as a whole,[37] the building of the second runway enabled direct action protesters to reproduce and reconstruct this identity through new protests. It was not surprising, therefore, that many of the environmentalists who had held media attention at the A30 protest at Fairmile arrived at Manchester. These included 'Swampy', 'Animal', 'Muppet Dave' and 'Ian', four of the five 'moles' from the Fairmile 'Big Momma' tunnel.

This focus on group identities, *à la* Dunleavy, goes some way to providing an important condition for the emergence and formation of groups and movements. However, the mobilisation of both local residents and green activists cannot be dissociated from the importance of embedded social networks and the presence of political entrepreneurs. There was a strong and active conservationist tradition in the villages that facilitated the exploitation and mobilisation of the residents' exogenously defined group identity. As early as the 1970s, village amenity groups in the area south of the Airport, especially in Knutsford, Mobberley and Styal, had been aware of the implications of economic growth and the expansionist zeal of the City of Manchester and its Airport. The Styal Action Group was formed in 1973 when it successfully fought the original plans for a new runway. The Mobberley Village Society was another well-established civic association that facilitated the emergence of the working group of residents in Mobberley opposed to the runway project. The leaders of these associations were instrumental in the formation of KAMJAG and MAJAG, the umbrella organisation that represented all ten local villages at the public inquiry.[38]

In addition, the leaders of MAJAG were, on the whole, local councillors or prominent members of the village communities, who were able to call upon the support not only of politicians and certain local authorities around the Airport, but also of professional people, such as lawyers, architects and risk consultants, who committed substantial expertise and resources to the campaign. These contributions lowered the costs of the campaign, while providing the campaign with important policy brokers. In sum, the leadership of MAJAG was able to call upon considerable resources to reduce its collective action difficulties. At its peak prior to the Public Inquiry, the supporters of MAJAG and its affiliated groups numbered an estimated ten thousand. The campaign itself raised over £300,000 during the run up to the Public Inquiry. The bulk of this fund-raising occurred at events, such as the summer ball in the grounds of Hill House, one of the listed buildings threatened with demolition.

Similarly, the rapid mobilisation of green activists at Manchester owed much to the prior existence of institutionalised networks of green activists in South Manchester. The Campaign Against Runway 2 brought together the different cultures and strategies of Manchester Friends of the Earth, and the environmental activists of Earth First!, the Green Party and Manchester Wildlife, as well as the Manchester Airport Environment Network. This diverse network of environmentalists was crucial to the mobilisation of militant green activists as the pre-established social networks which structure the green movement were exploited to trigger the flood of activists into the Bollin Valley. The camps had been planned for some time before the end of the Inquiry, with campaigners undertaking 'protest walks' along the proposed construction site for over twelve months, dropping off leaflets in the airport terminals and advertising the occupation of the site on the Internet. (The only secret was the exact timing of the occupation and the location of the camps.) In other words, the likes of 'Swampy' did not simply stumble upon the Manchester campaign, but were alerted through the communication structures and community networks of environmental activists.

As in the case of the residents' campaign, local political entrepreneurs played important policy broker and support roles throughout the campaign of direct action. Logistical support for the campaign came from more institutionalised actors. Throughout, the Manchester Friends of the Earth office became a focal point for dealing with press inquiries, holding meetings and co-ordinating responses to the actions of Manchester Airport. Jeff Gazzard, for instance, a local resident initially associated with MAJAG, who later acted as the chief co-ordinator for the Campaign Against Runway 2, was able to act as a critical hinge between the differently oriented groups in the campaign of direct action. Not only did he legitimise the roles of the different groups involved, he was also able to orchestrate the all-important media coverage of the events at the local and national levels.

Overall, the mobilisation of local residents and green activists owed much to the role of exogenous and endogenous group identities, the existence of strong social networks, and the presence of strategically placed policy entrepreneurs, who were willing to bear the costs of collective action in the hope of some future return. Indeed, the distinct group identities of local residents and environmentalists helps to explain the difficulties of mobilisation experienced by MAJAG at later stages of the campaign. Thus it is plausible to argue, following Olson, that the existence of an exogenously defined group identity held together by location and property interests produced a sub-optimal mobilisation of local residents. As the campaign progressed, both identity and interest cleavages emerged within the local residents' campaign. Jeff Gazzard split from KAMJAG because he wished to extend the media campaign of MAJAG over and beyond its submission to the Public Inquiry. This strategic question was not unrelated to issues of collective identity. As a leading member of MAJAG put it, 'he [Gazzard] was not Middle England'.[39] Additionally, in the absence of an endogenously generated identity amongst local residents, Manchester Airport was able to fragment their opposition by brokering compromises that appealed to their narrow individual or sectional interests. Symbolic concessions were made to the Styal Action group and rifts were engineered by making 'acceptable' offers to homeowners threatened by the new runway. In fact, given the sub-optimal mobilisation of local residents and their 'Middle England' identities, it is somewhat surprising that local residents supported and showed solidarity with the radical environmentalists. It is to the dynamics of this alliance that we now turn.

Forging alliances: 'Vegans and Volvos'

The plans to build the second runway 'dislocated' local residents and made possible the forging of new political identities. However, in preparing their submission to the Public Inquiry, residents were able to displace the disruptive effects of the Airport's proposals and reinscribe their traditional conservative social and political identities. Nevertheless, the most decisive dimension of the dislocation was the decision of the Public Inquiry to permit the construction of the runway. MAJAG supporters had invested great faith in their case and in the Inquiry to deliver a 'fair' judgement.[40] Their legal team, and the opinions and advice of the experts they consulted, gave them reason to believe that they had a powerful, almost unassailable, case. In theory, moreover, a Public Inquiry is the legitimate and impartial way for interested parties to make representations. However, here (as in other inquiries) it undermined confidence in the value of such procedures. As a leading campaigner put it to us, 'the Inquiry encouraged participation, but was in no way democratic'.[41] It was this recognition, by middle-class protesters, that established democratic channels were unreliable at the local and national levels, which goes a long way towards explaining the symbolic identification of many residents with more radical forms of protest action. But how are we to explain the construction of a tactical alliance between the groups and move-ments? Three main arguments can be adduced.

In the first place, connections were forged by the pro-Manchester Airport campaign. Initially, the eco-warriors were presented as different from, almost a danger to, the local residents. Graham Stringer, ex-leader of the Manches-ter City Council and head of the Airport, described them as 'a threat to the local community', adding later to the *Daily Telegraph*: 'It makes me very angry that young southerners come and stop people getting off the dole queue.'[42] As the campaign gathered momentum, both elements were pre-sented as equally threatening to the Airport and its interests. Stringer described a leading local protester as a 'lunatic, violent, and a liar'.[43] Tarring the legitimate interests and forms of protest of the middle-class residents with the same brush as those of the eco-warriors solidified and created a degree of identity between widely divergent groups and forms of campaign-ing. This ideological branding of its enemies as 'anti-airport' and 'anti-progress' was reinforced by the residents' own perceptions of the tactics employed by the Airport. The presence of black-shirted and balaclava-wear-ing evictors, the alleged heavy-handed methods of the private security guards, rumours of phone tappings and personal insults increased the sense of outrage. Claims that opposition to the new runway would endanger the creation of 50,000 jobs in the region also angered the residents' groups, whose members resented the accusations that they were rich Cheshire NIM-BYs opposed to economic growth. The emergence of an opposition between a dynamic Manchester seeking to expand its regional influence and an anti-growth movement that alluded to the Cheshire idyll thus structured the terms of the debate. It served to make manifest the distinction between the forces favouring regional growth and those who managed, at least for a while, to establish some common purpose to upset the developers' project, in spite of the campaigners underlying differences and aims.

Secondly, the media's consistent association of the residents and eco-war-riors served to crystallise the antagonistic constructions between the opposi-tional forces and the pro-Airport lobby. Images of eco-warriors and local residents side by side in their confrontation with the Airport authorities served to fix this unlikely linkage in the minds of the residents. Whatever the wider political consequences, one result was to legitimise the eco-warriors and their case. Just as New Labour courted the popular press, so did the direct action protesters. 'Swampy' may have been turned into an unlikely and, at times, unwilling media celebrity, but the attention certainly gained the protesters an audience previously denied them. He attracted major coverage from traditionally right-wing newspapers and tabloids, such as the *Daily Mail*, the *Daily Express*, the *Daily Telegraph* and the *Times*, ending up for a time as the 'new darling' of the popular press. A front-page *Times* story was entitled 'Swampy digs for victory',[44] the *Daily Express* printed a lifestyle story on him, complete with pictures of the new hero in Armani clothes, and even the *Telegraph* described him as 'the 23-year-old tunnel-digging star of Newbury'.[45] In sum, even though there was a good deal of personalisation and even trivialisation of the protesters and their lifestyles, the overall impact was literally to make 'Swampy' a household name, as well as altering public perceptions of new environmental movements and their objectives.

Finally, once again, local political entrepreneurs played important policy broker and support roles throughout the campaign of direct action, functioning as policy brokers between residents and eco-warriors. Jeff Gazzard was able to act as a critical link between the differently oriented groups in the campaign, despite his departure from the leadership of KAMJAG. However, new actors emerged to provide support and resources for the campaign of direct action as it benefited from the support of a network of local residents. The Mobberley Women, headed by Gaynor Trafford and Sylvia Selfe, established a support group for the environmental activists, providing deliveries of free bread and cakes and organising, among other things, a rota for recharging mobile phones and car batteries. Yet, the most significant and high-profile support came from Terry Waite, patron of MAJAG, who having written against the runway to John Prescott, the newly ensconced Deputy Prime Minister in the Blair government, led a procession of protesters to the site on 23 May 1997. It was behind the media profile of Waite that the campaigns of the residents and the green activists merged. Waite possessed the legitimacy necessary to mobilise the residents of Mobberley behind the demonstrations of the tunnellers. His end of May march around the security fence, accompanied by 300 residents, was both the clear manifestation of the 'Vegans, and Volvos' alliance and the last desperate attempt of residents to stop the King Kong of Manchester invading the Cheshire Green Belt.

In short, the dislocation and threat to the identity of local residents, the contingent construction of antagonisms, and the role of strategically placed entrepreneurs enabled local middle-class residents and the self-named eco-warriors to construct an unlikely working alliance against the Airport's plans. However, faced with the disappointment engendered by the Public Inquiry, it is somewhat puzzling that the outcome of the Inquiry did not foster more involvement of local residents in the campaign of protests and direct action. In comparison to other campaigns in the 1990s such as that against the export of live animals at Brightlingsea, relatively few local residents engaged in direct action. On the whole, local residents limited themselves to providing logistical support for the eco-warriors, so that even the march led by Waite around the construction site kept within the restrictive rules and conventions of legitimate demonstration.

Explaining the dynamics and breakdown of the campaign

For local residents and eco-warriors alike, the campaign induced the inevitable highs and lows of citizen protest. Given the emergence and formation of the 'Vegans and Volvos' alliance in the first part of 1997, one surprising fact is the rapid breakdown of the campaign by the middle of the year. How are we to account for this? With respect to the direct action protesters, the rapid disbanding of their resistance is not surprising. The eco-warriors regarded the defence of the Bollin Valley as one instance in an overall struggle to prevent the planning and implementation of large-scale, environmentally damaging infrastructure projects. Their campaign was a last-ditch attempt to prevent physically the building of the runway, to increase the costs of its construction, and to win broader ideological and political support in society. As the anarchist magazine *Aufheben* puts it, the key political objective of direct action campaigns was the 'creation of a climate of autonomy, disobedience and resistance'.[46] Hence, they were geared up for a 'final' confrontation with the police and Airport authorities, fully expecting to be forcibly removed from the site. The fact that the building of the runway, in contrast to road-building projects, took place in a confined space meant that this final confrontation was intense, but short-lived. As soon as the eco-warriors were removed, their campaign was effectively over.

But what of the local residents? They, after all, were still affected by the Airport's plans and had legitimate fears about the longer-term consequences of Airport expansion in the Cheshire Green Belt. To explain their actions, let us go back briefly to the moment of the Public Inquiry decision. The Inquiry decision finally dispelled the residents' faith in the legitimacy and credibility of normal channels of representation and interest intermediation, and revealed the full impact of the dislocation of their existing social and political identities. Borrowing from Hirschman's useful typology, the 'dislocated' residents were faced with the choice between 'exit' and 'voice', or a combination of the two, as the two primary mechanisms of redressing the falling benefits from their participation in the campaign. Recourse to 'voice', more likely in cases where individuals demonstrate high degrees of loyalty or attachment to the campaigning organisations, would enable residents to express their dissatisfaction with the campaign led by the MAJAG and KAM-JAG. 'Exit' from the campaign, which could be employed in combination with 'voice', was available to local residents in more than one way. They could transfer to a rival group, take up a completely different issue, or drop out of collective action altogether.

In actual terms, a handful of residents were sufficiently radicalised to exit from their existing organisations, to voice their disagreement with the existing strategies and tactics, and to link up with the direct action protesters. These residents became the crucial linchpins of the 'Vegans and Volvos' alliance. Most residents, however, even though they were prepared to identify symbolically with the direct action protesters, remained formally loyal to their existing associations and organisations, and in keeping with this elite mode of politics, continued the established pattern of opposing the construction of the runway. Nevertheless, most residents, including much of the leadership of MAJAG, were profoundly disillusioned and disaffected not only by the campaign, but by the entire political process, the rules of which they assumed to be in their interests and in keeping with their identity. (It is worth noting in this regard the election of Martin Bell as an Independent 'anti-sleaze' candidate in the local Tatton constituency and the widespread and popular support he commands amongst residents, despite the fact that the Tatton constituency has always been a staunch Conservative stronghold.)

It is necessary, therefore, to explain why the outcome of the Public Inquiry led to the widespread demobilisation of local residents as they dropped out of the campaign (and became disaffected with politics in general), rather than triggering more involvement of local residents in the campaign of direct action. To begin with, the relative demobilisation of the local residents' campaign after the Public Inquiry can be explained by the dislocation of the local residents' identities, and the failure of the residents' leadership to capitalise on the disruptive effects of the decision by putting forward a bold new strategy and approach. The shock was intensified, precisely because most residents believed that the inquiry system was rational and impartial, and that legitimate means of interest representation constituted the essence of the political rules of the game. This elite form of campaigning was consonant with the social and political identities of the residents, and also flowed directly from the ways in which they had overcome their collective action problems. In other words, it depended crucially on the activities of key personages in the villages and rested largely on activities such as fund-raising, the occasional village meeting and the signing of petitions.

In an important respect, of course, this was too late, and it can be plausibly argued that the horse had already bolted by the time the Inquiry announced its decision. However, there were other strategic and tactical options that were available prior to the Public Inquiry decision; in particular, a media-oriented campaign of lobbying, not only at the local level, but also at the national level, directed specifically at Westminster. These tactical debates about the use of the media did provoke an important strategic disagreement amongst the residents, when more radical elements argued that the campaign should downplay the Public Inquiry and concentrate on the lobbying of sympathetic MPs at Westminster, as well as a high-profile media onslaught. (This latter position was later vindicated when direct action activists were able to exploit media interest to further their interests.) Yet, while some campaigners were aware of the importance of publicity at both the local and national levels, most were reluctant to extend the scope of the protest, believing that the rationality of their arguments would win through at the Inquiry. For instance, outside the leadership of MAJAG and KAMJAG, Jeff Gazzard was able to act as a linchpin between the campaign of local residents and the eco-warriors, while attracting massive media attention about the issue. However, even his attempts to publicise and encourage crossover between the different aspects of the campaign were compromised by the history of his own prickly relations with the leadership of MAJAG and KAMAG. Moreover, Terry Waite could only mobilise individuals insofar as he represented legitimate forms of protest and mobilisation. The actions of Waite thus answered the demands of local residents for continued activism without requiring them to exit into other forms of protest. However, it is possible that a bolder strategy after the decision could have won greater concessions from the Airport.

The failure of political entrepreneurs to construct new forms of strategy and political identification at different points in the campaign was accentuated by the elite form of protest politics associated with the residents' campaign. As we have suggested, while group formation and mobilisation did occur, the residents were always under-mobilised, relying heavily on the existence of intrinsically cautious and apolitical conservationist networks, as well as political entrepreneurs willing to bear the costs of collective action to increase their status and esteem in the community.

A third factor is what Chong has called the 'bandwagon effect', that is, the 'bandwagon' towards 'exit' that results from the failure of a campaign to obtain concessions from the authorities. The decision of some residents to exit sparked a chain reaction, forcing the remaining activists to recalculate possibilities of success in light of their recent defections. These calculations caused other activists to lower sufficiently the chances of success for the campaign, thereby causing them to exit. This new round of withdrawals triggered another round of recalculations and new withdrawals, and so on. This bandwagon thus explains how the mobilisation of the residents stumbled after the decision to go ahead with the construction of the second runway. More so, the bandwagon was not countered by the entrepreneurship of the MAJAG leadership, who failed to reinvigorate the campaign with new ideas and new aims. Again, the final move by the MAJAG leadership to contest the legality of the tendering process for the construction of the second runway did not deviate significantly from the strategy pursued by the group from its inception. In other words, it remained wedded to traditional and more legitimate channels of participation in the policy process.

Finally, it is possible to argue that the campaign faltered because of the absence of an empty signifier to unite fully the different sections of the 'Vegans and Volvos' coalition. From this perspective, local residents and the eco-warriors were unable to construct an empty signifier around which the distinct identities and demands of the two groups of activists could unite. Opposition was thus weak, carrying no positive identification with which to articulate a collective will. The campaign of local residents itself was fraught with internal splits and personality clashes that betrayed the weakness of the collective identity of the residents. In fact, the absence of an empty signifier contrasted powerfully with the pro-runway lobby where the call for a 'Greater Britain, Greater Manchester' united a diverse coalition behind growth and economic modernisation. Indeed, although the campaign of Manchester Airport might have forged connections between some local residents and green activists, the Airport acted equally strategically to split the residents' opposition, thus revealing the paucity of their collective identity.

Conclusion

This chapter has sought to provide a rich description of certain aspects of the campaign against Manchester Airport's proposed second runway. We have developed a conceptual model based upon a particular understanding of the relationship between interests and identity in an effort to articulate insights from resource mobilisation theory and the new social movement literature. This model enables us to explore the ways in which different groups overcame their collective action dilemmas; set out reasons for the establishment of a temporary alliance between groups; evaluate the strategies and tactics employed by protesters; and account for the overall failure and breakdown of the campaign. In conclusion, are there any more general inferences that can be generated, and then 'tested' in other cases, from this microanalysis of one instance of protest? One important issue concerns the nature of the alliances established between NIMBYs and eco-warriors. How can it be characterised? Our research has vacillated between two opposing viewpoints. On the one hand, it is evident that the alliance was little more than a tactical marriage of convenience organised by short-term interests to oppose the second runway. On the other hand, however, there did exist a level of symbolic identification between the two groups, as local residents recognised the inadequacies of traditional forms of politics, and the just cause propagated by their more radical partners. Indeed, more radical sections of the residents actively identified and supported direct action, and continue to play an active role in environmental movements in Manchester and the North-West region. Our tentative conclusions reveal a symbiotic and supplementary relationship between the two sets of actors in the campaign against the second runway. In other words, each side of the alliance performed an important role for the other in making possible and legitimising collective action. In a sense, the eco-warriors were parasitic on the demands and grievances of the local communities they defended, as they were able to piggy-back on an existing issue. Moreover, their attempts to hegemonise local residents legitimised their broader political aims of opposing large-scale infrastructure projects, and enabled them to disseminate their alternative communitarian lifestyles and visions. For the local residents, on the other hand, the eco-warriors and the high-profile actions of important personages such as Terry Waite vindicated the moral dimension of their campaign, enabling them to 'live out' the fantasy of political conflict and confrontation. For them, the campaign was a kind of surrogate form of political protest without real cost.

A second issue concerns the public inquiry process. Here again there are opposed interpretations of the inquiry process in the UK (and other democratic societies). From one perspective, the inquiry system is little more than a window-dressing exercise designed to buy off opposition and legitimise unjust and controversial decisions. Another approach has suggested a more open-ended 'arena without rules' in which the development and execution of informed strategies by opposition groups can influence public decision-making.[47] Our analysis has suggested that in the Manchester case, the former picture is more accurate, but needs some qualification. First, the decision by residents to hire a leading London law firm to conduct its case and to pursue a submission built around technical planning issues was probably misguided. (A fact exacerbated by the scathing attitude of the eco-warriors, who refused to engage in any public negotiations whatsoever.) Secondly, the Airport authorities and negotiators proved highly successful in articulating and implementing a strategy to isolate and weaken the residents. For them, the Inquiry was indeed an 'arena without rules' and they used their entire bargaining and strategic prowess to pursue their case with ruthless efficiency, not least the negotiation of an environmental mitigation package approved by Cheshire County Council. Ultimately, therefore, the mounting financial and emotional costs of participating in a lengthy inquiry process weighed heavily against the campaign of the local residents. Indeed, such was the structural imbalance of resources between the Airport and local residents, even down to the minor status granted to lay expertise during the proceedings themselves, that the Inquiry was, in the words of the residents' solicitor, a 'David versus Goliath struggle', degenerating with each passing day into a 'fiasco'.[48]

Notes

1 Earlier versions of this chapter were presented to the 'Green Direct Action in the UK' Conference at Keele University in October 1997 and to the ECPR Workshops at Mannheim in March 1999. The authors would like to thank the participants of these workshops for their stimulating comments and criticisms.

2 B. Doherty, 'Paving the way: the rise of direct action against road-building and the changing character of British environmentalism', *Political Studies*, 47:2 (1999), 275–91.

3 E. J. Feldman and J. Milch, *Technocracy versus Democracy* (Boston, Auburn House, 1982); D. E. Apter and N. Sawa, *Against the State* (Cambridge, Harvard University Press, 1984); C. Buchanan, *No Way to the Airport* (London, Longman, 1981); D. McKie, *A Sadly Mismanaged Affair* (London, Croom Helm, 1973); D. Perman, *Cublington* (London, Bodley Head, 1973).

4 *The Times*, 19 May 1997.

5 M. Olson, *The Logic of Collective Action* (Cambridge, Mass., Harvard University Press, 1965).

6 *Ibid.*, p. 2 (original emphasis).

7 *Ibid.*, p. 51 (original emphasis).

8 A. Oberschall, *Social Conflict and Social Movement* (Englewood Cliffs, Prentice Hall, 1973), p. 159.
 9 K. Dowding, *Power* (Buckinghamshire, Open University Press, 1996), pp. 38–41.
10 *Ibid.*, p. 85.
11 In a famous footnote, Olson explicitly rules out explanations based purely on non-material incentives, arguing that these other motivations can be explained by recourse to material selective incentives. Olson, *Logic of Collective Action,* p. 61, n. 17.
12 P. Dunleavy, *Democracy, Bureaucracy and Public Choice. Economic Explanations in Political Science* (London, Harvester Wheatsheaf, 1991).
13 D. Chong, *Collective Action and the Civil Rights Movement* (Chicago, Chicago University Press, 1991).
14 A. O. Hirschman, *Shifting Involvements* (Princeton, Princeton University Press, 1982).
15 M. Castells, *The Urban Question* (London, Edward Arnold, 1977); N. Smelser, *Theories of Collective Behaviour* (London, Routledge & Kegan Paul, 1962).
16 For a discussion of the latter, see D. Howarth, 'Post-Marxism', in A. Lent (ed.), *New Political Thought* (London, Lawrence & Wishart, 1998), pp. 126–42.
17 A. Touraine, *The Voice and the Eye: An Analysis of Social Movements* (Cambridge, Cambridge University Press, 1981), p. 61.
18 *Ibid.*, p. 77.
19 A. Touraine, 'An introduction to the study of social movements', *Social Research,* 52:4 (1985), 760–1.
20 M. Castells, *The City and the Grassroots* (London, Edward Arnold, 1983); A. Melucci, *The Nomads of the Present* (London, Hutchinson, 1989).
21 D. McAdam, J. D. McCarthy and M. N. Zald, 'Opportunities, mobilizing structures, and framing processes – toward a synthetic, comparative perspective on social movements', in D. McAdam, J. D. McCarthy and M. N. Zald (eds), *Comparative Perspectives on Social Movements* (Cambridge, Cambridge University Press, 1996), pp. 1–23.
22 A. Scott, *Ideology and the New Social Movements* (London, Allen & Unwin, 1990), p. 68.
23 E. Laclau and C. Mouffe, 'Post-Marxism without apologies', in E. Laclau, *New Reflections on the Revolution of Our Time* (London, Verso, 1990), p. 118.
24 In this respect, our analysis has some affinities with the various sociological critiques of resource mobilisation theory put forward. See M. Castells, *The Power of Identity* (Oxford, Basil Blackwell, 1997); Melucci, *Nomads of the Present,* pp. 31–4.
25 S. Hall, 'Introduction: who needs identity?', in S. Hall and P. du Gay (eds), *Questions of Cultural Identity* (London, Sage 1996), p. 6.
26 This is a central dimension of what Laclau and Mouffe call the construction of antagonistic relations. See E. Laclau and C. Mouffe, *Hegemony and Socialist Strategy* (London, Verso, 1985), pp. 122–7.
27 E. Laclau, 'Why do empty signifiers matter to politics?', in J. Weeks (ed.), *The Greater Evil and the Lesser Good* (London, Rivers Oram, 1995), p. 171.
28 For a fuller analysis and application of this concept, concentrating specifically on the way 'blackness' functioned as an empty signifier, see D. Howarth,

'Complexities of identity/difference', *Journal of Political Ideologies*, 2:1 (1995), 55–78.
29 A. Weale, *The New Politics of Pollution* (Manchester, Manchester University Press, 1992), p. 61.
30 In fact, it might be argued that the issue stretched back to 1973, when local residents successfully opposed earlier proposals to expand the Airport.
31 For a discussion of such tactics, see B. Doherty, 'Direct action against road-building: some implications for the concept of protest repertoires', in J. Stanyer and G. Stoker (eds), *Contemporary Political Studies 1997* (Nottingham, Political Studies Association, 1997), pp. 147–55.
32 For a discussion of 'exit', see A. O. Hirschman, *Exit, Voice and Loyalty* (Cambridge, Harvard University Press, 1970).
33 I. Taylor, 'Fear of crime, urban fortunes and suburban social movements: some reflections from Manchester', *Sociology*, 30:2 (1996), 329–30; I. Taylor, K. Evans and P. Fraser, *A Tale of Two Cities* (London, Routledge, 1996).
34 Submission to the Public Inquiry into the Manchester Airport's Proposed Second Runway, North-West Regional Office, 1997; Manchester Airport, 'Gateway to the real Britain' (Manchester Airport plc, Manchester), p. 2.
35 Interview with T. Greaves, Executive Member of KAMJAG and J. McRae, leader of Mobberley Parish Council, 15 June 1998.
36 For an important discussion of these benefits, see G. Jordan and W. Maloney, *The Protest Business* (Manchester, Manchester University Press, 1997).
37 Aufheben, 'The politics of anti-road struggle and the struggles of anti-road politics: the case of the No M11 Link Road campaign', in G. McKay (ed.), *Party and Protest in Nineties Britain* (London, Verso, 1999), pp. 100–28. See also Derek Wall, *Earth First! and the Anti-Roads Movement* (London, Routledge, 1999).
38 The ten associations which MAJAG brought together included KAMJAG, MVS, Styal Action Association, Stockport Campaign Against Runway Extension (SCARE), Ashley Action Group, Mere Residents' Association, Handforth Ratepayers' Association, Knutsford Civic Society, Hale, Altrincham and Bowdon Action Group, and Heald Green and Long Lane Ratepayers' Association.
39 Interview with B. Hepburn, Executive Committee member of MAJAG, 30 September 1998.
40 This is evident in correspondence between the leaders of MAJAG and their lawyers and advisers.
41 Interview with J. Gazzard, 30 January 1998.
42 *Daily Telegraph*, 2 April 1997, 11.
43 Interview with Graham Stringer, 8 June 1999.
44 *The Times*, 1 April 1997, 1.
45 *Daily Telegraph*, 2 April 1997, 11.
46 Aufheben, 'The politics of anti-road struggle', p. 107.
47 G. Dudley and J. Richardson, 'Arenas Without Rules and the Policy Change Process: Outsider Groups and British Roads Policy', *Political Studies*, 46:4 (1998), 727–47.
48 Interview with B. Greenwood, 8 June 1999.

Provisionalism and the (im)possibility of justice in Northern Ireland

The current peace process in Northern Ireland is widely thought to represent the best chance for a lasting settlement since the formation of the six-county state in the early 1920s. The British government has let it be known that it sees its role in this process as that of a neutral arbiter[1] between the two communities in Northern Ireland. It will facilitate any agreement that the two communities reach as long as it can command the support of a majority of the people in the province. It claims that the only principles that inform its role are those of ensuring parity of esteem, equality and consent. It claims, in other words, that its democratic credentials are impeccable and that such a starting point should be acceptable to all good democrats and those committed to peace and justice. However, for many in the republican movement, which shares the objective of establishing the conditions for justice, the policy of the British government, far from representing a pure and unfettered democratic position, has a conspicuous 'blind spot' lurking behind its rhetoric concerning conciliation, justice and consent. When the republican community hears the demand for it to enter into dialogue on the democratic 'level playing field' it detects that all is not quite as it seems. What it detects is the prospect of dialogue in which power has already played an unacknowledged role in articulating a framework of assumptions structuring how that dialogue should proceed.[2]

For the Provisional movement, there are two significant manifestations of this dimension of power within the present situation. The first is the *consent principle*, which states that the constitutional status of Northern Ireland will not change unless a majority of citizens within the northern state vote for it. Far from this being a self-evident democratic principle, the Provisionals believe, quite legitimately, that it is an entirely contingent political ruling. For the Provisionals, however, this debate about which constituency has the right to determine the future of Northern Ireland serves to obscure an even more fundamental democratic failure, namely, that of the *inherently* unjust and undemocratic nature of the Northern Ireland state itself. For the Provisionals, therefore, what is really problematic about the current peace process is its central tenet that a democratic and just peace is possible in the context of a partitionist state. For all the other participants in the ongoing peace process, including the nationalist Social Democratic and Labour Party (SDLP), this proposition represents the cornerstone of the entire initiative, and it is clear that if it were not widely accepted the peace process in its present form would not exist at all. It is precisely this possibility of justice within a partitioned state, however, that the Provisional movement has consistently denied. It may now be prepared to accept interim structures such as a Northern Assembly coupled with cross-border bodies,[3] but its view that a united Irish state is a necessary condition for the realisation of justice and democracy remains axiomatic. Although Provisionalism has changed in many ways between 1970 and 1999, this remains a crucial article of faith and provides the movement with its most enduring dimension of continuity.[4]

In this chapter I examine this claim and argue that, although the pursuit of Irish unity is a legitimate political aspiration, the way in which it is articulated within Provisional discourse is problematic for precisely the same reason that the Provisional movement identifies in the structure of the peace process, that is, it seeks to deny the dimension of *power* inherent within it. Although Provisionalism is now engaging in a dialogue according to rules laid down by its political adversaries, throughout its existence, it too has sought to impose the terms of its own ideology under the guise of 'the natural order' of justice. It too has been involved in the attempt to hegemonise the space of justice and democracy, to decontest[5] the meaning of these signifiers, to force others to enter into dialogue with it in the context of *its* interpretation of the nature of the conflict. It is, of course, this struggle for hegemony that characterises all political engagement and in this sense the protagonists in the conflict in Northern Ireland are not remarkable.[6] However, if we are to understand the nature of this or any other conflict, it is important to reveal the fragile threads that preserve the ideological unity of the dominant discourses comprising it, and it is for this reason that a discourse theory approach to the study of Provisionalism is necessary.

The literature on the Provisional movement includes many impressive and detailed studies, but it is characterised almost entirely by the lack of a coherent theoretical framework in which its central claim concerning justice can be examined. This is not to suggest that within the literature the question of justice is not considered at all. It is, rather, that it is not examined in a context in which its relationship with wider strategic changes in the movement can be analysed. This is because most of the historical accounts[7] focus on issues such as personalities, organisational changes within the movement, the tension between militarism and politics, new political ideas or tactics and the growing realisation within the movement during the 1970s and 1980s of the importance of class struggle and politicisation as a means of advancing the struggle. McIntyre has objected to many of the texts on Provisionalism on the grounds that they either presume an exclusivist militarist ethos and mindset within the movement[8] or that they fail to locate strategic shifts 'within a broader dialectic of republican/British state conflict'.[9] I agree with McIntyre's claim that changes in Provisional discourse have to be understood in a broader context. His analysis, which insists on the essentially reactive nature of Provisionalism, is instructive but it does not take us any further in understanding the crucial relationship between justice and the movement's strategic/tactical changes. It is this relationship that is vital if we are to understand the nature of modern Irish republicanism, as it is only when we examine how Provisionalism's perception of justice is subverted by changes to other aspects of its discourse that we can understand this most complex political movement and come to terms with what remains its principle *raison d'être* – the struggle for justice.

It is specifically in this context of the relationship between Provisionalism's conception of justice and the strategic changes it experienced throughout its history that the value of a discourse theory approach can be clearly seen. By analysing how the movement articulated the links between justice and issues such as the British Army presence or socio-economic grievances, a discourse theory approach can show how these links, rather than being seen as *natural*, actually constitute and embody a moment of power in which two or more dimensions of the conflict are brought together in such a way *as if* each were only intelligible in the context of the other. In the same way that Marxist approaches to the study of Northern Ireland[10] gave an ontological primacy to the dimension of class struggle, Provisionalism cannot see beyond the unresolved national question and the subsequent denial of justice. By using a discourse theory approach it is possible to see how, within Provisional discourse, different dimensions of the conflict are stitched together in such a way as to appear seamless. Understanding how these dimensions are grafted together allows for a much more nuanced understanding, not just of the way Provisional discourse itself has been constructed, but of the nature of contemporary politics generally.[11]

Provisional discourse and the logic of the supplement

The basic premise of my argument is that there are two distinct levels of analysis within Provisional discourse. The first relates to the aforementioned transcendental claim that it is only in a united state that justice and democracy can be realised. The second relates to the three strategies the movement has followed between 1970 and 1999 in order to achieve its objectives. From 1970 to the mid-1970s the movement relied exclusively on a strategy of physical force. The dominant assumption within the movement in these early years was that this would be enough to secure victory. The lack of a tenable political solution, coupled with increased nationalist resistance due to British Army policy and loyalist reaction, would, or so it was hoped, be enough to convince any doubters that there was no solution other than unification of the state if justice were to be achieved.

In the second period, from the mid-1970s to approximately the mid-1980s, the strategy changed but the end remained the same. During this time, in addition to the original strategy of physical force, the movement embarked on a policy of 'social republicanism'. This dual approach was identified by a senior republican at the time, Danny Morrison, as the 'ballot box and armalite' strategy. The idea behind this was to demonstrate to the nationalist communities, both north and south of the border, that the social, political and economic grievances they were experiencing were the *necessary effects* or *symptoms* of partition.

When, by the late 1980s, this policy of agitation was deemed to have run its course, the movement abandoned it in favour of a third strategy that sought to establish links with the hitherto despised constitutional nationalist parties, primarily the SDLP and Fianna Fáil, in order to campaign collectively for Ireland's legally established right to self-determination. The course of the Provisionals' evolution in this context is neatly summarised by McIntyre:

> British state strategy brought into being against itself the only form of political struggle that republicans insisted could work to end partition. It did not work and republicans consequently felt compelled to adopt the stance of constitutional nationalism, which they had persistently claimed could not work.[12]

Now, although all of these strategies identify issues that are clearly linked to the constitutional question, this is a far more complex relationship than perceived by the Provisionals. Although we have to acknowledge and understand the causes of the very real sense of injustice experienced by the nationalist community in Northern Ireland since the inception of the state, this is not the same as holding to the view that there is an *inherent* link between partition and injustice. Therefore, any attempt to set absolute limits to the democratic potential of Northern Ireland has to be treated with some suspicion. If this is accepted, the relationship between Provisionalism's central claim about the conditions for justice and the issues highlighted in their different strategies seems at once more nuanced.

I want to suggest that the specific issues around which Provisional strategies mobilised have to be understood, not as reducible to, but as constitutive of the movement's central claim identifying the contradiction between partition and justice. It is in this specific sense that these issues can be seen as *supplementing* that central claim. But, if this is the case, that central claim is immediately subverted. If the intelligibility of Provisionalism's claim concerning the conditions for justice depends on a number of overdetermined factors, such as British state-sponsored violence, sectarianism, differential rates of unemployment or what is at best a series of ambiguous international rulings about self-determination, we uncover the possibility of seeing that claim, not as a logical, a priori statement about the immutable conditions for justice, but as the articulation of an ideological position constructed and mediated in a very specific political environment.

It is, therefore, the concept of supplementarity, taken from Derrida and given its political articulation in discourse theory, that is decisive. In the *Tain of the Mirror* Gasché attempts to uncover the two heterogeneous meanings harboured by the term 'supplement'.[13] The first meaning understands the supplement as 'something that adds itself ... a surplus, a plenitude enriching another plenitude, the fullest measure of presence. In this sense, the operation of supplementation is not a break in presence and plenitude but rather a continuous and homogenous reparation and modification of both.'[14] The other meaning of the supplement is given its clearest articulation by Derrida:

> [t]he supplement supplements. It adds only to replace. It intervenes or insinu-ates itself in the place of; if it fills, it is as if one fills a void ... Compensatory (*suppleant*) and vicarious, the supplement is an adjunct, a subaltern instance which takes – (the) – place (*tient-lieu*). As substitute, it is not simply added to the positivity of a presence, it produces no relief, its place is assigned in the structure by the mark of an emptiness. Somewhere, something can be filled up of itself, can accomplish itself, only by allowing itself to be filled through sign and proxy.[15]

In the next section I will show how the strategies pursued in the three distinct phases in the evolution of Provisionalism have to be understood as that which gave meaning and form to the argument linking nationhood and justice. In other words, I will show that because the content of these strategies (for example, the focus on political or economic discrimination) was both exterior to *and* necessary for the idea of nationhood = justice to have meaning, those strategies must be seen as supplementing that idea and, as a result, revealing its incompleteness. In other words, these strategies were performing the role of 'filling in a void', of providing the 'empty signifier'[16] of justice with an intelligible and positive content. This theorisation of justice as an empty signifer is important. It is precisely because it is a signifier that can accommodate so many different interpretations that it must always be understood as empty or, at least, partially empty in that, although its meaning will always be contested, at any time there will always be a dominant discourse that will be controlling and delimiting its meaning.

Three phases in the evolution of Provisionalism

When the Provisional IRA emerged in Northern Ireland in the late 1960s it was widely believed within the movement that the violent reaction prompted by the civil rights movement had finally exposed the contradictions inherent within the northern state and that, as a result, its demise was imminent. Following a British withdrawal, Irish unity would follow thus allowing for the emergence of a just and democratic society based on the principles of equality and fairness within a self-determining and sovereign nation state. The Provisionals' hope that the disintegration of the state witnessed in this early period would lead to early victory is captured well in the following observation:

> [t]he beauty of the Army's presence from the point of view of Gerry Adams is that when the Army came in, 'ambiguity', as he puts it himself 'went out of the window.' A community, which even in revolt, had a complex sense of its own identity, including its relationship to Britain, had the ambiguities literally knocked out of it ... this process was and is a blessing for the IRA ... if there is to be peace in Northern Ireland, getting it will be a process of letting the ambiguities that went out of the window 25 years ago back in the door.[17]

This demonstrates clearly the relevance and importance of supplementarity as a means of understanding Provisionalism in the 'pre-political' years of the early 1970s. It was the almost total absence of ambiguity within the republican community during this period concerning its perception of the meaning of the British presence in Northern Ireland that sustained and gave form to the Provisional view that peace with justice could never be won as long as that presence remained. In addition to what was perceived as an increasingly hostile and threatening army presence, nationalist opinion was also being influenced by the dramatic upsurge in sectarian tension between the two communities during this period. Of course, opinion differed concerning who was to blame for the collapse of the government[18] and the general descent into anarchy witnessed at this time, but what was significant about this period from the Provisionals' point of view was the reinforcing of the impression that the northern state was a failed entity which was incapable of providing to its citizens a peaceful, stable and just environment. It is a widely held view that the failure to disband the Stormont parliament when the Army was sent into Northern Ireland in 1969 'was the greatest single mistake of British policy during the troubles. The effect was to allow the Provisionals to present the British Army as the tool of the "Orange" Stormont ascendancy regime.'[19] It is, however, precisely because decisions such as this that were both highly contingent and yet so significant in contouring and structuring[20] the conviction that the northern state was inherently antithetical to justice, that we need to understand them in the context of supplementarity. In other words, it was events and decisions such as this, which were entirely avoidable, that reinforced and gave form to the Provisionals' central claim about justice and its conditions. This point can be seen more clearly by remembering how Gerry Adams recalled these early years of the conflict:

> [t]he state at any time could have undermined the civil rights agitation by moving swiftly on what were normal democratic demands; and perhaps in the global sense if wider issues had occurred earlier, the natural consequence of EEC membership would have been to modernise the state. But movement came

too late. In fact, whatever civil rights reforms were granted were only granted after the holocaust, after the whole thing was up in the air.[21]

This is significant in the sense that it acknowledges that the Provisional movement could have been outmanoeuvred if a more astute strategy had been followed by both the British and successive unionist governments at Stormont. But here Adams does not follow through with the logic of his own argument in that he does not acknowledge that the Provisionals' central ideological claim concerning the conditions for justice was, like the survival of the movement to which he refers, *itself* similarly dependent on a series of related but quite distinct phenomena such as British Army tactics or the escalating sectarian tension of the time.

When, by the mid-1970s, the Provisionals' desired course of events had failed to materialise, elements within the movement began to reassess republicanism's teleological strain that harboured the promise that one day Ireland would be free and the contradiction between partition and justice unraveled. As a result, a new strategy was devised in order to make *more* explicit the democratic deficit inherent within the existing constitutional framework. Thus, by the mid-1970s, a significant division had emerged within the movement separating those who thought that a campaign of armed struggle would suffice to win the war from those who recognised that justice could only be attained as a result of a process of politicisation.[22] Sean McStiofain, the Provisionals' original leader, summarised his antipathy to the policy of agitation being followed by republicanism's Marxist leadership in the 1960s as follows:

> [i]n addition to it being incapable of effecting what our people want, parliamentary agitation is in a thousand ways demoralising. Even if it could win our independence, independence so won would do no good; for freedom to do good must be gained with difficulty and heroic sacrifice, in the face of perils and death … Platform movements are necessarily unmilitary and consequently bad for a nation that wants to free herself from a foreign yoke. In short, no more insane and wicked idea would enter the brain of fools and knaves than the notion of reviving the system of agitation.[23]

McStiofain was just as intensely opposed to the new strategy being developed in the early to mid-1970s. For the new group challenging McStiofain's leadership, which increasingly became centred around the leadership of Gerry Adams and Martin McGuinness, what was necessary for the movement in the mid-1970s was precisely to revive the system of agitation by developing a new hegemonic strategy designed to make clear the absolute and inextricable link between partition and the concrete experience of injustice.

This division within the movement between the military purists and their political counterparts has retained a resonance to this day. However, although there were significant differences between these groups about the future direction of the struggle and the most appropriate strategy to adopt, both remained unshakeable in their conviction that the northern state was profoundly dysfunctional and inherently unjust. The militarists based in Dublin and the emerging and more politically radical northern elements centred around Gerry Adams remained firm in their conviction that there was a fundamental contradiction between partition and the realisation of a just and democratic political order. This position is articulated throughout all internal Provisional publications. In his book, *A Pathway to Peace*, Adams stated that:

> [w]e cannot have justice and peace in Ireland because we do not have a society capable of upholding them. Instead we have a system based on coercion, violence, sectarianism and exploitation. By its very nature British rule cannot be just or peaceful and, while this is so, revolutionary struggle will continue to strive to overthrow it in pursuit of true justice, peace and happiness.[24]

So how did the new Provisional leadership try to ensure that its understanding of the nature of the struggle would become the dominant one? In political terms the priority was to broaden the struggle from the republican ghettoes in the north to the southern electorate:

> [i]n pursuing a strategy in the 26 counties, Sinn Fein, which is a revolutionary party, therefore has to consider two major aspects. First of all it has to retain its republican analysis of partition as the major block to the development of a nation which can achieve political, economic, social and cultural justice. It therefore has to campaign against the present negations of that justice and attempt to build a revolutionary awareness of cultural pride and development, social freedom and economic independence – the reverse of the partitionist strategy – not in a vague or general way but on the specific issues.[25]

The same theme is echoed in the following:

> Sinn Fein should now get back to devoting itself to the painstaking work of building a strong radical republican political organisation. In the areas where it has influence Sinn Fein has to give leadership to the people in their everyday struggles in a capitalist society – the cost of which is high unemployment, poor housing and burdensome living standards, all of which sufferings are further compounded by the greater evil of partition.[26]

This strategy of social republicanism, which was the leitmotiv of the movement from approximately the mid-1970s to the mid-1980s,[27] took the form of an articulation of political frontiers.[28] The most important of these frontiers was that separating the equivalential chain unity = justice = democracy = freedom from partition = injustice = the continuation of social, political grievances. However, this attempt by the Provisionals to reduce the experience of everyday social, political and economic grievances to the wider constitutional question of partition was to prove problematic for the movement in that there was no *necessary* link between them. The difficulties faced by the Provisional movement during this period were summed up by Gerry Adams:

> [t]he overriding question is of course the national question, but there are many issues affecting people in the Free State in which we should be showing a lead – issues which are linked to the national question and which can only be solved when it is solved, but issues which people do not relate to that issue.[29]

This need to show a clear linkage between the broader national question and more local issues is also evident in the following: '[i]t is fine to support issues but to be socialist and democratic MUST involve integrating these struggles into the anti-imperialist one'.[30] What is clear from this, however, is that the Provisionals' awareness of their difficulty in this respect was a recognition of specific empirical or political limits which did not entail a questioning of the purity of the partition = injustice equivalential link. The Provisionals' problem was not, therefore, a crisis of faith but a lack of converts to it. What had become clear during the 1980s was that for many nationalists it *was* possible to imagine a just, normal and democratic society in a constitutional framework other than that of a united Ireland. Although nobody could be in any doubt over the systematic abuses of power committed in Northern Ireland since its inception, for many nationalists this did not justify condemning the province as an inherently unjust political entity.[31] In addition, social republicanism can now be seen to have been profoundly counterproductive in terms of the realisation of Provisionalism's objectives. It was precisely because the movement conceived of the relationship between the national question and social, political and economic grievances in a reductionist context that it overinvested in the potential and utility of a political campaign to make the structural links between them transparent.

In the context of the 'armalite and ballot box' period it could be argued that the category of supplementarity is doubly significant. In other words, to sustain the impression that the northern state was inimical to justice, in addition to the continuation of armed struggle, the movement now also relied on highlighting the 'social and economic ill-effects of partition'. What is important to remember here is that, although the experience of such grievances was not wholly unrelated to the national question, they did constitute quite a distinct problem. The fact that they were invoked by the movement as a necessary part of the strategy to demonstrate the inherently unjust nature of the northern state shows clearly the vulnerability of that claim. Let me be explicit about what is at stake here. The Provisionals regarded the experience of such grievances as intelligible only inside the context of the national question. My argument is that these grievances were overdetermined by a range of other factors and that, as a result, they need to be understood as being both inside and outside the context of the national question. However, because these grievances were necessary in order for the link between justice and the national question to be intelligible, the Provisionals' claim about the absolute nature of that link is problematised. In other words, because that claim needed to be supplemented *from outside* in order for it to function effectively in a acutely antagonistic political environment we can see it as a specifically *political* formulation and not a statement about the universal conditions for justice.

It was during this period of social republicanism that the Provisional movement finally crossed the rubicon and accepted that political progress would involve it participating in the electoral process.[32] However, after a series of encouraging results, particularly in the wake of the hunger-strike period, it had, by 1988, become increasingly clear to the leadership of the movement that its attempt to effect the transition from 'myth to imaginary'[33] had failed.[34] Its attempt to establish grievances as symptoms of a broader structural contradiction had not been successful. By the end of the 1980s, therefore, the Provisional movement finally accepted the limits of its electoral appeal. This period, therefore, witnessed a marked shift in their discourse. The socialist vocabulary that had suffused the pages of its main publicity organ, *An Phoblacht*, predicting a worker-led social and political revolution, had, by 1988, almost totally disappeared.[35] The new strategy now to be adopted involved the movement forming a broad front or pan-nationalist alliance with its sworn enemies – the 'class traitors' of the SDLP and the political establishment in Dublin. The Provisionals' rallying cry now became the right of all nations to self-determination. Although their 1992 document 'Towards a Lasting Peace in Ireland' contains the same position being articulated concerning the importance of ending British rule in order to achieve justice, the change in the movement's vocabulary is clear:

> [t]hose in Ireland who claim to seek permanent peace, justice, democracy, equality of opportunity and stability cannot deny that the abiding and universally accepted principle of national self-determination, in which is enshrined the principle of democracy, is the surest means through which to further those social and political aims and once having achieved them, of maintaining them.[36]

This new strategy, however, is no less problematic than its predecessors. This is because it is a *specific* interpretation of the internationally recognised principle of self-determination. From the perspective of unionism the same principle can be invoked. Here, however, its moment of application does not entail Irish unity – in fact it entails the very opposite, that is, unionists' right as a nation to self-determination. As the peace process unfolds it is this claim to national self-determination that continues to provide the Provisional movement with its sense of moral unity and purpose. The future, however, remains uncertain. At the time of writing the central political question in Northern Ireland is whether David Trimble's Ulster Unionist party will be able to form an executive with Sinn Fein short of any initiatives of decommissioning. However, what is clear is that the cursory overview of Provisional history outlined above raises a range of complex theoretical and political questions, and it is to some of these that I now want to turn.

Conclusion

I have argued that *within the terms of Provisional discourse itself* there is a
tension. The reason for this tension is that within this discourse there are two
quite separate dimensions. First, the communitarian claim that justice and
democracy require the emergence of a united Irish nation-state and, second,
that without the realisation of this nation-state a number of injustices will
persist, for example, harassment of nationalists by Army/RUC,[37] economic
and political discrimination or the denial of the Irish people as a whole to
their right to self-determination.

My argument throughout has sought to suggest that these denials of justice, rather than being reducible to the national question, are actually constitutive of it, and it is in this specific sense that they can be seen as
supplementing or giving form to that claim. Therefore, it is precisely
because, within Provisional discourse, these two dimensions were articulated
as if they were two sides of a given totality that an aporia or tension exists.
If this were not the case, it could be asked why the Provisionals constantly
felt the need to change the specific terms of their discourse in order to
demonstrate what for them was a self-evident and timeless truth. It could be
argued that all movements involved in political struggle change their strategy
in accordance with changing circumstances. It would indeed be foolish not
to do so. But there are theoretical consequences that follow from such
changes. I want to suggest that one of those consequences in the context of
the Provisional movement is that its central claim concerning justice at once
appears as a specifically political or ideological assertion.

It could also be argued that just because an ideological claim is articulated
in a deeply antagonistic political environment does not mean that it is not
right, that it is not a serious moral argument with substantive critical pur-
chase. In other words, one response to my argument could be, so what? This
is a fair point. After all, it would be reasonable to assume that most people
would want to argue that any meaningful conception of justice must have certain minimum requirements. And, if it is the case that any such reckoning can
only take place in a culturally and politically specific context, then do not all
of our arguments about justice fall prey to similar 'deconstructive' attacks?
The only answer to this question is yes, they do. There will always be radically different accounts of the nature of justice and the most apposite political environment in which it can be realised. Any account that does become
hegemonic will always have been the result of some mechanism of power and
exclusion. In other words, any dominant conception of justice will only attain
its meaning by referring to some 'spectre of otherness' that lies beyond it.

This point concerning the incalculable nature of justice is developed by
Derrida. In his discussion of the relationship between law and justice, Derrida argues that the most important condition for the realisation of justice is
a commitment to its essential contestability:

[e]very time that something comes to pass or turns out well, every time that we placidly apply a good rule to a particular case, to a correctly subsumed example, according to a determinate judgement, we can be sure that law (droit) may find itself accounted for, but certainly not justice. Law (droit) is not justice. Law is the element of calculation, and it is just that there be law, but justice is incalculable, it requires us to calculate with the incalculable; and aporetic experiences are the experiences, as improbable as they are necessary, of justice, that is to say of moments in which the decision between just and unjust is never insured by a rule.[38]

How is this relevant to the discussion about politics and, more specifically, the Provisional movement and the logic of the supplement? What is clear is that politics, despite the fact that it always takes place in a specific and mediated environment, always seeks to transgress the rule that justice is incalculable.[39] It seeks to do this by decontesting the meaning of a range of signifiers such as justice, democracy, unity or truth. However, in order to accomplish this task, a number of 'sleights of hand' have to be employed. What discourse theory allows for is a critical examination of how certain 'myths of unity' are created, thereby enabling a particular discourse to hegemonise the meaning of these signifiers. I have argued that, in the case of the Provisional movement, the dominant strategy was to establish an explicit link between the national question and a number of other phenomena such as reaction, sectarianism or discrimination. However, because these dimensions were not reducible to each other, and yet the intelligibility of the claim about justice and the national question relied on its articulation with these other phenomena, the political nature of that claim is revealed. This is an important argument because in Provisional discourse the claim about justice and its conditions is made as if were an eternal metaphysical truth. What I have tried to do, by using the category of supplementarity, is to demystify this claim, to show it for what it is: an ideological assertion. In a 1990 commentary, Johnathan Culler stated that Barthes's *Mythologies* 'stand at the beginning of a tradition of demystification, which he hoped would have political results'.[40] It is not at all clear what political results could or should result from this or any such attempt at demystification. Perhaps if it does no more than remind us of our inexorable capacity to mistake our particular values as universally true it will serve in some small way the causes of understanding and democracy.

Notes

1   This has been the position of successive British governments for some time. It was given its clearest articulation by Peter Brook in 1990 when, as Secretary of State for Northern Ireland in the last Conservative administration, he stated that Britain had no military, strategic or economic interest in remaining in Northern Ireland. This became a more formal aspect of British policy in December 1993 with the publication of the *Downing Street Declaration* (Northern Ireland, HMSO, M200 12/93 29254).

2 Loyalists would, of course, make the same argument. They, however, would maintain that the terms of the peace process are structured in favour of the republicans.

3 The assembly and power-sharing executive, coupled with new cross-border (Northern Ireland/Republic of Ireland) institutions, provide the basis for Northern Ireland's new constitutional framework.

4 This position is rooted in a communitarian ethic and is much discussed in the literature on Provisionalism. Jennifer Todd, for example, has argued that the 'dominant northern nationalist concept of justice is best understood in neo-Aristotelian terms. The social and cultural character of the individual is seen as central to his or her being; it must be respected in a just society and its reproduction should be fostered.' J. Todd, 'Northern Irish nationalist political culture', *Irish Political Studies*, 5 (1990), 31–44, p. 39. For a fuller discussion of the role of myth, mysticism and legend in sustaining the Provisionals' conception of nationhood, see C. C. O'Brien, *Ancestral Voices* (Dublin, Poolbeg Press, 1994) and R. Kearney, 'Myths of Motherland', in *Postnationalist Ireland: Politics, Culture and Philosophy*, (London, Routledge, 1997), pp. 109–22.

5 This notion of decontestation is elaborated by Freeden, who characterises the work of ideology as specifically to attach a single meaning to a political term: '[u]ltimately, ideologies are configurations of *decontested* meanings of political concepts … [i]n concrete terms, an ideology will link together a particular conception of human nature, a particular conception of social structure, of justice, of liberty, of authority, etc' (original emphasis) M. Freeden, *Ideologies and Political Theory: A Conceptual Approach* (Oxford, Clarendon Press, 1996), p. 76.

6 What I mean here is that all politics can be seen as the attempt to exact a form of violence by seeking to terminate the process of signification. For Hamacher, this is also true of law. He remarks that '[w]hile all that is law must rest on a law-making, law-positing, law-imposing violence, and such law-imposing violence is represented in all law-preserving or administrative violence, the idea of justice cannot depend on the law's changing powers of imposition. Justice must therefore belong to a sphere equally distant from the law on the one hand, and from the violence of its imposition and enforcement on the other.' W. Hamacher, 'Afformative, strike', *Cardozo Law Review*, 13:4 (1991), 1133–57, p. 1134.

7 Many of the texts on the Provisional movement could be categorised under the heading of 'liberal history'. By this I mean that they focus on accounting of events without working towards any theoretical or general conclusions. The main examples of this approach are P. Bishop and E. Mallie, *The Provisional IRA* (London, Heinemann, 1987); K. J. Kelley, *The Longest War* (London, Zed Books, 1988); B. O'Brien, *The Long War* (Dublin, O'Brien Press, 1993); H. Patterson, *The Politics of Illusion* (London, Hutchinson Radius, 1989). These texts all adopt as their substantive object of analysis the tension between a continuing commitment to armed struggle and Provisionalism's attempt to adopt a political profile. Patterson's book is particularly effective in this respect. His conclusion is that republicanism depends on the existence of social grievances but that it cannot manage to combine its role as political representative at the same time as seeking the overthrow of the state.

8 This is the leitmotiv of works such as J. Bowyer-Bell, *The Secret Army, The IRA 1916–1979* (Dublin, Academy Press, 1979) and T. P. Coogan, *The IRA* (London,

Pall Mall Press, 1980). M. L. R. Smith, in his *Fighting for Ireland* (London, Routledge, 1995), seeks to portray the movement as caught up in a 'logic of escalation' mentality in which it could no longer rationally assess the continuing utility of armed struggle. M. O'Doherty's *The Trouble with Guns* (Belfast, Blackstaff Press, 1998) portrays armed struggle as a means of rendering impossible the success of any internal solution.

9 A. McIntyre, 'Modern Irish republicanism: the product of British state strategies', *Irish Political Studies*, 10 (1995), 97–121, p. 104.

10 Two of the best-known studies that look at the modern conflict from this perspective are E. McCann, *War and an Irish Town* (Harmondsworth, Penguin, 1974) and M. Farrell, *Northern Ireland: The Orange State* (London, Pluto, 1980). The argument here is that a capitalist conspiracy is preventing the emergence of normal class politics by keeping the Protestant and Catholic working classes apart. The two main methods used to effect this outcome were to 'beat the sectarian drum' by warning of Roman Catholic plans to overthrow the state or by pursuing a policy of 'differential discrimination'. See J. Whyte, *Interpreting Northern Ireland* (Oxford, Clarendon Press, 1990), pp. 175–93.

11 By revealing how the component parts of a particular discourse are articulated together as if they were naturally linked, we gain some insight into how any relatively sedimented set of ideas or values is similarly shot through with the traces of contingency and power. For example, in what has become known as Blairism, economic justice has now been effectively decoupled from any notion of collectivism or neoliberalism. It is now articulated in the context of the 'third or middle way', as if this were entirely self-evident.

12 McIntyre, 'Modern Irish republicanism', p. 104.

13 R. Gasché, *The Tain of the Mirror* (Cambridge, Mass., Harvard University Press, 1986), p. 208.

14 *Ibid.*

15 J. Derrida, *Of Grammatology* (Baltimore, Johns Hopkins University Press, 1967), p. 145.

16 The concept of the empty signifier is examined in a number of books and articles. See, for example, E. Laclau, 'Why do empty signifiers matter to politics?', in *Emancipations* (London, Verso, 1996). There are two aspects to the functioning of empty signifiers that need to be identified. First, signifiers such as justice can provide a discourse with a focal point and unity. If a discourse succeeds in becoming hegemonic, then that conception of justice will also function as the general horizon which provides the society with a representation of its collective identity. Secondly, and crucially, as there is no necessary relation between any specific discourse and that which functions as the embodiment of a society's absent fullness, signifiers such as justice can be seen to be partially empty.

17 F. O'Toole, *Guardian*, 13 August 1994.

18 The Stormont Parliament was prorogued in 1972 in the aftermath of 'Bloody Sunday'.

19 P. Bew and P. Gillespie, *Northern Ireland, A Chronology of the Troubles 1968–1993* (Dublin, Gill & Macmillan, 1993), p. 19.

20 Lefort's work seeks to show how the institution of particular forms of society always coincide with an attempt to conceal the traces of its discursivity. Thus political science is misguided in that '[it] emerges from an attempt to objectify,

and it forgets that no elements, no elementary structures, no entities (classes or segments of classes), no economic or technical determinations, and no dimensions of social space exist until they have been given a form. Giving them a form implies both giving them meaning (*mise en sens*) and staging them (*mise en scène*). They are given meaning in that the social space unfolds as a space of intelligibility articulated in accordance with a specific mode of distinguishing between the real and the imaginary, the true and the false, the just and the unjust, the permissible and the forbidden, the normal and the pathological.' C. Lefort, *The Political Forms of Modern Society: Bureaucracy, Democracy, Totalitarianism* (Cambridge, Mass., MIT Press, 1986), pp. 11–12.

21 G. Adams, *The Politics of Irish Freedom* (Dingle, Co. Kerry, Brandon Books, 1986), p. 31.

22 This is not to suggest that there were no political murmurings in the movement prior to the north/south faultline that emerged in the mid-1970s. As the memoirs of Maria McGuire show clearly, there was a sensitivity within elements of the movement in the early 1970s to the need to develop a political strategy. It was not until later in the 1970s, however, that these elements were taken seriously. See M. McGuire, *To Take Arms: A Year in the IRA* (London, Macmillan, 1973).

23 S. McStiofain, 'Constitutional humbug!', *An Phoblacht*, January 1967.

24 G. Adams, *A Pathway to Peace* (Dublin, Mercier Press, 1988), p. 62.

25 'A state but not a nation', *Iris*, November 1983. There is a clear Gramscian resonance here. In a letter to Togliatti, Gramsci offers a clarification on the distinction between 'war of movement' and 'war of position'. The latter was a much more subtle and nuanced strategy that had to be adopted by revolutionary parties in advanced capitalist societies in order to confront and overcome their political superstructures. See W. Adamson (ed.), *Hegemony and Revolution* (Berkeley, University of California Press, 1980), p. 86. It was precisely such a shift in appreciation of the nature of the revolutionary task faced by the Provisional movement that informed its decision to embark on a programme of politicisation.

26 'Opening up new fronts', *An Phoblacht/Republican News*, 17 January 1981.

27 I would argue that, although Adams and McGuinness were vocal in their demands for a process of politicisation in the late 1970s, this did not actually begin to assume a coherent form until the early 1980s.

28 This concept of the frontier represents an important dimension in Laclau and Mouffe's work on hegemonic politics. Their argument is that the frontier 'is internal to the social ... [e]very society constitutes its own form of rationality and intelligibility by dividing itself; that is, by expelling outside itself any surplus of meaning subverting it'. E. Laclau and C. Mouffe, *Hegemony and Socialist Strategy* (London, Verso, 1985), pp. 136–7.

29 G. Adams, *Republican News*, 22 May 1976.

30 'The Bread and Butter Blind Alley', *Republican News*, 7 January 1978 (original emphasis).

31 It neds to be said here, however, that even if we cannot state a priori that a particular political situation is *inherently* unjust it certainly does not mean that it is easily open to reform or rearticulation. This is the point made by Connolly: '[t]here are obdurate contingencies, and it is a mistake to assume that the constructed character of a self-identity automatically implies its susceptibility to

reconstruction'. W. Connolly, *Identity\Difference. Democratic Negotiations of Political Paradox* (New York, Cornell University Press, 1991), p. 176.

32 The impetus for this development were the hunger strikes of 1980 and 1981.

33 Laclau identifies two possibilities in terms of the theorisation of the relationship between *myth* and *imaginary*: '[t]he first is the complete hegemonisation of the surfaces of inscription by what is inscribed on them ... the moment of inscription is eliminated in favour of the literality of what is inscribed. The other possibiity is symmetrically opposite; the moment of representation of the very form of fullness dominates to such an extent that it becomes the unlimited horizon of inscription of any social demand and any possible dislocation. In such an event, myth is transformed into an imaginary.' E. Laclau, *New Reflections on the Revolution of our Time* (London, Verso, 1990), pp. 63–4.

34 The *Anglo-Irish Agreement* (London, HMSO, Cmnd. No. 9657) of 1985 was designed to stem the flow of support from the SDLP to Sinn Fein. By the end of the 1980s this initiative was widely believed to have been successful. Garret Fitzgerald claimed that the impact of the AIA was to reduce Sinn Fein's electoral support in the June 1987 election to less than 11 per cent of the total Northern Ireland poll and 27.5 per cent of the Catholic vote. This dropped to 9 per cent of the total vote and 23.5 per cent of the Catholic vote in the 1989 European election. G. Fitzgerald, *Fortnight*, 332 (1994), 12–15, pp. 13–14. There were, of course, other reasons why the Provisionals faced an uphill struggle to establish a foothold beyond the traditional republican heartlands. The tacit support for a policy of armed struggle was always likely to offend those who advocated a constitutional way forward. Also, their socialist rhetoric was never going to prove popular with middle-class nationalists who felt that they had a worthwhile stake in the existing system.

35 Kevin Bea has characterised the abandonment of this strategy as the shift towards 'republican realism' – essentially the acceptance that the the Provisionals were not going to emerge as the necessary agents of emancipation. K. Bea, 'Occasional papers in Irish Studies' (University of Liverpool, 1992).

36 'Towards a Lasting Peace in Ireland' (Belfast, PSF, 1992), p. 2. This was an election manifesto presented to the Sinn Fein *ard fheis* (annual conferenc).

37 The Royal Ulster Constabulary, the police force of Northern Ireland.

38 J. Derrida, 'Force of law: the mystical foundation of authority', in D. Cornell (ed.), *Deconstruction and the Possibility of Justice* (New York, Routledge, 1992), p. 16.

39 This is essentially the point made by Michael Walzer when he claimed that all thin or universal conceptions of justice always issue from thicker and more local environments. See M. Walzer, *Thick and Thin. Moral Arguments at Home and Abroad* (Notre Dame, University of Notre Dame Press, 1994).

40 J. Culler, *Barthes* (London, Fontana Press, 1990), p. 40.

The Mexican revolutionary mystique

The twentieth century has brought widespread change. The decline of the great 'meta-narratives' has resulted in serious challenges to intellectual trends such as the Enlightenment. On a world scale, economic and political power has been continuously readjusted, as the global market economy permeates and is contaminated by its contact with local processes. In this context, new cultural and ethnic voices have emerged, and local narratives and political utopias have been reorganised. This chapter investigates the Mexican revolutionary discourse as a particular instance of such a local and national narrative.[1] My interest in the ordering of social relations produced by the Mexican revolution, as well as its system of representation, hinges upon the mystical traces of a collective imaginary constructed in the revolution.

My claim is that the revolutionary narrative operated as an articulating mystique that strengthened the different movements involved in the revolution, while fusing them into a unit. Different social agents tried to domesticate its meaning by presenting themselves as the depositories of its destiny and meaning through the official party. It is the mystical discourse that incarnates the idea of unity and transcendental selfhood that has conferred an identity to the revolution and its successive interpretations.

Some say the Mexican revolutionary system of representations is long dead, while others say it died after the Second World War. My view is that it still lives; though could be expiring. Of course, this depends on how the national political forces react to this decline, but is also conditional upon the way in which the revolutionary system of meanings is understood and characterised.

Some interpretations of the revolution suggest a teleological process led by a privileged social agent instituting a 'radically new' regime. However, the Mexican Revolution cannot be explained teleologically, as it does not fit any predicted revolutionary subjectivity, nor does it achieve a predetermined result. I will argue that in order to understand this process the circulation of meanings and political forces has to be grasped, as well as the processes whereby these meanings and political forces are fused into a ruptural unity.

Moreover, I will demonstrate that instead of a predetermined revolutionary agent, one has to recognise that the articulation of political subject positions in the construction of revolutionary agents does not obey a necessary economic, political or historical law. In sum, I will attempt to show that the Mexican Revolution was an overdetermination of various social movements articulated by a mystical discourse in which heterogeneous agents and political practices produced a unified but not homogeneous process.

Mapping the debate

Although the literature on the Mexican Revolution is abundant, I shall consider only those analyses published since the late 1960s. I will delineate the main positions by focusing on three main areas. These are the social character of the revolution, the unitary character of the revolutionary process, and the overall status of the revolution. The main issue with respect to the social character of the revolution concerns the class character of the revolutionary process. Analysing the stage of capitalist development, discussion concerns whether it was a bourgeois or a proletarian revolution.[2] By characterising the social composition of the movements and its leaders, or examining the political orientation of the new ruling bloc, some claim that the bourgeoisie was the leading force,[3] while others argue that it was a 'bureaucratic class' that was triumphant.[4] Finally, there are those that claim that the middle class led the revolution and were the victorious social class.[5] Moreover, for those who have concentrated their research on the main revolutionary documents, whether in the form of political agreements, plans, programmes or laws, the debate has been amongst those who portray the revolution as an instrument for the development of capitalism,[6] those that maintain it was an eclectic programme showing no consistent orientation,[7] and those that present it as a *populist* programme.[8]

The representation of the Mexican Revolution could have been raised in this discussion. However, little interest was awakened by this issue and it has either been treated as ideology[9] or it has been easily said that the revolution failed because it was lacking a mystique.[10] This simply ignores the fact that images are invented in revolutions to give meaning to the social dislocations, narratives of universal utopias emerge awakening passion to defend them and hatred to whatever may challenge them.[11] These images and narratives constitute imaginary formations such as mystical discourses.

The second aspect of the debate focuses on the unitary character of the revolutionary process, and centres around three main positions.[12] Regional historians argue that there were many revolutions, each with their own particularity and leadership.[13] Others claim that there were no leaders at all,[14] and a third group suggests that there was no revolution at all, only a disconnected set of armed movements or rebellions.[15]

The final focus of the debate concerns the very status of the process.

Again, three main positions can be distinguished. Those that argue that it was a genuine revolution,[16] those that it was merely a rebellion,[17] and those who see it as a set of disconnected upheavals with different means and ends.[18]

In short, while some interpretations recognise the diversity of agents, social demands and political orientation of those engaged in the revolution, and tend thus to diffuse the unity of the process by disregarding the changes at a national level, those accounts which attempt to reinforce the unitary character of the revolution tend to overlook the geographical and social heterogeneity of the social movements and political leadership conducting the revolution, as well as the overall outcome of the struggle. Finally, while some idealise the political and social outcomes of the revolution, others question whether it was a revolution at all.

The position I will defend in this debate about the character of the revolution is that it was an overdetermination of social movements articulated around a mystical discourse, which in turn shows the emergence of a research field: the system of representations produced in the Mexican Revolution.[19] A series of questions that need to be answered arise out of this conception. Is it possible to interpret the multiplicity of social dispersed movements as constituting the Mexican Revolution? Is it possible to characterise it as a single revolution while having these differential features in the North and in the South? Is there a single political utopia bonding together this variety of social and political demands? If so, how can we account for the diverse sources of its social and political demands?

Overdetermination, mystical discourse and identification

In order to address these questions and to provide the conceptual tools to justify my interpretation of the revolution as an overdetermination of initially dispersed social movements unified by their identification with a mystical discourse, I will introduce the concepts of *overdetermination* and *mystical discourse*. The two basic operations involved in the concept of *overdetermination* are the logics of *displacement* and *condensation*. The former refers to the continuous circulation of meanings and identities between different social movements, agents and agendas. It shows that no identity is pure and uncontaminated, but always involves traces of other identities, thus displaying the relational character of the social. The latter logic involves the precarious fixation that temporarily stops the flow of signification by fusing different elements in a 'ruptural unity'.[20] The logic of condensation thus helps us to understand that fixations are never definitive, but result from the welding of diverse elements into precarious units which do not completely eliminate the particularity of what has been condensed.

These two logics allow us to understand revolutions not as a necessary moment in the self-unfolding of history, in which predetermined social agents accomplish a historical mission (in short, ruled by necessity). Rather it is a process permeated by *a lack of a necessary and sufficient ground*, the objectivity of which cannot be predicted by rules, reason or algorithms but is always susceptible to ruptures dislocating the very identity of the process (contingency). In other words, it is a process conditioned by a constitutive tension between necessity and contingency.[21] However, once the historical mission incarnated in a pure and predetermined social identity is challenged by the contingent articulation, how do we account for the strong links and commitment required in any revolution? In my view, it is mystical discourse that provides a powerful sense of belonging magnifying the importance of the political enterprise involved.

Mystical discourse can be understood as an ordering of representations of the origins, the sense and transcendence of collective identities in history.[22] It therefore shares common features with the Lacanian concept of the imaginary.[23] In other words, both discourses emerge to compensate for a 'lost fullness' and both offer a reorganising principle when identities have been dislocated, concealing the contingent 'origins' of social institutions. However, some differences between these two concepts must be identified.

On the one hand, the mystical discourse operates around an *empty signifier*, and its strength is related to the intensity of the sense of lack and disruption experienced by the subject, the universality it claims, and the expansion of equivalencies it allows.[24] It operates as a powerful device for the successful interpellation of the agents and their identification as subjects of the mystical project. I will argue that the Mexican revolutionary discourse was constituted as a mystical system of representations providing a strong sense of belonging, unity and commitment. This is why, despite its failures, it maintained its popular appeal for so many years.

On the other hand, an *imaginary* system cannot be properly understood when separated from two other concepts that form a triangular interconnected relationship. I am referring to the *symbolic* and the *real*.[25] The symbolic shares with the imaginary register the form of signification; however, it differs from the latter in that the imaginary operates as that which conceals the open-ended character of the symbolic. The imaginary compensates for the gap that forever shows that all symbolic registers are structured by a constitutive lack, something that is missing and paradoxically exceeding the system, something escaping symbolisation, that is, the real. The real breaks the symbolic, dislocates the identity system, and it is in this complex triadic interconnectedness that a mystical discourse emerges as a supreme sense of an absolute union with a transcendental energy.

As against the idea of a predetermined revolutionary agent, evident in the dominant interpretations of the Mexican Revolution, I will argue that the revolutionary agent was not a pure, predetermined social class, but rather a heterogeneous composite of different social groups whose articulation was precarious, and whose identity changed during the different phases of the process.[26] This means that their identity was constituted through successive processes of *identification* with images provided by plans, manifestos, demonstrations, emblems, music and even forms of clothing that signified the revolution.[27] It was constituted in a relation where a subject was negated by another (for example, the *antagonism* between the landowner and the landless peasants) in which an enemy was pinpointed and political frontiers established. However, it was also constructed by a sense of belonging to a similar social group (for instance, the oppressed peasants and industrial workers). This was possible through the construction of equivalencies among different social groups, all of which signified their demands in a similar way. The very possibility of producing this sense of belonging emerges in the designation of a common enemy (for example, the government), and thus the shared construction of a plan to annul it, and a proposal to compensate and heal its oppressive effects. This whole process of reciprocal negativity, frontier demarcation, equivalence between the different groups and identification with the images provided by a political project, is what Laclau and Mouffe call *hegemonic articulation*, and it helps us to understand the constitution of the Mexican Revolutionary agent as the people.[28]

Historical background

Having presented the conceptual tools to support my interpretation of the Mexican Revolution, I shall now turn to the historical background that makes possible a full account of its particular logic. Without providing an exhaustive empirical account of the revolutionary process, I will highlight the key aspects of the existing literature, and those required by the analytical tools presented above.[29]

In 1910, President Porfirio Díaz had ruled Mexico for thirty years. He was a liberal who promoted capitalism, modernisation and progress, as understood by the foreign companies monopolising the railroads, mining, banking and other important sources of wealth. His liberalism had the peculiarity of being quite conservative in moral and intellectual terms since, although Positivism and the separation of State and Church had been promoted in 1856, it had later been rearticulated around an authoritarian and prejudiced, narrow-minded and intolerant morality. Thus, the Catholic Church had an extended moral and intellectual leadership within the population, regardless of their social belonging, and it was compatible with the dominant productive and the political system of this regime.

Agriculture was one of the most important sources of income for the popular sectors, and was controlled by a rather small group of large estate owners (*latifundistas*) who kept their workers in deplorable conditions. Landless peasants could be distinguished by their degree of dependence in relation to the landlord. They ranged from being the landlord's property to working free in exchange for half of an acre to exploit, or for *in-kind* payment. Right up until 1900, the almost unlimited prerogatives of landlords *vis-à-vis* 'their' workers resembled those between the lord and his serfs. By 1905, these provided fertile conditions for the constitution of peasant guerrilla movements in the northern, central and southern states of the country. The famous peasant leader Pancho Villa headed the *División del Norte* and Emiliano Zapata conducted the peasants of central southern states. Impoverished, illiterate, hungry, untrained and poorly equipped landless peasants mainly constituted this militia. Some small-property owners also participated in this agrarian force. Many of these different groups of peasants were highly religious, as could be inferred from their emblems and banners. Although the landless peasants initially backed Madero in the elections against the *Porfirista* dictatorship, they were soon disappointed by Madero's performance, and by 1911 had reorganised their strategies. Peasants remained supportive until 1915 around plans and proposals demanding land, justice, freedom and the rule of law, as these values underpinned their request for agrarian property and development, labour rights, roads and schools, as against the prevailing quasi-feudal conditions. For many of them, this was a struggle of the poor and destitute against the rich, and they organised around the idyllic view of a new society.

Industrial workers enjoyed no better conditions during the early phases of Mexico's capitalist development. They endured long working hours, no social security, low wages, poor labour rights, miserable working conditions, and lack of provision for casualties and hygiene. Incipient political organisations such as trade unions and workers' federations emerged to fight against factory owners, entrepreneurs and employers, who were in turn supported by laws and gunmen. Major strikes at the Cananea and Río Blanco factories, where industrial workers were violently repressed, played a key role in fomenting resistance on the eve of the revolution. Their intellectual leaders were represented by the Flores Magón brothers, who headed the Liberal Party combining anarchist and unionist principles. By 1906, they had called both the agrarian and industrial workers to combat dictatorship, ushering an egalitarian, laic and libertarian programme articulated around the slogan 'Reform, Freedom and Justice'. Many represented their struggle as a manifestation of 'the international proletarian class struggle against world capitalism'.[30]

Professionals such as lawyers and schoolteachers, and intellectuals such as politicians, civil servants and artists constituted another social sector opposed to the *Porfirista* regime. Some of them came from the northern states such as Sonora, while others were rooted in the central region and a few proceeded from the southern states of the country. Madero, who was the antagonistic candidate in the elections against the dictatorship, initially had a strong support from these sectors, which although politically diverse (socialists, liberals, democrats), all opposed Díaz and his allies, that is, the Catholic Church, foreign capitalists, national landlords and entrepreneurs. Some of them joined the *Partido Anti-Reeleccionista*, which was founded in

1909, while others participated independently, and some would later set up the *Constitucionalista* group. However, together they can be considered a source of political programmes where plural social demands were condensed. The destruction of *latifundio*, education and social security for the workers, women's rights, administrative reorganisation and political reform were the key issues risen by them in the Revolutionary Convention in 1916. For many within this sector, the representation of this struggle was the fight for democracy against dictatorship. Its horizon was very much inspired by the French revolution, German socialist ideals, US liberalism and Spanish rationalism, amongst the most traceable influences.[31]

The logic of the Mexican revolution: overdetermination and hegemonic practices

This brief sketch confirms that the revolutionary agents and agendas of the Mexican Revolution were politically, culturally, socially and geographically heterogeneous. In addition, their articulation changed during the different moments of the revolutionary process. Three basic features of the revolution can be discerned. First, the initial intellectual leaders were liberals, anarchists and socialists who were linked with industrial workers. Secondly, the initial military leaders directly linked with the effective supporters of the armed movement (that peculiar combination of agrarian workers) were a handful of landowners (for intsance, Carranza) and, to a great extent, a number of quasi-illiterate peasants themselves (for example,Villa's and Zapata's peasant guerillas), tired of the *latifundista's* unlimited violence and despotism. Thirdly, the frontal enemies identified by these sectors were represented by four groups. These were Porfirio Díaz and his *Científicos* cabinet, and their diverse repressive forces; the oligarchy (basically formed by the large estate owners, *latifundistas*, and their gunmen, the *Guardias Blancas*; the hierarchy of the Catholic Church; and the bourgeoisie (bankers, businessmen and factory owners).

   In addition, this setting was not the same during the years of military action. Other political configurations reorganised the antagonistic poles. For example, when Madero, having won the elections, failed to meet demands of those who had supported the armed movement, especially the peasants and industrial workers, or those who intellectually and politically had re-enforced his position, a political frontier emerged between them. Another significant change occurred in 1915 when the peasants who initially were articulated to the industrial workers did not give up their weapons, and the workers' Red Battalion, urged by Obregón, antagonised the agrarian movement. Thus, no predetermined and uncontaminated class-centred revolutionary agent can be derived from these heterogeneous and mobile political groupings.

   Instead, as I have suggested, the process can be understood as an overdetermination of different social movements organised around a mystical discourse. This was made possible because of the existence of conditions for constructing equivalences between them. In the first place, the movements were organised around antagonistic poles, in which agents were polarised in terms of the *oppressor* and the *oppressed*. Thus landlords were opposed to landless peasants, factory owners to industrial workers, dictatorship to liberal democracy, and the Church to rationalist teachers. Secondly, the displacement of the signifier 'oppression' to these different antagonistic sites made possible the construction of equivalences amongst them as the *oppressed*. This permitted three further discursive moves: the condensation of binary chains of equivalences, as the enemy was represented as the oppressor who could be impersonated by the government ≈ the dictator president Porfirio Díaz ≈ the *Científicos* cabinet ≈ the Church ≈ the landlords ≈ the entrepreneurs, and so forth; the substitutability of the enemy, as any of the signifiers of the chain could represent the enemy even if it was not the direct antagonistic pole of this social group; consequently, the revolutionary agent as 'the people' ≈ *the oppressed* was constituted as a heterogeneous social composite. Thirdly, the availability of emancipatory discourses, such as anarchism, socialism, liberalism, rationalism, and so forth, was engraved in the system of representations of the new regime which operated as a surface of inscription. The promising images of identification provided by these discourses articulated many of the social sectors' differential demands. Finally, there existed a nodal point in which different struggles, demands and expectations could be fused into a unity. This was the *Plan de San Luis Potosí*, enunciated on 20 November 1910, which represented a symbolic event invested with intense and multiple signification. It operated as a key articulatory episode, as well as the beginning of a 'new' imaginary horizon, namely, the Mexican Revolutionary Mystique.[32]

The social composition of the new ruling bloc was the outcome of negotiations during the last phases of the process. The social category that emerged involved individuals and groups of diverse social extraction (and can hardly be reduced to a social class). Wealthy northern liberals, *Constitucionalistas*, *Agraristas*, old military involved in the armed movement, intellectuals, teachers, worker and peasant leaders and even the odd industrial worker and peasant, were all accommodated within this heterogeneous ruling bloc. Moreover, the intellectual and political composition that emerged from this unity of diversity was characterised by hybridity and eclecticism, which permeated the revolutionary national programme. It involved social demands as expressed by its popular bases, the political conceptions informing specific plans of each social sector, intellectual traditions differently rooted in geographical areas, and last but not least, the inescapable common sense dwelling in *Mexican idiosyncrasy*. The latter, in turn, combined religious fanaticism, as well as its anticlerical counterpart, national chauvinism and *malinchismo*, naive optimism and sour pessimism.[33]

This hybrid system of signification of the Mexican Revolution emerged and operated as a mystical discourse. It came to provide a strong feeling of belonging and transcendental union; it gave meaning to the sacrifice and the loss, offering a horizon of compensation and an idyllic image of the future. It provided new images of identification for indigenous groups, peasants, industrial workers and schoolteachers, as well as the champions of the revolution, whose dignity was restored to its correct position. It cemented the dispersed agents and ideals involved in the armed and political movements, and operated as the ultimate source of legitimacy and proof of the righteousness of policies, laws, rituals, budgets, and so forth. Considering the constitutive fanaticism of the population it is not surprising that the symbols of this mystical discourse came to occupy the sacred positions formerly devoted to religious emblems. It is neither surprising that the new ruling bloc later became aware of this and has strategically benefited from it. The Mexican revolutionary mystique was inhabited by legendary heroes and epic events[34] being later immortalised in literature,[35] murals,[36] popular and classical music, agrarian and school rituals, unionist agendas and later, the film industry.

Let us now turn to the other key question concerning the status of the process. The variety of social movements involved in it can neither be overlooked nor should be conceptually reduced. Different timings, geographic areas, political programmes, social demands and expectations, intellectual leaders, participation and effects characterise this process. Regional and local historians have provided detailed information of these differences.[37] Nonetheless, at a national level, transformations have been documented authorising a legitimate interpretation of the process as *one* revolution. I will summarise them in the following three features. To begin with, there was a genuine mass participation; political frontiers were created thus constructing the classic binary opposition friend versus enemy. Furthermore, there was a systematic struggle over the power *loci*, the Presidency, Federal Government, Cabinet, states governments, strategic positions, and both domestic and international alliances. Finally, there were consequences affecting the nation as a whole, even if in an unequal degree. Taking different realms, I will focus on four aspects. On the *political* level, a new hybrid ruling bloc was constituted that not only changed those in positions of power, but also transformed the political system itself. Thus in 1917, the supreme law, the Mexican Constitution, was rewritten. The state as an institution increased its branches. Relations between the Church and the State were modified; the *de jure* separation between their domains, which was already at work since 1856, and during the Porfirista regime blurred, was reinforced to be again a *de facto* situation. In *economic* terms, the feudal agrarian system was strongly undermined, though not eliminated completely, as laws, institutions, political organisations, financial support, and infrastructure were developed. Industrial workers were also involved in the new order, as rights and laws, political organisations and working conditions were all reconsidered. The internal market was broadened, and the conditions for the process of industrialisation were strengthened. In *intellectual* and *moral* terms, changes took place concerning the Church leadership, which although not being extirpated, was strongly put into question by the new official discourse. The State launched a monumental educational programme, which at least competed with the previous monopoly of Roman Catholicism, and fostered a sense of national belonging articulated to the revolutionary conquests. Fourthly, on a *social* level, there was a recomposition of the groups participating in politics and the distribution of goods and services. In addition, different social identities were fostered that 'revalued' the peasant, the worker and the indigenous person by means both of art (music, literature, and painting), as well as financial support, rhetorical eulogy and caring institutions.

Conclusion

I will now conclude by pulling together the different arguments of the chapter. My examination of the available literature has shown that the current conceptual frames overlook the heterogeneity of the revolutionary process, as well as its national character. Moreover, theory has tended either to operate as a straitjacket on historical narratives, or else erases all idea of a national process in the name of fragmentation. Accordingly, different conceptual tools were needed to read this process in such a way that these problems could be overcome. By deploying the logics of overdetermination and hegemony, I have been able to develop an interpretation that both acknowledges the unforeseeable heterogeneity and mobility of the revolutionary process, while still preserving its national character. The presentation of a limited amount of historical detail about the social movements, political agents, goals, programmes and representations, struggles and negotiations that constituted the revolution has enabled me to contextualise and substantiate the account I have elaborated.

The displacement of political meanings amongst different and initially dispersed social movements facilitated the construction of equivalences between them. In turn, this helped the constitution of a heterogeneous revolutionary agent, and the national project that emerged from the ruins of the previous symbolic system. The available emancipatory discourses and the social demands expressed by popular groups articulated this heterogeneous agent around a unique system of representations which has operated as a mystical discourse. This revolutionary mystique gave a strong sense of union and commitment to the disparate outcomes of the process; today, after more than seventy years, it is endlessly re-signified,[38] manipulated and undermined. In short, the Mexican Revolution is still partly constitutive of the Mexican political imaginary.

Notes

1   The concept of discourse has some particularities, which will be presented later.
    I will now just say that it refers to socially instituted systems of meaning and
    involves linguistic and non-linguistic practices. See E. Laclau and C. Mouffe,
    Hegemony and Socialist Strategy. Towards a Radical Democracy (London, Verso,
    1985) and 'Post-Marxism Without Apologies', in E. Laclau, *New Reflections on
    the Revolution of Our Times* (London, Verso, 1990).
2   P. González Casanova has claimed it was an 'unfinished democratic bourgeois
    revolution', since the feudal system had not been yet overtaken by a bourgeois
    structure. See his *La democracia en México* (Mexico D.F., ERA, 1964). On the
    contrary, J. Cockroft has sustained that it could not be a typical bourgeois revo-
    lution since the previous regime was based already in a capitalist system; for him
    it was a 'miscarried proletarian revolution'. See *Intellectual Precursors of the
    Mexican Revolution 1900–1913* (Austin, ILAS, University of Texas Press, 1968).
3   A. Córdova also agrees that a capitalist system was already at work; however, he
    adds that the *Porfirista* bourgeoisie – former economic and political leadership –
    lost political control in their struggle against the peasants. See *La ideología de la
    revolución mexican* (Mexico D.F., ERA, 1980). Ruiz also considers it as a bour-
    geois movement readapting the capitalist system. See E. Ruiz, *La gran rebelión*
    (Mexico D.F., ERA, 1986).
4   On his part, Gilly has also accepted that the bourgeois revolution was long
    before 1910, and thus characterises the Mexican Revolution as 'a miscarried
    peasant revolution combined with a petit-bourgeois political revolution in a
    Bonapartist fashion'. The new ruling bloc was for him a bureaucratic class. A.
    Gilly, *La revolución interrumpida* (Mexico D.F., El Caballito, 1971).
5   Because Falcón landowners and the middle class led the revolutionary process.
    See R. Falcón, 'Los orígenes populares de la revolución de 1910. El caso de San
    Luis Potosí' *Historia Mexicana*, 29 (Mexico D.F., El Colegio de México, 1979).
6   González Casanova sustains that precisely in the Mexican Constitution an exem-
    plary instrument for capitalist development can be verified (*La democracia*).
7   According to F. Tannembaum, its eclecticism would show the lack of a proper
    political leadership. See his *Peace by Revolution. Mexico After 1910* (New York,
    Columbia University Press, 1966).
8   For Córdova this legislation is precisely the proof that a new political force was
    emerging: the *constitucionalistas*, with a brand new programme, populism.
9   In a random sample of more than three hundred entries on the key words 'Mex-
    ican Revolution', not a single research concentrated around the system of repre-
    sentations of this process. The closest work deals with it in terms of ideology,
    which, on the other hand, is not the idea I am interested in. See Córdova, *Ide-
    ología de la Revolución Mexicana*.
10 This is precisely J. Silva Herzog´s position. See his *Breve historia de la revolución
    mexicana* (Mexico D.F., Fondo de Cultura Económica, 1960).
11 F. Furet, *El pasado de una ilusión* (Mexico D.F., Fondo de Cultura Económica,
    1995), pp. 28–34 (my translation).
12 Although Wilkie claims there were three revolutions (i.e. the political, the social
    and the economic), he does not fragment the process and thus I will not consider
    him within this group. See J. Wilkie, *The Mexican Revolution. Federal Expendi-*

ture and Social Change Since 1910 (Berkeley and Los Angeles, University of California Press, 1970).

13 R. Falcón, who researched on San Luis Potosí, claims that the popular sectors were not an autonomous force in the process, and therefore a single national revolution could not be assumed (see 'Los orígenes). Aguilar Camin stresses the landowners in Sonora were the key leaders in the northern movements and in the new ruling bloc. See H. Aguilar Camín, *La frontera nómada: Sonora y la Revolución Mexicana* (Mexico D.F., Siglo XXI, 1987). F. Paoli and E. Montalvo, in *El socialismo olvidado de Yucatán* (Mexico D.F., Siglo XXI, 1977) and G. Joseph, in his *Revolution from without: Yucatan, Mexico and the United States 1880–1924* (Cambridge, Cambridge University Press, 1982), concentrating in Yucatán, also show the regional particularities (hemp landowners, Spanish Rationalism, *Alvarado's* socialism and the cultural question). Martínez Assad (ed.), *La revolución en las regiones* (Guadalajara, Universidad de Guadalajara, 1986), also concentrates in the diversity of social and political processes in each zone of the country.

14 For Tannembaum, this heterogeneity was a sufficient reason to show an absence of political leadership.

15 In pointing at this diversity R. Ruiz stresses the idea that a single revolution is rejected, fostering rather the interpretation of disconnected armed movements or rebellions. See his *La gran rebelión* (Mexico D.F., ERA, 1986).

16 A. Knight claims that the Mexican Revolution involved a genuine mass participation, the struggle between rival ideologies, and a consequent struggle for political leadership and authority. According to him, these features amount to a revolution. See his 'La revolución mexicana: Burguesa, nacionalista o simplemente una gran rebelión?', *Cuadernos políticos,* 48 (Mexico D.F., 1986).

17 For Ruiz, as we said above, it was merely a rebellion improving, updating and modernising the prevailing capitalist structures.

18 The official interpretations of the revolution would assert the homogeneous and unitary character of the process, putting aside the heterogeneity stressed by those historians dealing with the local particularities. Those who do not agree on the popular and mass character of the movement, namely the 'regional historians' (see note 11), do not accept it was a rightful revolution but, as we said above, merely a set of disconnected upheavals with different leaders, programmes and objectives.

19 In 1986 I started a research on this subject. See R. N. Buenfil, 'Politics, hegemony and persuasion: education and the Mexican revolutionary discourse during World War II', (Ph.D. thesis, University of Essex, 1990), and R. N. Buenfil, *Revolución mexicana, mística y educación* (Mexico D.F., Torres Asociados, 1997).

20 Althusser was the first to introduce this logic and the expression 'breaking or ruptural unit' in political philosophy. See 'Contradiction and overdetermination', in L. Althusser, *For Marx* (London, Allen Lane, 1969).

21 By contingency, I mean on the one hand that the conditions of existence of any entity are exterior to it and that it is not possible to fix them with precision as a necessary and sufficient ground; and on the other, that the link between the blocking and simultaneous negation of an identity introduces an element of radical undecidability in the structure of objectivity and an ineradicable impurity of the identity thus produced (Laclau, *New Reflections on the Revolution of Our Time*, pp. 19–21).

22 It shares with the mythical space that emerges as a principle reordering a dislocated structure, incarnating the form of fullness, and, as such, allows the incorporation of almost any social demand. It operates as a surface of inscription. Laclau's *New Reflections on the Revolution of Our Time*, p. 66 and E. Laclau, *Emancipation(s)* (London, Verso, 1996).

23 See chapter VII in J. Lacan, *The Seminar of Jacques Lacan*, Book I (Cambridge, Cambridge University Press, 1988).

24 By *empty signifier* I mean one of two sides of a discursive operation: on the one hand, that a sign never reaches an isomorphic relation between its elements (signifier and signified) but there is always some degree of flotation; on the other, that full signification is structurally impossible, that what makes it possible instead of a positive kernel, is exclusion, an 'empty essence' (see E. Laclau, 'Why do empty signifiers matter to politics?', in Laclau, *Emancipation(s)*).

25 See J. Lacan, with W. Granoff 'Fetishism: the symbolic, the imaginary and the real', in M. Balint (ed.), *Perversions, Psychodynamics and Therapy* (New York, Random House, 1956).

26 The concepts of identity and revolutionary subjectivity have already been challenged on different fronts: psychoanalysis, genealogy and deconstruction, *inter alia*. See S. Hall, 'Who needs identity?', in S. Hall and P. Du Gay (eds.), *Questions of Identity* (London, Sage, 1996). However, the literature on the Mexican Revolution has not incorporated this conceptual income yet.

27 See J. Laplanche and J.-B. Pontalis (London, Hogarth Press, 1985) *The Language of Psychoanalysis*.

28 Laclau and Mouffe, *Hegemony and Socialist Strategy*.

29 There are excellent historiographical narratives, document collections, abundant interpretations and debates. See, for instance, the series issued by El Colegio de México: *Historia de la Revolución Mexicana* (Mexico D.F., El Colegio de México, 1977–95); or Comisión de Investigaciones Históricas de la Revolución Mexicana (ed.) and J. E. De Fabela (dir.), *Documentos históricos de la Revolución Mexicana* (Mexico D.F., Fondo de Cultura Economica and Editorial Jus, 1960).

30 See Plan del Partido Liberal, cited in Silva Herzog, *Breve historia*, pp.156–60.

31 Many documents such as plans, programmes, manifestos and other documents show this intellectual and political diversity; see Comisión de Investigaiones Históricas de la Revolución Mexicana (ed.) and De Fabela (dir.), *Documentos históricos*.

32 A detailed account of the emergence of this mystical revolutionary discourse can be consulted in Buenfil, 'Politics, hegemony and persuasion'.

33 *Malinchismo* is a rather unfortunate Mexican word meaning the overvaluation of the foreign and underestimation of the native, which became a constitutive feature of Mexicans during the colonial period, and although being bitterly criticised, it has not been eradicated.

34 See, for instance, the splendid collection of pictures produced by the Fondo Casasola and edited by P. Ortiz Monasterio, *Jefes, héroes y caudillos*, Fototeca del INAH (Mexico D.F., Fondo de Cultura Económica, 1986).

35 See J. Rutherford, *An Annotated Bibliography of the Novels of the Mexican Revolution of 1910–1917*, in English and Spanish (Troy, NY, Whitston Pub. Co., 1972).

36 C. Pellicer and R. Carrillo Azpeitia, *Mural Painting of the Mexican Revolution* (Mexico D.F., Fondo Editorial de la Plástica Mexicana, 1985).
37 Information provided in note 13.
38 I sustain elsewhere that, during the first half of the twentieth century, the Mexican revolutionary mystique had three crucial processes of signification: its emergence (1908 to 1917), its radicalisation (1933 to 1938) and its 'rectification' (1940 to 1946). See Buenfil, *Revolución mexicana, mística y educación*.

On the emergence of Green ideology: the dislocation factor in Green politics

Although the 1990s witnessed a vast proliferation of publications attempting to analyse Green politics and Green ideology, some of the basic questions that shaped this whole field of research remain crucial and largely unanswered. Most prominent among these questions are surely the following. What is the background against which the need for the articulation of Green ideology emerges? Why does that need arise, and how? More generally, to what reasons does Green ideology and Green politics owe their emergence, and what factors can account for their development? In this chapter I shall try to move beyond standard but, to a large extent, unsatisfactory answers to these questions, towards an analysis of the emergence and development of Green ideology informed by discourse theory and particularly by what I shall call a theory of dislocation.

What I mean by 'theory of dislocation' is a set of theoretical assumptions and analytical tools articulated around the concept of dislocation as it is introduced by Ernesto Laclau. A theory of dislocation, which is here understood as an integral part of 'discourse theory', differs from other more traditional forms of analysis in the sense that it elevates to the epicentre of our discourse what is foreclosed in more traditional approaches. It focuses on the element of negativity inherent in human experience, on the element of rupture and crisis threatening and subverting our social – ideological – forms, the field of social objectivity. Starting from a negative ontological framework, according to which all human constructions constitute attempts to institute an impossible object (society) and master an eccessive element (the real in Lacanian terms) which always escapes our means of representation, theory of dislocation belongs to a type of theorisation and political analysis which is based on the assumption that understanding social reality is not equivalent to understanding what society is (describing the positive forms our social constructions take) but what prevents it from being.[1] What prevents it from being what it promises to be is the force of dislocation; which is also –this is the crucial part for the analysis developed here – what generates new ideological attempts to reach this impossible goal.

Before moving to the main body of my argumentation a set of conceptual and theoretical points which constitute its conditions of possibility have to be spelled out. As I have already pointed out, the main focus of this chapter is the emergence of Green ideology. Since, however, this emergence, as well as the development of Green ideological forms, coincides with the emergence of the general field of Green politics of which it forms an integral part (Green ideology can only be the ideology of a Green movement or a Green party), the two terms will be used sometimes interchangeably or side by side. However, in order to avoid confusion the following clarifications are pertinent at this point:

1 In this chapter we understand 'ideology' in a broad sense as encompassing all meaningful constructions (belief structures, constructions of reality, discursive practices) through which social reality is produced and our action within it – especially our political action – acquires cause and direction. Ideological constructions of reality attempt to provide a final symbolisation of the world around us and thus articulate themselves 'on the basis of closure, of the fixation of meaning', by repressing any recognition of 'the precarious character of any positivity, [and] of the impossibility of any ultimate suture'.[2] The ideological is thus constitutive of our constructions of reality since there is no reality without some sense of closure. It does not exhaust though the whole of human experience. Beyond ideological articulation there is dislocation, beyond positivity there is negativity, beyond reality there is the *real*, in the Lacanian sense of the word (that which cannot be symbolised, the impossible). In that sense, a rigorous theoretical approach to the analysis of ideology has to take into account the fact that ideological construction emerges in a dialectic with something that exceeds its symbolic and imaginary boundaries. The fantasy – the illusion – supporting all ideologies is that they can master this excessive element.[3]

2 The way ideologies attempt to master this escaping real and suture dislocation is by articulating a chain of signifiers (previously belonging to other, now dislocated discourses) around a new nodal point (accepted as) incarnating an ultimate fullness of meaning and thus as suitable to hegemonise a certain discursive field and appeal (as an object of identification) to the respective audiences to which it is addressed (electorate, party membership, public opinion, and so on).

3 We can conclude, on the basis of this schema and of the political experience from the 1960s onwards, that there is a separate ideological form which can be called 'Green ideology' the same way we speak about liberal political ideology, and so on. This ideology has emerged from the 1960s and 1970s onwards as a result of the articulation of a series of socio-political elements (decentralisation, direct democracy, post-patriarchal principles, and so on) around a certain conception of nature. Its novel character is due to the location of this Green signifier which, perhaps for the first time, becomes the nodal point of a whole ideological frame (although the various

elements hegemonised by its central position have preexisted their new articulation).[4]

4 What are the implications for our analysis from understanding ideology and Green ideology in particular in these terms? It follows that Green ideology is restricted to the different versions of parties, movements, groups and ideologues putting forward a radical environmental agenda; something characterising mostly first-world situations. It seems that in all other cases the Green element remains on the periphery of the ideological chain. Similar is the case with most versions of eco-feminism, eco-socialism and even eco-fascism where, although the Green element aquires a prominent place, it usually remains hegemonised by another principle (feminism, socialism and fascism, respectively) without, however, the existence of impure forms being ruled out a priori. Some of the reasons accounting for this political radicalism and localisation of Green ideology will be sketched in the following pages.[5]

Do we really need a new framework for the analysis of Green ideology and its emergence? Encircling the dislocation factor

The need, however, for an alternative, or rather complementary, analysis of Green ideology can only be founded on the realisation of the limits of more 'traditional' approaches. Let us discuss and explore the value of some of them as briefly as possible. Let us reconsider, in other words, some of the standard answers that are usually being given to the aforementioned question in the relevant literature: What led to the formation and influences the development of Green ideology and Green politics in general?

1 The first rather naive answer was proposed by the first wave of 'new social movements' theorists such as Touraine who, in the late 1960s and early 1970s, identified the Green movement as the new historical subject of our age; a historical subject in the teleological sense of the word, taking the place of the proletariat in the emerging post-industrial society. This idea does not take into account the fact that the ultimate failure of every single attempt to promote a sense of a historical subject within the framework of a secular eschatology – be it Hegelian, Marxist or of any other kind – not only puts in question the identity of the particular historical subject but subverts this whole eschatological logic. Due to the realisation of this fact and to the instability of Green politics it was very soon realised that the explanatory power of this idea was very limited: ideological struggle is not following any predetermined course but is always conditioned by the contingent nature of political antagonism.

2 Another 'naive' answer is the one reducing the emergence of the Green movement and Green ideology to environmental crisis itself as an 'objective' factum. This idea brings to memory the Marxist idea of a base/superstructure model: the base here is the order of objective nature which is conceived as

determining its political and ideological manifestations. Such a view remains trapped in a representationalist problematic which has proved to be catastrophic for the theory of ideology.[6] Besides being theoretically outmoded, its empirical validity is also extremely limited. For example, it is not true that environmental degradation directly leads to the development of some sort of Green consciousness, to a Green concern or to Green action. Clive Ponting describes the example of the inhabitants of Easter Island, which is typical: the people of Easter Island cut down almost all the trees on their island in an attempt to transfer their gigantic statues from one part of the island to another. This led to gross environmental degradation and, finally, to the environmental and physical destruction of Easter Island's flora, fauna and culture. It seems, though, that in the course of this mass suicide no 'Green' concern has arisen.[7] Environmental degradation, then, was not unknown in primitive cultures as it is usually believed. To give another example, the Maori of New Zealand caused the extinction of many species of birds without any Green reservations. What is shown by these two examples is that Green concerns and reservations are historically and discursively constructed, a created set of normative and empirical claims, principles and prescriptions. They are not something 'ahistorical', 'transcendental' and 'objective' and thus available to all human societies regardless of when they exist. Finally, to give a more contemporary example, the lack of any environmental movement of considerable organisation and influence in Athens proves that environmental degradation does not directly lead to the emergence of a Green concern or a movement. Simply put, a strong Green concern can be present in countries and contexts with minimal environmental problems and absent in countries with major environmental degradation. One then should agree with Yearley's assertion that 'objective conditions in themselves ... are [not] enough to promote' environmental awareness and action.[8] In fact 'objective' conditions 'may not and theoretically need not' be necessary at all, as Kitsuse and Spector have argued.[9] The idea of a direct connection between 'objective' nature and our representation of it remains trapped in an essentialist conception of nature as something outside culture and discourse, a positive unchanging reality that can be mirrored in a particular type of discourse. Nature is understood as an object to be discovered, and described and not to be constructed. Today, however, this sort of essentialism is proved untenable by the increasing hegemony of the various versions of social constructionism.[10] Nature, meaning our representations of nature, is no longer accepted as something 'already there' but is understood as the result of a slow and complex process of historical and social construction.[11]

The question, though, remains: What are the conditions that lead to the emergence of a Green – ideological – concern? There is an increasing consensus that what is needed beyond any 'objective' crisis is the construction of a sense of crisis at the level of discourse as a social problem. As Yearley points out, following Kitsuse and Spector, 'the existence of social problems depends

on the continued existence of groups or agencies that define some condition
as a problem and attempt to do something about it'.[12] Thus, Yearley stresses
the importance of environmentalist groups and the media for constructing
and promoting environmental issues and generating the Greening of the public. What is necessary, then, for the development of a certain environmental
consciousness is the social availability of the symbolic resources permitting
the construction of the environment as a pressing social problem. These
resources are missing when a society is hegemonised by a mythic or other ideological structure explaining things in a different way. In any case, as Andrew
Dobson has argued, these developments (the discursive production of environmental crisis) may only be viewed as preconditions for the emergence of
Green ideology and do not provide any reason for the transformation in
question, namely the radicalisation of environmentalist discourse and its
investment with political significance, a transformation that takes place in the
1970s.[13] In other words, even if we have explained part of the 'how' we still
have not located the 'why' *vis-à-vis* the emergence of Green ideology.

3 Equally insufficient is the explanation according to which the emergence of Green ideology is the effect of the shift to a set of post-materialist
values. Even if these constitute another precondition, they cannot account
for the fact that at a certain point a bundle of post-materialist and other more
traditional ideas are articulated around a Green concept and transformed
into a cohesive ideology.[14] Besides, a lot of well-grounded objections, both at
the theoretical and at the empirical level, have been raised against Inglehart's
theory of a *Silent Revolution*.[15] One has to agree with Kuechler and Dalton
that 'Inglehart's data provide overwhelming evidence that the new movements have developed in a favourable context, with a fairly large segment of
the population principally endorsing their goals. Yet, they do not sufficiently
account for the emergence of these movements.'[16] In his recent work Inglehart has acknowledged himself the limited explanatory power of his theory.[17]

4 The emergence and development of Green politics and Green ideology have been also attributed to the whole framework of opportunities and
constraints, the so-called opportunity structure that characterises a given
institutional setting. Surely it cannot be denied that the character of the electoral system can help explain the emergence of a Green party by creating
extremely favorable conditions for its electoral success. But although it is
certain that an electoral system of proportional representation can help the
emergence of Green parties this has not taken place in a variety of cases; it
is not a sufficient condition for the emergence of Green politics. The cases
of Denmark and the Netherlands are revealing: 'both countries have electoral systems which are unusually hospitable to small parties; yet neither has
been a pace-setter in the development of Green Parties'.[18] Besides, the
nature of the opportunity structure is not affecting only Green parties but
all small parties.

It is not, however, our intention in this chapter to stage a detailed critique of standard explanations of the emergence of Green politics and Green ideology. What is important, what is of interest from our point of view, is that there is a growing consensus that all these, and other available explanations to which we have not referred, are increasingly defined as, to a large extent, inadequate. Rootes points out, for example, that 'just as highly developed and widespread awareness of environmental issues, national or global, is no guarantee of the development of a successful Green party, neither is a decentralised political system operating under conditions of proportional representation'.[19] This argument is valid not only regarding the development – which is Rootes's explicit target – but also regarding the emergence of Green politics and Green ideology. Karel-Werner Brand, for his part, after presenting a list of current explanations of the emergence of new movements, a list slightly different but overlapping with the one presented here, also concludes that 'none of these single interpretations ... offers an adequate explanation of the mobilisation cycle of new social movements',[20] and Richardson refers to the 'relevance but overall inadequacy of the concepts of postmaterialism and postindustrialism in explaining' things.[21] On the one hand, then, it is true that no single factor can account for the emergence, the differential development and varying electoral success of Green ideology and Green parties.[22] On the other hand, however, it is also true that even if we take into account all the aforementioned factors still something is missing – the explanation is not adequate. And although perfect explanations are no more than utopian dreams, it might be possible for us to identify the missing link, the source of the inadequacy of our analyses, the trace of the real remaining outside our representations of political reality: 'It is this factor – the *contingent* balance of political competition – which makes theorising and prediction so difficult, because although one can point to the ways in which social, economic and political institutional considerations create the framework for political competition, *how that competition is worked out in practice depends on any number of the caprices of humanity and nature.*'[23] In that sense, any further advance in our understanding of Green politics and Green ideology depends on our ability to activate the theoretical tools that are going to permit us map and encircle these 'caprices of humanity and nature'.

Our inability to do that up to now should be attributed to the fact that what we were looking for was positively existing causes and rational explanations, whereas these 'caprices of humanity and nature' are located precisely where all these fail. Surely a caprice is something unexpected, something running contrary to 'normal' – ideologically sedimented – behaviour. Thus, it seems legitimate to link these caprices to the moments of an unexpected dislocation both at the strictly political level (the level of political ideology and ideological struggle) and at the level of nature (that is, of our representation of nature and environmental crisis). Dislocation is understood here in the way Laclau defines it, as the moment of failure and subversion of a system of representation (that is, a political ideology, a social paradigm or even a scientific explanation, and so on).[24] Dislocation introduces a rupture in a normal – or rather 'normalised' – order of things. Although dislocations are embodying a radical negativity – they have no positive content in themselves – and cannot be predicted by any kind of teleological philosophy of history, they have certain important consequences. This is due to the fact that besides their negative character they also entail a productive element. If on the one hand they threaten identities, ideologies and discourses, on the other hand, by creating a certain lack – which is not easy to bear – they generate attempts to rearticulate these dislocated ideologies and discourses.[25] Thus, dislocations and crises, although they do not constitute positively defined factors (they have no substance), can help us move beyond the current impasse in Green politics research. Dislocation as a complementary[26] explanatory factor can considerably enhance our understanding of the emergence and development of Green ideology.

Of course, this is not to say that the whole of the bibliography on this issue is outmoded. In fact, it has been argued lately that two parameters are essential for the analysis of the emergence of Green ideology. First of all, it has been realised that ideologies do not emerge like mushrooms, or according to any plan of predestination, but constitute responses to particular crises that cannot be known in advance and cannot be administered within the previous ideological configuration. Secondly, it has been recognised that far from being a piecemeal operation, the articulation, the emergence and the operation, as well as the success of an ideology – in our case Green ideology – depend upon the play of hegemony and its contingent punctuation. Robyn Eckersley, for example, has made considerable progress in these two directions. He asserts that environmental dislocation (at a so-called 'objective' level) can be constructed and has been constructed in a variety of ways bringing to the fore a crisis of participation, a crisis of survival and finally, and most importantly, a 'crisis of culture and character as an opportunity for emancipation'.[27] When environmental dislocation was constructed as a crisis of industrial culture, 'a new breed of ecopolitical theorists [Green ideologues] began to draw out what they saw as the emancipatory potential that they believed was latent within the ecological critique of industrialism',[28] Thus a concept of crisis and the initiation of a hegemonic project become inexorably related.

What is not, however, developed in Eckersley's analysis is the reason behind the motivation of various ideologues to reinvest the futures of radical politics in ecocentrism. My own argument is that in order to account for this development we have to posit another dislocation. In Eckersley's terms this would be a dislocation of emancipatory ideologies, a crisis creating the need for their rearticulation around a Green centre. This ideological dislocation has been very well documented, mostly in the part of bibliography devoted to the study of particular Green movements and Green ideologies. For instance, in analyses of the German Greens such as those of Hulsbergs and Papadakis, it is made clear that the emergence of Green ideology has been the result of an overdetermination of various struggles and movements under the umbrella of a Green core and as a response to the failure of the more traditional left. We shall return to these approaches in a while. For the time being let us just say that this is not a common-sense or trivial assumption. Take, for example, the following argument presented by Dobson: 'On the face of it, the Green movement could hardly have appeared on the political scene at a worse moment form the point of view of socialism'; he is referring to the moment of the critique of bureaucracy and of the socialist regimes, the moment of the crisis of social democracy and of the general crisis of the left exhibited in developments such as those of May 1968: 'In this context of an assault by the right, the last thing socialism needed, so the argument goes, was a challenge to its hegemony on the left hand side of the political spectrum.'[29] What is not realised here is that it is exactly because of the crisis, of the dislocation of the left, that a lack in the ideological level was created, a lack generating the need for a new articulation of radical ideological discourse, a process eventually hegemonised by Green ideology. In fact, a theory of dislocation is so important not because it is based on some difficult or obscure logic but exactly because it is based on an almost common-sensical assumption which, however, is often foreclosed from the theoretical and analytical terrain. For my part, and contrary to this foreclosure, I shall argue that besides all positively defined factors the emergence of Green ideology is due to a *lack* created by the dislocation of our (imaginary/symbolic) conceptions of nature by a feeling of environmental crisis, a lack that coincided with another lack created by the dislocation of certain currents of ideological discourse in the radical political spectrum.[30] Thus, Green ideology is not a single, direct expression or representation of nature but entails a new imaginary/symbolic answer to the dislocation of our previous conceptions of it. Furthermore, this new conception is invested with political significance because it coincides with a political dislocation and serves as an attempt to cover over, to suture, this dislocation also. Let me make clear at this point that I am not arguing that whenever we have these two dislocations we shall necessarily have the emergence of Green movements; this will depend on the particular contingent hegemonic play.[31] What I will try to show is that in our particular historical example these two dislocations were administered in a way that produced Green ideology.

Let me now present in a more detailed way the two dislocations that, as I argue, are related to the emergence and development of Green ideology. My argumentation will be supported by a variety of empirical examples taken from a number of mostly European contexts.

The first dislocation …

Surely, one 'necessary' dislocation is the dislocation of nature as exhibited in our perception of the ecological crisis. As we have already argued, this is not only a real experience of ecological crisis. It is primarily a dislocation of our imaginary/symbolic construction or mediation of our relationship to (the real of) nature and of the concomitant construction of environmental crisis as a pressing social problem.[32]

The field of our relationship to nature is one of the fields in which the real is continuously intersecting with our symbolic and imaginary reality, with our constructions of objectivity. It is in that sense that Žižek presents eco-logical crisis as initiating a period of continuous, everyday encounter with the real.[33] Here, the real, as introduced by Lacan, is that which always escapes our attempts to incorporate it in our constructions of reality, con-structions that are articulated at the level of the image (imaginary level) or the signifier (symbolic level). The encounter with this impossible is exactly what dislocates our imaginary/symbolic constructions (ideologies, para-digms, and so on). Ecological crisis is characterised by such a dislocatory dimension. In fact, the unpredictability and severity of natural forces have forced people from time immemorial to attempt to understand and master them through processes of imaginary representation and symbolic integra-tion.[34] This usually entails a symbolisation of the real of nature, the part of the natural world exceeding our discursive grasp of nature. The product of this symbolisation has been frequently described as a 'story' or a 'paradigm' about how the world works. We can trace such a story, or many competing stories, in any civilisation or cultural ensemble. In modern secular techno-sci-entific societies it is usually science that provides the symbolic framework for the symbolisation of nature. Predicting the unpredictable, mastering the impossible, reducing the unexpected to a system of control, in other words symbolising, integrating the real of nature, is attempted through the dis-course of science and its popularisation in the media.

Now, as we have pointed out, these discursive mediations instituting human reality are not eternal or transcendental but change over time. It seems that today we are witnessing such a gradual but important change. What is asserted by many analysts of the environmental crisis is that 'a new story about the relationship between humans and nature is emerging in west-ern societies that contrasts sharply with the story that currently dominates public discourse'.[35] Indeed if we call this story a paradigm, generalising the Kuhnian application of the term, if we understand it as a discursively con-structed belief structure that organises the way people perceive and interpret their relation to nature, then we could assert that we are witnessing a grad-ual paradigm shift.[36] It has been suggested that this is a shift from a Domi-nant Social Paradigm (DSP) to a New Environmental Paradigm (NEP).[37] Most importantly, this shift is produced by the dislocation of the old para-digm and the need for a new discursive structure to fill the lack produced by this dislocation.

At this point, it is important to keep in mind that the lack of meaning pro-duced by a dislocation can activate a plurality of reactions. As Žižek has put it, one can continue to stick to the old paradigm, pretending that the dislocation does not affect it, or engage in frenetic environmental activism, identifying with new paradigms, new stories, new ideologies.[38] The direction of the response depends on the course of action which seems to be more capable of neutralising the terrorising presence of this impossible real, more capable of covering over the lack of meaning in question and of providing the greater feeling of 'security'. This means that subjective responses to such situations cannot be predicted in advance nor do they follow any rational rules. In cases where the dislocation is severe and the symbolic means to articulate a new response are not *available* it is even possible for social actors to ignore its implications for their life. In fact, as Beck has put it:

> as the hazards increase in extent, and the situation is subjectively perceived as hopeless, there is a growing tendency not merely to accept the hazard, but to deny it by every means at one's disposal. One might call this phenomenon, paradoxical only at first glance, the 'death-reflex of normality'. There is a virtually instinctive avoidance, in the face of the greatest possible danger, of living in intolerable contradiction; the shattered constructs of normality are upheld, or even elevated, as if they remained intact.[39]

Beck quotes Patrick Lagadec who, in his exposition of major accidents and the reactions to them, continuously comes up against the phenomenon that the people most gravely affected by these accidents are frequently those who are most determined to repress them. Lagadec presents the empirical example of the Seveso accident and its victims: 'Many did not criticise those who denied the hazards arising from dioxin. On the contrary, they displayed a truly boundless trust in those who played the dangers down, while those who stressed the toxicity of dioxin but knew no appropriate counter-measures met with bitter and occasionally pedantic criticism.'[40] Lagadec continues:

> The populations' scepticism and indignation were most apparent when the people evacuated from the zone of greatest danger ... got into their cars on the morning of Sunday 10 October, and returned to Seveso. They broke through the barbed-wire fence and moved back into their homes. For hours the contaminated zone became virtually the theatre of an uncanny spectacle. In the black comedy that ensued, the actors played out their lives in the safe and familiar world of the past, the world prior to the disaster that had left the scene largely intact. The houses and gardens, the grass and the countryside – it all looked so hospitable! People invited each other to dinner or picnics. This 'authentic' spectacle only came to an end when the police and gendarmes were deployed, and when the provincial and regional authorities appeared.[41]

Sticking to the old paradigm, to the old symbolisation, is not, however, the only response to such a catastrophe or a crisis. In fact, as far as it concerns the general environmental crisis, it could be suggested that one of the dominant responses to this dislocation has been the identification of the public with what we have called a 'New Environmental Paradigm'. This paradigm is built on the dislocation of the previously dominant view of our right to dominate nature, this domination being fantasised as an operation with no hazards and no limits. What is shown by the current environmental crisis, the environmental dislocation, is in fact that there are some limits, limits to growth and economic expansion, limits imposed by the real of nature to which the public is becoming sensitive.

This productive/ontological character of dislocation is not something surprising. Milbrath, at the end of his analysis, an analysis very near to our own, asks the following question: 'nature can use its fury to get us to listen, even when we do not wish to. Must we always learn the hard way, by death and destruction?'[42] The answer must be affirmative, although this affirmation is something we easily forget. Dislocation, with all its disruptive power, can be found at the root of all paradigm, discursive, or ideological shifts. Even the romantic idealisation of nature in the late 1800s, which generated the first wave of conservationist environmentalism, can only be understood as a reaction to the social dislocations of the period. The idealised conception of nature provided a source of stability and harmony that attempted to cover the lack produced by these dislocations.[43] It was, again, dislocatory events such as Chernobyl that reinforced the current wave of environmentalism, initially produced by environmental problems such as acid rain, toxic waste, and so on. As Dalton has put it, 'the Chernobyl nuclear disaster in 1986 may be the event which finally changed the course of contemporary European politics on environmental issues'.[44] Wiesenthal has also pointed out that events with great dislocatory power, such as Chernobyl, bring forward a 'that's enough' logic which can facilitate a paradigm shift, an identification with a new discursive ensemble. It is these striking incidents that prompt new innovative interpretations, and suggest new routes of action.[45]

People involved in Green politics seem to be aware of the tremendous power of such dislocations in facilitating a change in the direction of 'Greening' public opinion. The introduction of radical environmentalism in Denmark presents a paradigmatic case. In a society which largely neglected environmental issues, Green activists chose to *simulate* environmental dislocation, anticipating that this violent event would result in an identification with radical environmentalism. They enacted the following happening in a meeting of a respectable natural history society at the University of Copenhagen (NOA) in March 1969. This is how one of the participants describes the events:

> We locked them all in. We were about twenty people. After we had locked the doors, we cut off the ventilation and started to poison them. It was pretty violent. We got up on the stage and talked about air pollution. We burnt garbage and tobacco in large quantities. We poured waste water from a nearby factory in an aquarium with goldfish who slowly died ... And we had taken along a wild duck which we covered with oil. 'Come and save it', we screamed. 'You talk about pollution. Why don't you do anything about it?' Finally we cut off

its head to end its suffering, and we walked down along the first row of chairs so that all who were sitting there got blood on their clothes. After an hour we opened the doors and said that we wanted to start an environmental movement, and that the founding meeting was being held in the next room.[46]

Environmental dislocation, however, is not a sufficient condition for the emergence of Green politics and Green ideology. Nor is it enough to administer such a dislocation in the direction of constructing a New Environmental Paradigm. There is no necessary link between the development of so-called 'environmental consciousness' and Green politics *per se*, or the construction of a Green political ideology. This so-called Greening of consciousness can be articulated within pre-existing ideological discourses. Besides, environmental dislocation can be administered in ways not leading to the Greening of a society. Although Green ideology cannot be articulated before the traumatic experience of environmental dislocation because without it nature is not cathected with any importance, this dislocation does not lead directly to the emergence of Green ideology.

... and the second

In fact, it has been argued that wherever Green identifications occurred, the experience of environmental dislocation was coupled with another fear resulting from social and political dislocations. Dickens's analysis of the *Mass Observation Archive* leads to such a conclusion:

> for some people, analogies are being made between on the one hand unpredictable natural disasters and on the other hand the feeling of insecurity deriving from increasingly globalized economic and social conditions. This suggests that some people are, albeit unconsciously, projecting their personal fears in the social world out to the natural world ... . It would be difficult to argue, therefore, that the deterioration of the physical environment is, on its own, the cause of the recent resurgence in environmentalism. Rather, such politics are at least as much a commentary on people's social circumstances, analogies being made between these circumstances and their sense of alienation from other aspects of society.[47]

This view is supported by various personal histories depicted in interviews contained in the archive. The implication of this is that an increasing number of people look for a solution to problems such as unemployment and economic deterioration in Green ideology. Now, although this is undoubtedly true, this moment in fact *follows* the emergence of Green ideology, and concerns its hegemonic appeal. What is not mentioned here is another important dislocation. If today people are increasingly looking to Green ideology in order to solve these problems this means that previously hegemonic identifications (from the labour movement up to the limits of the radical tradition, not to mention the right wing of the political spectrum) have been dislocated.

Our argument then runs as follows. For Green ideology to emerge, what was needed, besides environmental dislocation, was the dislocation of a certain political tradition or ideological field (it was the radical tradition which happened to perform this role), a dislocation which was partially resolved by making nature or the NEP the core of a new ideological rearticulation. This process produces an appealing new object of identification as a potential solution to the social problems around which hegemonic struggle currently takes place.

What I am arguing, in other words, is that a dual dislocation is the necessary precondition for the emergence of Green ideology. This is not a metaphysical point. This emergence was not a necessity but a contingent development which, however, had very precise conditions of possibility. Dislocation is the concept we can use in order to facilitate an analysis of the conditions of possibility related to this area of contingency. This is also stressed by Adrian Atkinson if one connects his conception of crisis with that of dislocation. Atkinson speaks of two crises: 'amongst those who do perceive our age as one of crisis there are two almost completely different sets of notions as to what is involved'.[48] The first of these crises is what we have been calling the environmental dislocation, a growing concern and fear that the way in which our society is making use of the biosphere is not sustainable even in the medium term. The second one is a political dislocation. Atkinson especially stresses, in this respect, the collapse of social democracy, socialism and communism. One should not underestimate the effect of these dislocations on the identity of people involved in left-wing politics:

> For many these changes have precipitated personal crises that turned to new
> opportunities or resignation, but the general reaction has not been one of the
> kind of tension associated with crisis but rather of a quiet falling away of value
> structures into a life process that seems effortlessly to carry all along with it. In
> so far as this has generated a sense of crisis, this has been one of intellectual
> concern with the wisdom of the changes in train and an anxiety with regard to
> the ultimate social, political and cultural settlement that might evolve out of the
> current rapid metamorphosis.[49]

Atkinson has very successfully shown how the fear produced by these dislocations initiated a quest for new identifications and new ideologies that would fill this ideological lack.

In that sense, Atkinson's view is very close to the idea that in the basis of the emergence of Green ideology one can detect a dual dislocation. A dislocation of the way our relationship to nature has been symbolically negotiated up to now, and a second dislocation, the dislocation of a political tradition. The first dislocation elevates the idea of nature to a virtual nodal point, a potential master or empty signifier that contingently came to articulate around it a whole ideological edifice as an answer to the second dislocation. The crisis of the left – a contingent coincidence – created the need for a rearticulation of radical politics, and nature, as constructed within the NEP, was historically *available* as a potential nodal point with enormous power and social appeal.[50]

This is, then, the logical structure of our argument regarding the second ideological dislocation. Green ideology did not exist in the 1920s or the 1940s. The fact that it has become an object of identification can only mean that previous identifications have failed. The need to identify with something new can only arise after the failure/dislocation of our previous identifications (in the same sense that we have argued that the articulation and the identification with the NEP can only be understood as following the dislocation of an older social paradigm that regulated our relationship to nature). But this logical argument is not enough. One has to show that it holds true in different concrete cases. What is, however, the empirical evidence for this second political dislocation? Although the argument presented here suggests that such a dislocation can be found wherever a Green ideology is articulated, I will limit myself to presenting only a couple of examples from different political contexts.

In Hulsberg's analysis of the German Greens, it is evident that one of the factors that most strongly influenced the emergence of Green ideology and of the German Green party has been the failure of the Marxist left and the left in general during the 1960s. Far from being a purely ecological phenomenon, Green politics and the formation of the German Green party was much more the result of the concrete social situation in which a crucial role was played by the failure of the Comintern models of revolution and the erosion of the potential force of the labour movement and social democracy in general.[51] It is true that in the German context, the 1960s and 1970s have signalled an acute disillusionment of the left which led to phenomena such as left-wing terrorism and had a profound effect on German society.[52] More so for the politically active younger generation: 'violence, fruitless theoretical discussions and conflicts with their immediate surroundings led many students to search for a new context in which to overcome their own isolation. The ecology movement provided an important outlet for them to express their dissatisfaction.'[53] This failure/dislocation of the left has been a central ideological theme also for the movement of the *Spontis*, a source of great inspiration and powerful influence for the Green movement: 'the left, argue the *Spontis*, has failed to take part in the revolt of life against the world of death, which they describe as prisons, lunatic asylums, family structures, schools and war. This failure is caused by its overestimation of analysis and knowledge.'[54] The role of the Green party as filler of the lack produced by the failure of the left has been also reinforced by the particular German political setting. The German Greens 'filled a gap in supply of a kind that was unknown in the political systems of other western European states, namely, the specific German lack of a socialist opposition, resulting from the division of the country, the cold war, and the semi-official anti-communism'.[55]

It is the case of the Netherlands, however, that is essential to our argument. Here the articulation of a Green ideology and the emergence of a Green party followed the dislocation of dominant left ideologies, ideologies that were previously expressed by a series of Dutch parties, namely, the Communist Party of the Netherlands (CPN), the Pacifist Socialist Party (PSP), the Political Radical Party (PPR) and the Evangelical People's Party (EVP). Here, as in Germany, the emergence of the new 'Green Left' party, which resulted from the merger of these parties, followed the dislocation of their respective ideologies, 'notably, the abandonment of the class struggle as the sole engine of history and the dislocation of the idea of the vanguard of the working class'. In any case, 'cooperation among these parties started in the 1970s, stimulated by the introduction of new left ideas and the rise of new social movements, combined with the declining electoral fortunes of the parties themselves'.[56]

Our argument that the emergence of Green ideology and Green politics presupposes a dislocation in a certain part of the ideological spectrum, to which it constitutes a response, is further reinforced by the failure of a 'pure' Green party to develop despite the favourable social and political conditions. This is what Voerman has described as a *paradox*: 'Despite the low electoral threshold (a party requires only 0,67 per cent of the vote to obtain a seat in the national parliament) and the presence of a large electoral reservoir in the shape of relatively strong new social movements in the 1970's and early 1980's, a Green party did not enter the Dutch parliament.'[57] In fact, when a deep Green party was set up in 1983 'it suffered failure after failure'.[58] It did develop only as a result of the *rapprochement* of already existing parties as part of their attempt to rearticulate their ideology and enhance their electoral prospects. This is what Voerman calls the second Dutch *paradox*. He even concludes his paper with the expression of an *aporia* which shows the inadequacy of standard theoretical approaches to Green politics: 'In theory, then, there remains room in the political landscape of the Netherlands for a deep Green party. In practice, it has been demonstrated that such a party will not grow in the present Dutch electoral climate.'[59] The paradoxical puzzle in which Voerman finds himself and the inadequacies of his theoretical tools to approach political practice are due to the fact that, as I have tried to suggest, the deciding factor in this case is the factor of dislocation. The successful Dutch Green party ('Green Left')[60] owes its 'success' to the fact that its development was stimulated by a very real need for rearticulation, the need for a new ideological construction following the dislocation of the ideological profiles of the radical parties that were united or merged to form it. No other 'pure' Green party managed to develop, besides the favourable conditions, because it did not correspond to any preceding dislocation in the ideological spectrum; there was no room or real need for it.[61]

Conclusion

To recapitulate, our hypothesis concerning the emergence of Green ideology runs as follows. Green ideology is articulated as a result of the temporal and contingent coincidence of two dislocations. These dislocations constitute its *conditions of possibility*. The first is a dislocation of our previously hegemonic mode of symbolising the real of nature. This dislocation of what has been called the 'Dominant Social Paradigm' led to the articulation of a 'New Environmental Paradigm' simultaneously investing the signifier 'nature' with major social importance. The second is a dislocation of the Western radical tradition. For a variety of reasons at some point in time radical ideologies can no longer perform the job of every ideology, that is to say, to master the real of society – the impossibility of society – in other words to provide 'credible', hegemonically appealing answers to social dislocations taking the form of 'social ills' such as unemployment and inequality. This dislocation produced a lack in the ideological level which had to be covered over if the radical side of the political spectrum still wanted to appear as a hegemonic force, an administrator of social dislocations. In order to do that the radical tradition was in need of a rearticulation, a new investment of its potential. This new articulation was performed around 'nature', a highly cathected signifier of public discourse and discussion; a signifier with a radical potential. What emerged was Green Ideology; and this is probably the closest we can get to the caprices of humanity and nature and their relation to Green politics.

Notes

1 E. Laclau, *New Reflections on the Revolution of Our Time*, (London, Verso, 1990), p. 44.
2 *Ibid.*, p. 92
3 For a detailed conceptualisation of ideology along these lines see Y. Stavrakakis, 'Ambiguous ideology and the Lacanian twist', *Journal of the Centre for Freudian Analysis and Research*, 8 & 9 (1997), 117–30.
4 Y. Stavrakakis, 'Green ideology: a discursive reading', *Journal of Political Ideologies*, 2:3 (1997), 259–79.
5 For a detailed analysis of Green ideology through the theoretical frame adopted here besides Stavrakakis, 'Green ideology', see Y. Stavrakakis, 'Green fantasy and the real of nature: elements of a Lacanian critique of Green ideological discourse', *Journal for the Psychoanalysis of Culture and Society*, 2:1 (1997).
6 Stavrakakis, 'Ambiguous ideology', pp. 120–1.
7 C. Ponting, *Green History of the World* (London, Penguin, 1991), especially pp. 1–7.
8 S. Yearley, *The Green Case* (London, Harper Collins, 1991), p. 49.
9 J. I. Kitsuse and M. Spector, cited in *ibid.*, p. 50.
10 See, in this regard, some of the recent studies on the social construction of nature: N. Evernden, *The Social Creation of Nature* (Baltimore, Johns Hopkins

University Press, 1992) and K. Eder, *The Social Construction of Nature* (London, Sage, 1994).

11 Laclau, *New Reflections on the Revolution of our Time*, p. 102.

12 Kitsuse and Spector in Yearley, *The Green Case*, p. 50.

13 A. Dobson, *Green Political Thought* (London, André Deutsch, 1990), p. 34.

14 M. Robinson, *The Greening of British Party Politics* (Manchester, Manchester University Press, 1992), p. 46.

15 See, in this respect, S. Flanagan, 'Value Change in industrial society', *American Political Science Review*, 81 (1987); M. Kuechler and R. Dalton, 'New social movements and the political order: inducing change for long term stability', in R. Dalton and M. Kuechler (eds), *Challenging the Political Order: New Social and Political Movements in Western Democracies* (Oxford, Polity, 1990).

16 M. Kuechler and R. Dalton, 'New social movements', p. 286.

17 R. Inglehart, 'Values, ideology and cognitive mobilisation in New Social Movements' in Dalton and Kuechler, *Challenging the Political Order*, pp. 43–4.

18 C. Rootes, 'Environmental consciousness, institutional structures and political competition in the formation and development of Green parties', in D. Richardson and C. Rootes, *The Green Challenge* (London, Routledge, 1995), p. 242.

19 *Ibid.*, p. 241.

20 K. W. Brand, 'Cyclical aspects of New Social Movements: waves of cultural criticism and mobilisation cycles of new middle class radicalism', in Dalton and Kuechler, *Challenging the Political Order* , p. 29.

21 *Ibid.*, p. 20.

22 Richardson, 'The green challenge', in Richardson and Rootes, *The Green Challenge*, p. 20.

23 Rootes, 'Environmental consciousness', p. 248, my emphasis.

24 For a full elaboration of the logic of dislocation see Laclau, *New Reflections on the Revolution of Our Time*, especially pp. 39–45, and the introduction to this volume.

25 *Ibid.*, p. 39.

26 Complementary in the sense that it is not invalidating all other approaches although operating at a totally different level.

27 R. Eckersley, *Environmentalism and Political Theory* (London, UCL Books, 1992), p. 17.

28 *Ibid.*, p. 18.

29 Dobson, *Green Political Thought*, p. 172.

30 Exactly because ideological crisis has been deeper in the left during the period examined, most Green ideological forms emerge within the radical left political spectrum.

31 The place of contingency cannot be eliminated; it is impossible to make it entirely transparent. It is possible, however, to recognise its powers and take into account its structural causality.

32 If the real is beyond our symbolic means of representation then both our social behaviour and our analysis cannot be based on a positive symbolisation of this real. What we argue here is that we can experience, however, the causality of this real through the dislocation of our social constructions. Although the real is not graspable *per se*, the failure to grasp it (which is revealed in the moment of dislocation) can become the focus of our analysis. This failure is a productive

failure; its administration leads to the construction of new symbolisations. This is not applicable only to the real of nature but to all modalities of our encounter with the real.

33 S. Žižek, *Tarrying with the Negative* (Durham, Duke University Press, 1993).

34 For a brilliant account of the attempts of traditional societies to make sense of the dislocatory force of nature see M. Eliade, *The Myth of the Eternal Return* (London, Arkana, 1989).

35 L. Milbrath, 'The world is relearning its story about how the world works', in S. Kaminiecki (ed.), *Environmental Politics in the International Arena* (New York, SUNY Press, 1993), p. 21.

36 T. Kuhn, *The Structure of Scientific Revolutions* (Chicago, University of Chicago Press, 1962); Milbrath, 'The world', p. 23.

37 R. Dunlap and K. Van Liere, 'The new environmental paradigm', *Journal of Environmental Education*, 9:4 (1978).

38 S. Žižek, *Looking Awry* (Cambridge, Mass., MIT Press, 1991).

39 U. Beck, *Ecological Politics in an Age of Risk* (Cambridge, Polity, 1995), pp. 48–9.

40 Lagadec in *ibid.*, p. 49.

41 Beck, *Ecological Politics*, p. 49.

42 L. Milbrath, 'The world', p. 38.

43 R. Dalton, 'The environmental movement in Western Europe', in Kaminiecki, *Environmental Politics in the International Arena*, p. 43.

44 R. Dalton, 'The environmental movement', p. 58.

45 H. Wiesenthal, *Realism in Green Politics* (Manchester, Manchester University Press, 1993), p. 84.

46 A. Jamison, R. Eyerman and J. Cramer, *The Making of the New Environmental Consciousness* (Edinburgh, Edinburgh University Press, 1990), p. 66.

47 P. Dickens, *Society and Nature* (Hemel Hempstead, Harvester Wheatsheaf, 1992), pp. 171–2.

48 A. Atkinson, *Principles of Political Ecology* (London, Belhaven Press, 1991), p. 1.

49 *Ibid.*, pp. 1–2.

50 Which means that if the emergence of the NEP coincided with a crisis in the right of the political spectrum it is conceivable that Green ideology could emerge as a solution for the rearticulation of conservative politics. Needless to say, such a Green ideological configuration would be composed of different elements than the current one (of elements coming from the supposedly dislocated conservative discourses it would attempt to rearticulate).

51 W. Hulsberg, *The German Greens* (London, Verso, 1988), p. 218.

52 E. Papadakis, *The Green Movement in West Germany* (London, Croom Helm, 1984), p. 46. Consider, for example, the implications of the decree introduced by the Social Democrat chancellor Willy Brandt in the early 1970s and which forbade people with radical convictions to be employed in the public sector. Taking into account that this decree was most often exercised on the left, it is not very surprising that 'it caused many left-wing Germans, frustrated by this first social democratic government, to feel they had no political home'. D. Jahn, 'Green politics and parties in Germany', in M. Jacobs (ed.), *Greening the Millennium? The New Politics of the Environment* (Oxford, Blackwell/The Political

Quarterly, 1997), p. 174.

53 Papadakis, *The Green Movement*, p. 46.

54 *Ibid.*, p. 36. In that sense the emergence of the Greens is due to the integration of the 'ideologically homeless on the left with the anti-state sentiments anti-establishment initiatives of the young'. Jahn, 'Green politics', p. 174.

55 Wiesenthal, *Realism*, p. 195.

56 G. Voerman, 'The Netherlands: losing colours, turning Green', in Richardson and Rootes, *The Green Challenge*, p. 110.

57 *Ibid.*, p. 109.

58 P. Lucardie, 'Greening and un-greening the Netherlands', in Jacobs (ed.), *Greening the Millennium?*, p. 187.

59 Voerman, 'The Netherlands', p. 125.

60 Although Green Left is not considered a 'deep Green' political force it is definitely 'the greenest in the Lower Chamber of [the Dutch] Parliament' and is generally identified as the greenest party by various surveys (Lucardie, 'Greening and un-greening', p. 188). Most important, it has hegemonised the signifier 'Green' and managed to attach it to its own political platform. This is maybe another factor which influenced a lot the failure of the 'pure' Greens. When they emerged 'other parties had already claimed the colour green, literally in their election posters, or ideologically in their election platforms ... The Greens still resent the name Green Left' (*ibid.*, pp. 187–8). In other words, Green Left managed to construct a link between the rearticulation of the ideologies of the parties that formed it and the signifier 'Green' which became the 'necessary' nodal point of their 'rapproachment'. Thus its discourse could be constructed, according to our typology of Green ideology, as a Green ideological discourse, although not of the most radical kind.

61 Our hypothesis is that evidence from other countries reinforces this, albeit contingent, link between the dislocation in the left and the emergence and development of Green ideology in Western Europe and North America. Further research may reveal the validity of this claim. However, space limitations force us to conclude our argumentation here.

The construction of Romanian social democracy (1989–1996)

We Romanians will not copy that which, unprepared, some or other of our neighbours ... have done. The great demonstrations of these days, have called, in their slogans, for the removal of the dictatorship of Ceauşescu, for freedom, democracy, and have been firmly in favour of socialism, for the honourable principles of socialism, cleansed, for the property of the people, for real ethical norms and equality, untainted by the spirit of recklessness and political demagogy of Ceauşescu, as well as those who were for so many years his advisors. No one cried 'down with socialism', only 'down with Ceauşescu's dictatorship'.

Editorial, 'Trăiască libertatea, trăiască răspunderea', in *Scînteia poporului*, Bucharest, 23 December 1989, p. 1.[1]

Introduction

This chapter analyses the trajectory of ideological reform of the *Partidul Democraţiei Sociale Din România* (Romanian Social Democratic Party, PDSR).[2] It highlights the changes in its economic doctrine between 1989 and 1996, and their implications for its political ideology. The party's ideological roots in the tradition of east European communist revisionism[3] were seriously challenged after 1989 by the neoliberal ideology of new parties, such as *Partidul Naţional Ţărănesc* (National Peasant Party, PNŢ) and the *Partidul Naţional Liberal* (National Liberal Party, PNL). Henceforth, revisionism struggled to provide an ideological interpretation and meaning for the revolutionary events of 1989, and the social, political and economic dislocation and crisis of identity that followed. Neoliberal ideology, with its emphasis on cutting back the role of the state in society, seemed to fit well with 'anti-politics', the discourse of civil opposition to neo-Stalinism[4] in Eastern Europe.[5] But, neoliberalism also introduced into the political discourse, for the first time, a meaning of democracy that included a specific type of capitalism as a necessary condition, replacing the Marxist–Leninist conception of economic democracy. This neoliberal discourse was not transplanted unmodified into the east European political arena, but was rearticulated as 'transition theory', the best example of which is the work of the Harvard economist Jeffrey Sachs.[6]

This chapter charts the development of revisionist socialism in Romania, initially conceived as a democratising and socialist response to the neo-Stalinism of the Ceauşescu era. Over the years since the revolution, revisionist socialism has adapted to the challenge of neoliberalism, primarily through the simultaneous incorporation of notions such as 'social market' and 'privatisation' in their discourse. This has led to the gradual emergence of a distinctive social democratic ideology. Another major aspect of this process of adaptation has been the incorporation of the powerful metaphor of the 'transition' into this new ideology. The importance of this for Romanian politics lies in the existence of an ideology of the left that can articulate a positive socialist reading of the transition, and can contest the power of neoliberal discourse.

The collapse of the Ceauşescu regime, and the analytical categorisation of the 'transition' as a dislocation, provides a starting point for this chapter, which analyses the role of political discourse in the reconfiguration of the symbolic political order between 1989 and 1996. Most studies of contemporary Romanian politics tend not to analyse in detail the important role of ex-communist parties in constructing democratic post-communist political orders. Studies such as Tom Gallagher's *Romania after Ceauşescu* and Martyn Rady's *Romania in Turmoil* focus on the extreme nationalist and 'anti-democratic' aspects of ex-communist parties, rather than viewing the construction of post-communist democracy as a contested discursive terrain of political competition. Katherine Verdery's work on the construction of the post-communist political order is a necessary corrective to this tendency. This study is an endeavour to build on the work of Verdery, giving close attention to the role of ex-communist political discourse in defining the limits to the arena of contestation.[7]

The discourse of the PDSR has been chosen to provide a window through which the key issues of political conflict in Romanian politics during the 'transition' can be analysed. This party is still a major political force in Romania. Between 1989 and 1996, it was the party of government (first as the FSN, then as the FDSN, and most recently as the PDSR), winning a majority of the votes cast at elections.[8] Although it is no longer the party of government, it nevertheless maintains a strong electoral position. I analyse the discourse of the party from several perspectives. First, the evolution of strategies used in their discourse is analysed, in order to understand how the party attempted to, and succeeded in interpellating subjects.[9] Secondly, I draw a conceptual map of how the ideology has changed and evolved. This will achieve two things. It will, first, provide a sense of the new articulations involved in the rebuilding of Romanian politics following the disruption in 1989 of the neo-Stalinist surface of inscription. Secondly, it will outline the discursive production of political frontiers structured around the party's response to neoliberal economic theories.

Articulating the meaning of the 'people's revolution'

The social democrats in Romania emerged from the revolutionary success of a faction of the *Partidul Comunist Român* (Romanian Communist Party, PCR), which attempted to reform itself and its ideological appeal in the context of the social dislocation of 1989. The events of the December 1989 revolution left an ideological void, filled previously by the political imaginary of the Ceauşescu regime. According to Laclau and Mouffe, if an identity is constituted within an imaginary, then, if a crisis occurs within the imaginary, this leads also to a crisis of identity.[10]

How did the FSN seek to deal with or even to take advantage of this crisis? They proceeded by a novel reading of the experience of the revolution, one that placed the FSN at the centre of the 'revolution', giving it a preeminent role in the collapse of the regime. This was, of course, at odds with various other interpretations of the revolution that circulated. These representations were all loaded with political significance. Opposition to the FSN regarded the revolution as a spontaneous expression of popular feeling that had nothing to do with support for the FSN. This directly contested both the FSN's claims about the revolution, and by virtue of this the legitimacy of their claim to authority.

However, the production of a symbolic political order had to be at the same time something 'recognisable'. At this point it is worth mentioning the salience of a discourse which had a new political and revolutionary vocabulary, but at the same time operated from the basis of the previous imaginary which had collapsed. Some of the key characteristics of the Ceauşescu political imaginary give clues as to why the FSN was so successful in its interpellation of subjects in 1990, despite strong opposition from the new parties and student demonstrators. Ceauşescu's society was an extremely rigid one, with lack of personal choice over the smallest details of everyday life. Everything was the responsibility, and in the gift of, the bureaucratic apparatus.[11] A strict social hierarchy formed part of everyday life. This produced a lack of individual choice or action because the state was the nodal point and Ceauşescu was the father of the nation. The figure of Ceauşescu therefore functioned as a symbolic guarantor of the political continuity of the Romanian nation-state. The removal of Ceauşescu, and the collapse of the whole symbolic order of his regime, represented a crisis of that guarantee. The experience of this collapse threw many people into a state of unease and panic, documented widely by Romanian sociologists and social psychologists.[12] For example, many people found it impossible to associate a multi-party system with a strong state, and lamented the appearance of a new order that seemed to be marked by conflict and violence. Many associated multi-party competition with conflict and instability and, crucially, saw it as harmful to national unity. It was the Romanian reformed communists, organised initially as the FSN, who attempted to rearticulate that guarantee. This was achieved by the deployment of the symbolic resources of the revolution. The FSN invested the 'popular uprising' of December 1989 with meanings articulating the revolution as an expression of the need for work, national unity, and a strong, independent Romanian state.

During the period 20–23 December 1989, most Romanians were glued to *televiziunea română liberă*, or were attempting to glean information from what newspapers were at hand. The FSN, who came to be recognised later as the anti-Ceaușescu faction of the PCR, were busy consolidating their political control, making appeals to the population via the media networks, which were also firmly under their control. At this time the FSN defined and refined its political message, while constructing itself symbolically as the new guarantee of change and continuity. The effect was to render an image of the FSN as the legitimate political authority. This was pursued through the use of several discursive strategies. First, to give meaning to the events of 16–23 December 1989, 'the revolution', as a popular expression of support for the FSN and Iliescu. Secondly, to separate the FSN from the 'dictatorship' of Ceaușescu. Thirdly, to articulate the material and spiritual suffering of the population under the 'Ceaușescu dictatorship'. The following quotation is a good example of this strategy:

> It has been already highlighted by some members of the leadership of the Front [FSN], that it is pointless, inefficient and dangerous to look elsewhere for a model for a new organisation or movement. Because this [FSN] is the model of our lives in this historic hour. Its law is our life, our blood, our sweat, and our needs. The platform of the FSN is written in the blood of the revolution.[13]

The post-Christmas 1989 period is important in terms of the constitution of post-communist political ideologies, all of which were framed initially in terms of 'the revolution'. The dominance of the ex-communists under the aegis of the FSN can partly be attributed to their control of media networks and their pre-electoral constitution as the legitimate state power. This state of affairs also formed part of the ex-communist revolutionary myth. The FSN gave meaning to the revolution, equating itself with the events, and defined itself by virtue of this, as the legitimate decider of the future of the 'nation'. 'The platform of the FSN is written in the blood of the revolution.'[14] 'The organs of the new structures of democracy must urgently begin the work of rebuilding the country, subordinating themselves to the Council [FSN], and adopting measures of political, social, administrative and economic order, which are absolutely necessary for the first stages of the reconstruction.'[15] The meanings also defined the revolution as for socialism and against Ceaușescu: 'No-one cried "down with socialism" only "down with Ceaușescu's dictatorship".'[16] Thus, the legitimacy of their power derived from a discursive construction of the revolution, as being distinctly socialist and nationalist, and conservative and reformist at the same time.

Developments up to the May 1990 elections, and the extreme polarisation of the political arena, led to the exclusion of many elements from connection with the 'revolution' in the official discourse. The new parties, the PNȚ and the PNL, as well as people involved in anti-FSN demonstrations under pro-democracy banners were excluded by this discourse. The FSN was portrayed by its leaders as the new symbol of 'national unity', thus equating the FSN with the revolution, which was the symbol of 'national unity' *par excellence*. 'It was against the FSN that shots were directed in the cities and squares of Romanian martyrdom.'[17] This statement equates 'the people', in this case the opposition to Ceaușescu, with the FSN. Simultaneously, opposition to the FSN was articulated by their leaders, Petre Roman and Ion Iliescu, as being against the interests of national unity, labelled anti-revolutionary and reactionary enemies of the people and the nation. This formed the enemy around which the FSN platform of the 'revolution' and the 'nation' were articulated.

The reason the FSN were engaged in such articulations is connected primarily with their representation of certain conservative interests, but their interpellation of workers was also crucial. It was clear from the outset that free elections, one of the demands of the demonstrators during the revolution, would be impossible to avoid. Therefore, backed by security, bureaucratic and industrial interests, the FSN without hesitation set about appealing to their potential electoral base, state-sector employees. The radical reform proposals of the PNȚ and the PNL (shock therapy) were held up as examples of 'selling the country to foreigners', leading to economic disaster and mass unemployment. Thus, an appeal to national solidarity was also a message of conservatism to those in the bureaucracy who might otherwise have felt compromised due to their complicity with the Ceaușescu regime. At the same time the discourse contained a direct suggestion to state-sector workers that their livelihoods would be secure if they supported the FSN.

The excluded – including the new parties and the student demonstrators – were defined as counter-revolutionaries, hooligans, foreign spies and *agents provocateurs*. Their involvement in opposition parties and demonstrations challenging the FSN for having hijacked the revolution was portrayed in the FSN-controlled media as anti-revolutionary, and against the interests of national unity. The demands of the demonstrators, associated with the League of Students, outlined in the Proclamation of Timișoara ('birthplace of the revolution') of 20 March 1990, contested the power of the FSN. The accusation was that the FSN were the state and the party at the same time. 'Timișoara did not make the revolution in order to obtain larger salaries, or material advantages. For that a strike would have been sufficient.'[18] In the demonstrations following the revolution, the chant which replaced 'down with Ceaușescu' was 'down with Iliescu'.

The inclusion and exclusion of those defined through the events of the revolution, who were discursively constructed as 'good Romanians' and 'bad Romanians', were designed to exclude the 'bad elements' from the right to define the future. This is why the construction of mythologies surrounding the revolution was so politically salient, since they were used to justify the brutal treatment of anti-FSN demonstrators in June 1990.

The second '*mineriadă*' confirms conservative dominance

> Some nostalgic political forces, detached from the realities of Romanian society, promote ideas such as the restoration of the monarchy, capitalism gone wild, or of communism with a human face.[19]

In the May 1990 elections, the FSN won a landslide majority, with Iliescu elected as President and Petre Roman installed as the Prime Minister of an FSN government. However, differences over the reform agenda within even the FSN, between 'conservatives' and 'reformers', became clear after the fall of the Roman government in September 1991. This government fell after Iliescu called the miners from Valea Jiului to Bucharest to 'defend the revolution'. Roman was forced by the miners to tender his resignation as Prime Minister, or otherwise face the mob.

This incident, dubbed '*mineriadă*' highlighted the differences over economic policy between Iliescu and Roman, who had already carried out some economic reforms, such as price liberalisation. It is likely that the bureaucratic and industrial interest groups felt threatened by Roman's acts as Prime Minister. Iliescu's act of calling on the miners for support showed that he was still aware of the need for an electoral power base. The Party split into the FDSN led by Iliescu and the FSN led by Roman, with Iliescu's FDSN taking power. From this point onwards the FDSN began to create Romanian social democracy. This proceeded from the starting point of an integrated critique of neoliberal transition policies, such as shock-therapy reforms. The FDSN countered the discourses of the opposition parties (PNȚ, PNL and now also FSN) who wanted liberalising economic reforms by appealing to national and social values and 'economic rationality'. The FDSN halted moves towards radical economic reform after the fall of the Roman government in 1991, articulating their economic policy in terms akin to Hungary's *Kádárism*.[20] This policy in socialist Hungary sought to appease opposition by the efforts of the party to provide material benefits.

Therefore the delicate construction of a recognisable ideology at this time had to recognise the necessity of creating clear ideological boundaries between 'counter-revolutionary' forces on the 'left', and 'counter-revolutionary' forces on the 'right'. As with *Kádárism*, this was presented as, under the circumstances, the least bad policy available at that moment. Although the government's actual policy of the day was to minimise the suffering and hunger that had characterised the Ceauşescu era, this policy was discursively constructed as a third way. The FDSN were opposed to shock-therapy reforms such as those conducted in Poland, and placed heavy emphasis-on enterprise level reform rather than mass sell-off and reliance on foreign direct investment.[21]

The FDSN embarked on a public voucher privatisation of some enterprises. However, the state continued to hold the vast majority of shares in state holding funds, so bureaucratic control of enterprises was still secure. These essentially conservative economic policies, carried out to the benefit of the bureaucratic and managerial class of the Ceauşescu regime, were part of what has come to be known as 'nomenklatura capitalism'. This means that a process of privatisation takes place that allows state assets to be sold to insiders for much less than their real value. The insiders then become the owners. However, in Romania the privatisation took place in the context of unclear rules about property rights, and the continued availability of credit from the state to enterprises (otherwise known as 'soft-budget constraints').[22] These policies were articulated as 'reforms', true to the 'ideals of the December 1989 revolution', but not the same as 'wild capitalism', 'shock therapy' and 'selling the nation to foreigners'. This discursive strategy was used between September 1991 and the elections of 1992 as a way of countering the democratic, anti-Communist discourse of the PNŢ and PNL, now grouped together with several other smaller parties in an electoral coalition called *Convenţia Democrată* (Democratic Convention, CD).

The discursive construction of FDSN economic policy is of some interest. It was not rationalised only in economic terms, but also as serving the interests of the nation, as it was cited as being true to 'the ideals of the revolution'. As the revolution had been an expression of 'national unity', the economic policy was articulated as serving the interests of the nation. This was in opposition to those in the CD, who the FDSN accused of wishing 'to sell the country to foreigners'. The violent removal of the Roman government in 1991 was articulated by the FDSN as resulting from the failure of the Roman government's economic policy due to an 'under-appreciation of the role of the state', and also because of the anti-democratic and anti-revolutionary conduct of his government.[23]

The FDSN's attempt to hegemonise the Romanian political imaginary relied on an appeal to specific national values, which were equated in their discourse with their economic policy. This was how they fought CD discourse supporting privatisation, the free market and the introduction of democratic practices and institutions. The FDSN and their ultra-nationalist allies in *Partidul România Mare*, (Greater Romania Party, PRM) and the *Partidul Unităţii Naţionale Române* (Party for Romanian National Unity, PUNR), claimed the right to define the nation's values and their relation to the political future of the 'nation'.

The deployment of national values was accompanied by the exclusionary definition of the Hungarian minority as an enemy of the Romanian state.

This discourse was created and dissimulated by the PRM and PUNR and supported by the FDSN and Iliescu. The contestation of this discourse from the *Uniunea Democrată a Maghiarilor Din România – Romániai Magyar Demokrát Szövetség* (Democratic Alliance of Hungarians of Romania, UDMR/RMDSz) led to the aggravation of ethnic conflict in Transylvania. This had as its result the positioning of the 'nation' at the top of the political agenda, and ensuring the electoral dominance of the FDSN and the Romanian nationalists in the new context of competitive elections for the first six years since the revolution.[24] However, it is not enough to state that their success was a result of an appeal to national solidarity. The functioning and structure of the appeal had to have success in a specific social and political context, in this case the context of social dislocation associated with liberalising reforms, and a public receptive to an essentially conservative economic message. This relationship between the representation of a context (the revolution, the transition and reform), and its endowment with national meanings, is of central importance in accounting for the success of such discursive strategies.

Globalisation and 'The Nation'

> Continuing the conditions of Romanian Social Democracy, responds to a political necessity, and expresses the position of the PDSR, which in principle is to respect the feeling of national dignity, the history and culture of the country, the centuries long struggle of the Romanian people for national and social freedom, in defence of its identity, in favour of progress and civilisation.[25]

The autumn 1992 elections showed that the strength of the revolutionary message was waning, along with its memory, for many people. After these elections, the job of reconstructing the ideology of the FDSN began in earnest. This was carried out with the aim of getting rid of the ex-communist – apparatchik image of the party. The party renamed itself the Party of Social Democracy of Romania (PDSR). Although its ideological constructions were already heading in this direction, the elections were a sign that the discursive strategies of the CD, led by Emil Constantinescu of the PNŢ, were a danger to the conservative agenda of the FDSN. The opposition began to move from the positive interpellation of those who had somehow avoided complicity with the Ceauşescu regime to a more subtle appeal to 'reform' as opposed to 'stagnation'. 'Reform' became the empty signifier that every party sought to control. Despite the conservative economic policy of the FDSN government, bankruptcies of large enterprises were increasing, unemployment was rising, and inflation had become a serious problem. This was having a corrosive effect on the electoral base of the party.[26]

Since Iliescu had identified his party as the party of 'stability', the critique of his policy by the CD was dangerous. Ideologues in the PDSR, such as Adrian Năstase, began to engage more subtly with the neoliberal economic discourse of 'reform' being dissimulated by the parties of the CD.

In the discourse of the PDSR the context of Romania and its global economic relations contains a reference to the unjust results of the market, which provides the ideological justification for the conservative economic policy. This also allows the policy to continue to be articulated in terms of the 'nation'. The changed economic environment of globalisation provides the backdrop for the contemporary discourses of the 'nation', somewhat comparable to nineteenth-century discourses of the nation situated in contexts of foreign political domination. The economic policy of the PDSR is a small part of this tradition. By 1995, the party's programme pronounced that 'the material inequality of states and the global problems of humanity are not the result of local mistakes in political economy, but rather the result of the global system of exploitation, which favours the developed countries to the detriment of the less developed'.[27] This is clearly a response to the globalisation elements of neoliberal transition discourse. It answers the critics of the PDSR government with the notion that it is the world system that is responsible for Romania's economic weakness, and not 'entrepratchiks' and 'nomenklatura capitalists', the 'directocracy' that emerged as a result of PDSR policies.[28]

The creation of Romanian Social Democracy by the PDSR was accompanied by the abandonment of much of the Marxist–Leninist ideological dead wood by 1995. However the supplementary appeal to national values remained. In this sense it is possible to say that the ideology has been drastically reformed, but not into something unrecognisable from the Ceauşescu era, which interpellated subjects according to similar national values. This is where the discourse of the PDSR adapted the previous regime's discourse to fit the context of the transition. The interpellation changed to 'good Romanian European social democrats' from the previous 'good Romanian national communists'.

A reading of the transition was therefore produced which relied on universal values inherent in socialist ideology, such as economic equality between individuals, and fair division of labour, both between individuals and states. But this reading also relied on particular national values. The PDSR articulation of the post-communist transition encompasses a critique of neoliberalism based on the particularity of the experience of the Romanian nation after 1989. Thus, the appeal maintains the need for national unity and vigilance in the face of foreign predation. The meaning given to 'globalisation' provides, at the same time, the basis for an appeal to universal values such as 'social and economic justice'.

Conclusion

> Property is not a natural right; it is a social institution.[29]

In the first years of the party's development the discursive strategy was to appeal to the 'unity of the nation' and to the 'continuity of the revolution',[30] whereas recently the party has increasingly made appeals to 'social-democratic', 'national' and 'European' values.[31] The aim of this chapter has been to show how the use of various empty signifiers, such as 'revolution', 'reform', 'stagnation', 'democracy' and 'transition', has structured the ideological horizons of Romania's first post-communist years. The chapter has also pointed to the highly contested and fluid nature of political identities in this period. The specificity of Romanian political conflict is shown, evading categorisations, such as left and right, prevalent in western Europe. There is a radical reversal in meaning for Romanian social democracy, being conservative and nationalist in a specifically east European sense.

It is important to situate the ideological reconstruction of the PDSR in the context of the dislocation brought about by the transition. This opens up space for new discursive attempts to suture the symbolic horizon of politics. However, the basis for the contestation thus engendered is also tied to the availability of pre-existing discourses which have a long history of dominance in Romanian political life. The national independence and emancipation discourse of an economically peripheral people, with a history of oppression at the hands of various empires, collides with the discourse of economic and political liberalism of an elite, dating from the nineteenth century. The contemporary discourses concerning 'reform' and 'globalisation' are thus laden with historical meaning. The historical resonance of PDSR discourse lies in their dichotomous rhetorical invocation of a choice facing the nation, whether to be an independent nation-state, or whether to be a peripheral element of an international political and economic regime.

At the same time, the discourse of the PDSR shows their attempts to construct themselves as a democratically legitimate party of the left. This is situated in their specific narration of the globalisation phenomenon and its meaning for the Romanians.[32] The PDSR have been influenced in their reform by the necessity of creating a programme and discourse meaningful to an electorate who understand their social and political reality in terms of the dislocation of the transition.

The ideological reform of the PDSR has undergone several phases, and the phases suggest the failure of their initial attempts to interpellate subjects and identities according to the 'ideals and values of the Revolution of December 1989'. Initially FSN discourse was couched in the values of the revolution. Later, after the 1992 elections, the now PDSR began to appeal to stability as opposed to radical reform. More recently the appeal has become for transitional reform but of a 'social democratic' type. This is shown by the adoption of new discursive strategies through which the PDSR render a reading of the 'transition', directly contesting the neoliberal transition discourse of the Democratic Convention, by contesting the meaning of 'reform'. The transition as a dislocation in Romanian politics means that ideological attempts to suture the symbolic horizon are centred on making sense of this primary notion in contemporary east European politics. The challenge to the PDSR from the CD can be understood by their attempt to render a specific reading of the transition which equates it with free-market reform, Europe, progress, democracy and anti-communism. Under the pressure of the ideological challenge to their hegemony, unleashed after the events of the revolution, the PDSR have been engaged in a constant rearticulation of their ideology. Their identity as a party of former communist apparatchiks has necessitated their efforts to reconstruct themselves as social democrats, thus downplaying the perception of their complicity with the Ceauşescu regime.

I have also examined the ideological reconstruction of the left in Romania from the point of view of their attempts to interpellate subjects within an ideological framework of both a socialist and nationalist heritage. The meaning of these notions are laden with interpellations relating to social class, history, and the specificity of Romanian values as produced during the communist period. It would seem, from the analysis, that the discourse embodies a highly contested set of terms or signifiers deriving from international economic discourse, which are given their meaning and specificity from previous Romanian discursive systems and interpellations. When PDSR discourse speaks of 'social democracy' it is important to look further into how this name is shorthand for a whole series of ideological constructions with resonances specific to the political culture in which the signifier is situated. In the Romanian case, which has been our example, 'social democracy' embodies a whole set of ideological statements concerning the relationship between the economic, the political and the social spheres. The ideological formations of the PDSR follow patterns of mediation between the universal and the particular, which were established features of Romanian political discourse during the Ceauşescu years.[33]

In addition, the chapter has also indicated the centrality of economic discourses to the conceptions of politics in the discourse of the PDSR. The most powerful alternative to the discourse of the PDSR is the neoliberal solution to economic problems of the 'transition' period. Throughout the ideological development of the PDSR since 1989, the appeal is made on behalf of the positive results of their programme (A + B + C = social justice, national unity, equality, democracy and national independence), as opposed to the negative results of the neoliberal programme (A + B + C = inequality, mass poverty, dysfunctional democracy, national disunity, social injustice, and the dependence of the nation on outsiders). In 1989, therefore, when the party still maintained a need to preserve 'socialism', this 'socialism' functioned as a signifier that included economic rationality, production, moral values, national consensus and revolutionary values, as distinct from the unpure,

corrupted, tyrannical and inhumane Ceauşescu regime. By 1992, the pene-
tration of 'democracy' as an empty signifier, and its centrality to the discursive account of the neoliberal economic policies supported by the CD, led the
PDSR to provide a reading of democracy in opposition to neoliberal equa-
tions in use by the CD. This necessarily led the PDSR to contest neoliberalism by using economic language. However the system of equivalence
underpinning this new signifier changed only slightly to include a 'social market economy', which provided a just basis for 'democracy', thus giving a clear
economic meaning to democracy. The chapter has charted the growth of a
specific Romanian social-democratic ideology. It has been shown how the
notions of 'revolution', 'transition', 'European integration' and 'democracy'
have all played a role in the construction of the PDSR version of reality.
However, on a wider level, this chapter seeks to contest certain ideas current
in research that have a tendency to regard Romanian politics as being the politics of nationalism. I assert that, although the politics of the nation plays its
role in Romanian politics, it is the current context of the transition that
makes the politics of nationalism merely one tool in the armoury of conservative resistance to radical change.

Notes

I would like to express my gratitude to Maria Cra⁻ciun from the Institute of Central
European History of the University of Cluj, Romania, for her continued friendship and
support in connection with my research on Romania. A version of this chapter was presented at a conference at the University of Alba Iulia, Romania, November 1998, on
the Discourses of Nationalism and Religion in Romania. I am grateful to the participants of this conference for their comments and suggestions. I would like to thank
Aletta Norval for her extensive and helpful comments on drafts of the chapter. Aletta
Norval, David Howarth and Yannis Stavrakakis have suggested useful theoretical
approaches to this particular topic. Thanks go to Sarah Birch, Wendy Bracewell,
Frances Millard, Andy Wroe and Marina Popescu, who read and commented extensively on this chapter. I would finally like to thank the participants of the Ph.D. Collo-
quium in the department of Government at the University of Essex, and of the Ideology
and Discourse Analysis seminar for their comments, questions and suggestions.
  1 'We address the whole people with the solemn assurance that *Scînteia poporului*
     will be a newspaper of the people, of the whole truth.' I. Iliescu, *Scînteia poporu-
     lui*, Bucharest, 23 December 1989.
  2 PDSR is the most recent acronym for the party which was the National Salvation
     Front (FSN) until 1991, became the National Democratic Salvation Front
     (FDSN) until after the 1992 elections, when it became the Romanian Social
     Democratic Party (PDSR). The primary source materials used in this study are
     political pamphlets and speeches of the pre-1991 split *Frontul Salvării Naţionale*
     (National Salvation Front, FSN), *Frontul Democrat al Salvării Naţionale*
     (National Democratic Salvation Front, FDSN) and the PDSR. The author has
     selected representative examples of the party's discourse from a wide period of
     time and covering a wide range of issues.

3 L. Kołakowski, *The Main Currents of Marxism*, Vol. 3 (Oxford, Clarendon Press, 1978), pp. 450–522.
4 Neo-Stalinism here refers to the retrenchment and modification of the Stalinist political and economic model in some eastern European states, following de-Stalinisation after 1956.
5 D. Held, *Models of Democracy* (Cambridge, Polity, 1996), pp. 275–8.
6 See for example J. Sachs, *Poland's Jump to the Market Economy* (Cambridge, Mass., MIT Press, 1993). Jeffrey Sachs is probably the individual most associated with shock therapy. Not only was shock therapy an academic exercise, but Sachs lent his services as a special economic adviser to both the Polish and the Russian governments on how best to carry out shock therapy.
7 K. Verdery, *What Was Socialism and What Comes Next* (Princeton, Princeton University Press, 1996); T. Gallagher, *Romania After Ceausescu: The Politics of Intolerance* (Edinburgh, Edinburgh University Press, 1995); M. Rady, *Romania In Turmoil* (London, I. B. Tauris, 1992).
8 In 1990 the FSN gained 66.3 per cent of votes for elections to the Chamber of Deputies, and presidential candidate for the FSN, Ion Iliescu, gained 85.1 per cent at the first ballot on a voter turnout of 86.2 per cent. In 1992 elections the picture was somewhat worse for the FDSN, with their share of the vote for elections to the Chamber of Deputies being only 27.7 per cent, thus relying on parliamentary support from the two Romanian nationalist parties PUNR and PRM in order to form a government. Iliescu won 61.4 per cent of votes for the presidential elections at the second ballot. In the 1996 elections the PDSR were finally defeated with 21.5 per cent as opposed to the CD's 30.1 per cent. In the presidential elections of 1996, Emil Constantinescu of the CD defeated Ion Iliescu at the second round with 54.4 per cent to Iliescu's 45.6 per cent. See *Monitorul Oficial al României*, Bucharest, 1990, 1992 and 1996.
9 The discussion of the notion of ideological interpellation is based on Althusser's identification of this mechanism of subject identification. L. Althusser, 'Ideology and ideological state apparatuses (notes towards an investigation)', in S. Žižek (ed.), *Mapping Ideology* (London, Verso, 1994), pp. 100–40.
10 'If the subject is constituted through language, as a partial and metaphorical incorporation in a symbolic order, any putting into question of that order must necessarily constitute an identity crisis.' E. Laclau and C. Mouffe, *Hegemony and Socialist Strategy: Towards a Radical Democratic Politics* (London, Verso, 1985), p. 126.
11 See Katherine Verdery's synthesis of the political economy of neo-Stalinist regimes, and its impact on culture and politics. K. Verdery, *National Ideology under Socialism: Identity and Cultural Politics in Ceaușescu's Romania* (Berkeley, University of California Press, 1991).
12 A. Mungiu, *Românii după '89: Istoria unei neînțelegeri* (Bucharest, Humanitas, 1985), Ch. 4.
13 *Adevărul*, Bucharest, 25 January 1990.
14 *Ibid.*
15 From 'Comunicatul Consiliului Frontului Salvării Naționale', broadcast on Romanian Television, 14.35, 24 December 1989.
16 *Scînteia Poporului*, Bucharest, 23 December 1989.
17 *Adevărul*, Bucharest, 25 January 1990.

18 *România Liberă*, Bucharest, 20 March 1992.
19 FDSN, *Să Construim Împreună Viitorul României: Platformă-Program a FDSN* (Bucharest, 1992), p. 5.
20 *Kádárism* entailed 'a proposition that while the existing state of affairs in Hungary might have been imperfect, it was the least bad available at that particular moment. This was extraordinarily effective in disarming both domestic and external criticism. Potential domestic opponents of *Kádárism*, still traumatised by the aftermath of the failed revolution of 1956, were more than ready to go halfway to find a compromise with the regime. The regime, for its part, was similarly shell-shocked by having been swept away overnight in 1956 and understood that it would not be able to reimpose a hard-line, high mobilization system.' G. Schöpflin, *Politics in Eastern Europe 1945–1992* (Oxford, Basil Blackwell, 1993), p. 216.
21 'Reform through "shock therapy" in a country at the limit of poverty, and of social misery, will generate profound instability, the deterioration of the mechanisms of development, paralysis, and socio-economic collapse.' FDSN, *Să Construim Împreună* p. 20; Verdery, *What Was Socialism*, pp. 210–16.
22 *Ibid.*, pp. 210–16; Verdery, *National Ideology Under Socialism*, Ch. 2.
23 'The populist policy of some elements of the government led to a loss of control of the social and economic situation, and to their under-appreciation of the role of the state in the promotion of reform, and the organisation and leadership of society in the transition period.' FDSN, *Să Construim Împreună*, p. 8.
24 K. Adamson, 'The political functions of ethnic conflict: Transylvania in Romanian politics', in M.Crăciun and O. Ghitta (eds), *Ethnicity and Religion in Central and Eastern Europe* (Cluj, Romania, Cluj University Press, 1995), pp. 381–98.
25 PDSR, *Platformă, Program a PDSR* (Bucharest, 1995), p. 19.
26 See M. Shafir and D. Ionescu, 'Radical political change in Romania', *Transition*, Bucharest 3:2 (1997), 52–4.
27 PDSR, *Platformă, Program*, p. 11.
28 Verdery, *What Was Socialism*, pp. 210–16.
29 PDSR, *Platformă, Program*, p. 32.
30 'FDSN defines itself as a social democratic party of the centre-left ... in conformity with the ideals of the Revolution in December 1989.' FDSN, *Să Construim Împreună*, p. 9.
31 'In the opinion of the PDSR, Romania's integration in the EU represents the fundamental strategic objective of Romanian foreign policy, connected to the democratic, European system of values, and the creation of a viable competitive economy based on the principles and mechanisms of a social market economy.' PDSR, *Program Politic* (Bucharest, 1997), pp. 134–5.
32 'Contemporary history has created an integrated world system, in which national economies are embraced inside a network of interdependence and exchange of goods, and in this way, no country can now develop in isolation. At the same time, in the context of globalisation, we are witnessing the deepening of differences and a much more acute polarisation of wealth and poverty, both inside some states, and also at the level of the structure of the world system. Faced with the consequences of a system oriented only by market mechanisms and by profit, the most diverse societies are in search of a durable model of development, which can create a harmony between economic efficiency, social justice,

protection of the environment and human progress. In these conditions it is vital to opt for a model which will dominate in the world of tomorrow, and not to repeat the models and experiences which have overwhelmed the developed countries'. In, PDSR, *Program Politic*, pp. 12–14.
33 Verdery, *National Ideology under Socialism*, pp. 302–18.

9 *P. Sik Ying Ho and A. Kat Tat Tsang*

Beyond being gay: the proliferation of political identities in colonial Hong Kong

Identity politics in a colonial context

Homosexual identity is often conceived as something that an individual acquires, involving processes of self-definition and identification with the socially constructed categories of gay, lesbian or bisexual individuals. Identity, in this sense, is grounded primarily on the similarity that an individual believes he or she shares with other people as it is expressed in the discursive domain through particular signifiers.[1] Although most theorists agree that homosexual identity should not be taken as essential and referring to a homogenous group of individuals, in practice many analyses still resort to the convenience of a simple separation between homosexual and heterosexual categories. Costello, for example, tries to demonstrate that 'bisexual, lesbian, and gay families can indeed be distinguished from straight families'.[2] Burke tries to identify a technique for assessing the unique nature of homosexual stress.[3] Such studies, perhaps inadvertently, reinforce the practice of using simple binaries in the understanding of sexual realities. It assumes that the frontiers or sites of contestation are always located between heterosexuals and homosexuals, neglecting the presence of lesbigay individuals and groups who are engaged in contestations not exclusively based on sexual orientation. As will be shown later, lesbigay individuals and groups are involved in multiple agendas connected to issues such as ethnic identity, gender, lifestyle, religion, art, political orientation, occupation, and the like, and heterosexual people are not always automatically excluded.

The purpose of this chapter is to focus on conceptual issues concerning the diversities that intersect with differences in sexual orientation by elucidating the multiple strategies of identity creation and positioning. The constitution of social identities is a political act. As Laclau puts it, 'the constitution of a social identity is an act of power and that identity as such is power'.[4] Identity constitution is an empowering act for the individual as it gives him/her a position from which to speak and organise his/her life. At the same time, it also creates new social spaces. The existence of new names provides new resources for people to make use of and to develop alternative lifestyles and identities. When a number of people who find the same social category appealing organise themselves as an interest group, they may become a new power base which has the potential of altering the existing political dynamics in the public arena, for instance, by taking up concrete political actions, championing a new form of gay activism and fighting for particular rights. In this sense, the process of personal identity constitution is intimately tied to the politics of identification and the possibility of developing new strategies to expand political space.

Guided by this theoretical perspective, we argue that gay identity constitution consists of more than finding a social category to identify with, although the emergence of an identity has to pass through a name. It is a creative process which, although it implies the identification with a name (the signifier 'homosexual', for example) or a social category available in the sociocultural environment, also involves redefining the meaning of that social category. We argue that the very act of identification is a creative process, for it is always an individualised interpretation of a collective name and not a perfect imitation of a social category. There is always a misreading of the so-called pre-existing social category and reinterpretation of what is imagined to be there. It is a process that operates according to the form of logic that Derrida terms 'iterability'. It is Derrida's argument in 'Signature event context' that the unity of any signifying form is constituted by its iterability, that is to say, by the possibility of being repeated 'in the absence of a "determined signifier"'.[5] What is worth noting is that the manner in which repetition of elements is to be understood is never simply a repetition of the same. The idea of repeatability/iterability involves both elements of sameness and elements of alteration.

Furthermore, when an individual or a group of individuals finds the socially available categories for describing himself/herself inadequate or inaccurate to capture the 'essence' of who he/she is, he/she may appropriate a new name or choose to identify with a different social category by drawing elements from other discursive fields. A new identification is thus constructed in conjunction with other signifiers. This naming and renaming process is political, as it challenges the existing social order and destabilises fixed conceptions of what that identity is about. What is also gained by following this signifying and political play is emphasising the creative dimension of identification which is usually neglected in more traditional accounts: according to the discourse-theory approach developed here identification is discursive but not passive and, furthermore, it frequently entails the active expansion/rearticulation of the discursive space instead of passively reproducing the hegemonic limits of discourse.

The situation of Chinese lesbigay individuals and groups in Hong Kong is used in this chapter to illustrate how the politics of identification was played out in a colonial context, where personal and political space are closely monitored. Most authors in the West do not find it difficult to characterise agendas and actions of individuals and groups as political. Yet, in Hong Kong, colonial subjects are often described as apolitical,[6] as participation in explicitly political organisations and activities are regularly suppressed. For example, in the 1960s, organised political resistance challenging colonial authorities was brutally suppressed. The legislature in Hong Kong did not have elected members until 1984, and political parties were only formed in the final years of colonial rule in the 1990s. The entire population is fingerprinted and everyone is required by law to carry identification documents at all times. Police officers actually spot-check citizens on a regular basis. 'Homosexual conduct' was punishable by a life sentence until 1991, when homosexual behaviour between consenting adults in private was decriminalised. The Offences Against The Person Ordinance (1981), inherited from Britain and in force since 1901, prescribed punishment of up to life imprisonment for anal intercourse between men, between a man and a woman, and a woman or a man and an animal, and up to two years' imprisonment for any act of 'gross indecency,' that is, contacts of a sexual nature by a man with another man, irrespective of whether it is performed with or without consent in private or in public. Even after decriminalisation, the maximum penalty of life imprisonment remains in place for a man who commits buggery with a man under the age of twenty-one.[7] Many gay men are still arrested and prosecuted for 'homosexual buggery'. This political environment calls for a different understanding of political practice. The lack of explicit political claims should not automatically be confused with the absence of political intent or effect. It can be added that within such a colonial context, representing oneself as apolitical may be one of the strategies of resistance. The contestation which is linked with the language games around the signifiers 'homosexual', 'gay' and '*tung-ji*' show the continuous interplay between politicisation and depoliticisation in the Hong Kong context. An analysis of identity politics in colonial Hong Kong, therefore, requires a method which is sensitive to the presence of multiple political agendas associated with a variety of articulatory and discursive practices. It also demands a theoretical conceptualisation which can capture the fluid movements between the explicitly political and the more subtle political processes.

The dossier: methodological and historical background

In our analysis, the politics of identification amongst Chinese lesbigay individuals in colonial Hong Kong is taken as a *dossier*, which according to Foucault, is

> a case, an affair, an event that provided the intersection of discourses that
> differed in origin, form, organization, and function ... All of them speak,
> or appear to be speaking, of one and the same thing; ... But in their totality
> and their variety they form neither a composite work nor an exemplary text,
> but rather a strange contest, a confrontation, a power relation, a battle among
> discourses and through discourses. And yet, it cannot simply be described as a

single battle; for several separate combats were being fought out at the same time and intersected each other.[8]

This will be clearly, then, a dossier of discourses, an index of names, and interactions and power play between names. Drawing such a map of the interaction among discourses, providing such an index of names, naming strategies and procedures, can help us to avoid the misunderstanding that discursive political analysis entails locating the (single) dominant or hegemonic discourse within a historical configuration (a standpoint which reproduces the problems of the so-called 'dominant ideology thesis' paradigm). It can help us to demonstrate the delicate language games involved in identity constitution which can only be highlighted with the use of a sophisticated discourse theory framework. However, it also imposes certain restrictions on the methodology adopted here. It requires, for example, an inclusive approach to data collection. Government publications, academic writings, professional reports, newspaper stories, public documents, promotional material published by lesbigay organisations, interview records, personal comments, and so on are taken as texts that constitute multiple discourses.

Following Foucault's treatment of the case of Pierre Rivière, we take a dossier to be constituted by a wide range of sources without emphasising one dominant discourse but treating them as a series of contestations. There are also others who argue for a flexible approach to data collection. Fairclough, for example, suggests that the nature of the data required for discourse analysis should vary according to the project and the research questions, and that there are also various ways in which a corpus can be enhanced with supplementary data. This is partly a matter of knowing what is available, how to get access to it, having a mental model of the domain one is researching, as well as the processes of change it is undergoing.[9] Thus, the corpus should not be seen as constituted once and for all before one starts the analysis, but as open to ongoing enhancement in response to questions which arise in the analysis. As a result, the analysis is an interactive engagement between the researcher's conceptualisation and the material collected. Taking identity politics as the analytic focus, material was initially extracted to map out the major discourses around this issue. Tentative formulations were corroborated with available data. There were also situations in which such formulations demanded new information. For example, when publicly available information such as pamphlets did not provide the rationale behind the choice of the name for a new organisation, the researcher had to interview the leaders of the organisation to gain the necessary information. In situations where the voice of marginalised or excluded individuals was conspicuously missing and the discourse seemed to be dominated by elites, efforts were made to include diverse voices through individual interviews or focus groups. Such a method offers an opportunity to examine intersecting discourses and to challenge fixed notions, leading to a reconceptualisation of identity politics and strategies of resistance. Below, we will introduce the dossier and explore the meaning of different names adopted by the lesbigay individuals, groups and organisations in the context of colonial Hong Kong to illuminate the importance of naming in identity constitution.[10] This study also shows how the creative play of identification can be opened up even when there seems to be no possibility for invention left in a particular discursive field.

The context of decriminalisation: the MacLennan incident

The dossier should be prefaced by the 'MacLennan incident' in 1980. John MacLennan was a young Scottish Inspector with the Royal Hong Kong Police Force who was charged with gross indecency and anal intercourse, but was never arrested. When the police entered his flat, they found him dead. His death created a political crisis for the colonial government. First, a law enforcement officer was associated with a serious crime punishable by a life sentence. Second, it was believed that the officer knew of homosexual involvement of other senior colonial officers. Third, he was involved with young Chinese boys, some of whom were prostitutes. The population did not find it difficult to believe that MacLennan was murdered to prevent further disclosure of 'indecency' within the senior ranks of the colonial civil service. When the government proclaimed, after a brief internal investigation, that it was a case of suicide, the scandal simultaneously ignited explosive sentiments connected to deeply held values regarding sexual morality, the administrative integrity of the government, and interracial relationships in a colonial context. In response to the extensive criticism in the local media, the government formed a special Commission of Inquiry to reinvestigate the case. The Commission again concluded that the case was one of suicide and the system was in order.[11] As discussion in the media gradually died down, the government proposed to decriminalise homosexuality that, at the time, could attract life imprisonment according to the letter of the law.

The Law Reform Commission, an independent body formed by the government, recommended in its 1983 report the decriminalisation of consensual conduct between two males aged twenty-one and over.[12] But their recommendations were not acted upon. In 1988, a consultation paper was issued by the government to gauge public opinion on the matter.[13] The result of the exercise was never published. The matter was postponed until 1990 when the Legislative Council passed a motion in favour of removing criminal penalties relating to homosexual acts committed in private by consenting men who had reached the age of twenty-one. It was suggested that homosexuality should be decriminalised to make the law compatible with the proposed Bill of Rights which forced people to re-examine the need for privacy and civil rights. The Crimes (Amendment) Ordinance was enacted in July 1991 to give effect to these proposals and also to extend to men and boys the same protection from sexual exploitation that the Crimes Ordinance (Cap. 200) gave to women and girls. Public debate over the issue of homosexuality was again revived when the Equal Opportunities Bill (EOB), a Private Members Bill, was introduced in the 1994–95 legislative session. As part of the government's 'step-by-step' approach in tackling problems of discrimination, a series of studies were conducted on discrimination based on sexual orientation.[14]

Naming and renaming: gay individuals as objects and subjects of discourse

The colonial law was only concerned with homosexual conduct, and not the sexual orientation or identity of the parties involved. However, when the public discourse moved beyond the confines of technical legal language, the attention shifted from what men do, which is the business of the law, to describing who they are. In the heated controversy that followed the proposal to decriminalise homosexual conduct, Christian church leaders, health and legal professionals, academics and journalists usually referred to 'gay men' as a social category of human beings, and to 'homosexuality' as an orientation, instead of focusing on homosexual conduct as isolated legal incidents. Gay men as a social category was thus created by such discourse, even though it was not yet possible for them to come out and speak for themselves. In the subsequent discursive developments, especially after decriminalisation, lesbigay individuals and groups have become increasingly active in defining who they are. Their own naming and renaming, as we shall demonstrate, constitute the major site of engagement for the complex politics of identification within the colonial context. From the struggle over being and non-being, to those over visibility and invisibility, subject and object, author and script, lesbigay individuals resist the forces of definition that objectify and marginalise them by constantly reinventing themselves and multiplying the socio-political space they occupy.

In the early 1980s, lesbigay individuals were talked about as a group, and were usually referred to as 'homosexuals'. Public discourse then was dominated by professional elites, as there was not a single group of lesbigay individuals who had come out. Self-labelling, then not popularly adopted, had actually been started by early activists, who preferred the term '*tung-sing-oi-je*' (same-sex-love-person).[15] After decriminalisation, there has been a proliferation of new self-labels, some of them associated with new social organisations. As a result, lesbigay individuals are constantly being reinvented: they are 'homosexual', 'gay', '*gei-lo*' (gay-men) and '*tung-ji*' (comrades), 'lesbian', '*dau-foo-pau*' (beancurd women), '*gei-pau*' (gay women), '*jimooi tungji*' (sister-comrade). The use of these names and labels, while conditioned by the contemporary social context, often transforms the very conditions under which they are created. Groups of individuals create new names and bring into existence new social groups with which to identify themselves. Though not always intentionally, the creation of these new identity labels and new social organisations challenges and transforms the current social and political order and expands the space for alternative forms of life desired by lesbigay individuals. As Weeks says, they are there 'to reveal the macro and micro forms of domination that constitutes modern life', and also 'to demonstrate the possibilities of other forms of life that are not simply prefigurative of some imagined future, but are actually being constructed in the here and now'.[16]

These namings and renamings show a movement at work, strategies of inclusion/ exclusion, in lesbigay identity constitution and frontier creation, which is not just about defining themselves against the heterosexual community but also among themselves and with themselves. Their engagement in different forms of self-narration, including the acquisition of self-defined labels, formation of and participation in lesbigay groups, are strategies of intervention in cultural, social, economical and political practices by posing challenges to the dominant social order as they struggle to assert their very being and to claim critical space for alternative life styles. It is through such creativity in identity constitution that their power to resist the forces that subject them, while at the same time enabling them to become subjects through discourse, is revealed.

Let us engage in some detail with the creative dialectic of subjection and resistance through the naming and renaming of lesbigay individuals and groups. To the extent that identity is power, the creation of homosexuality as a problem category by the colonial government has, ironically, empowered lesbigay individuals. Although the superimposition of the colonisers' value and sexual categories was met with denial, neglect, subversion and contestation, the constitution of a social identity creates a site of resistance. As Foucault puts it, 'where there is power, there is resistance' and 'this resistance is never in a position of exteriority in relation to power'.[17] For Foucault biopolitics is a prime instance of the 'strategic reversibility' of power relations, or the ways in which the terms of governmental practice can be turned into forces of resistance. He describes this kind of politics as 'an ethics'[18] while Homi Bhabha treats it as 'a performativity'.[19]

The discretionary use of identities, including racial and sexual ones, is part of the practices of the self against the technology of power.[20] The formation of such new identities is not just about politics in the narrower sense but involves other forms of intervention to shape social practices. It is concerned with 'expanding the space of the individual and collective growth, and in broadening the basis of the public sphere'.[21] It entailed for example, in the Hong Kong context, a dramatic increase in access to information, contacts, emotional support, potential partners, and many forms of help and facilitation in work, pleasure, health, community participation and self-development. However, it is our view that the ultimate importance of these strategies goes beyond the confines of the lesbigay communities as they impact on the enveloping social context by making it necessary for other people to engage with lesbigay realities. These engagements have given rise to a wide range of social changes, including an equity policy[22] and the introduction of a sex education curriculum in secondary schools.[23]

Signifying contestations: from homosexual to gay/*gei* identity

Before British colonisation, homosexuals did not exist as a social category, although it was believed that homosexual relationships existed. The political significance assigned to sexual propriety can be construed as another important protocol which is part of the Western political etiquette,[24] while sexual licence was tolerated in traditional Chinese officialdom.[25] Homosexuality was thus created as a problem category by the colonial government, using the language of criminal justice. But the oppressive definition of male homosexual conduct in colonial Hong Kong created a space for articulation and contestation. This is the irony of colonial domination: it simultaneously suppressed and produced gay men as a social category, and subsequently led to the creation of multiple lesbigay identities. The following is an analysis that tracks the emergence of a diverse homosexual community in spite of close monitoring by a colonial government. It reveals the multiplicity of discourses on lesbigay identity constitution which challenge notions of fixed identities, and at the same time illustrates the political significance of sexual identity formation.

In all its official reports, the British colonial government in Hong Kong uses the word 'homosexuals' to refer to men whose sexual preference is for the same sex. No mention is made of lesbians, who are obviously not the concern of the administration. Even the English word 'gay', which has become part of the everyday language of Hong Kong people in the late 1980s and 1990s, refers largely to men. Gay is generally regarded by gay people themselves as a more positive identity, a self-imposed celebratory label, while the word 'homosexual' is considered a medical term and a sterile and old-fashioned label. The word gay also signifies a self-concept, style, politicisation and various modes of life with reference to the models provided by the Western countries. *Gei*, the Chinese term for 'gay', sounds exactly the same as its Western equivalent, but has a literal meaning of 'foundation' or 'basis'. This Chinese character was hijacked to refer to homosexual desire and people who are gay. The way this word was appropriated through its sound or transliteration is one of the commonly used strategies in translation to deal with Western concepts with no Chinese equivalents.[26] In such situations, the meaning of the word *gei* is gay rather than 'foundation', which is somehow displaced by the English word 'gay'. *Gei* is thus a hybridised signifier, a Chinese signifier signifying an English concept. However, *gei* does not exactly mean gay since the very meaning of the word has been altered through the translation process. The word '*gei*' has helped to put the idea of gay identity into wider circulation in the Chinese/Cantonese-speaking community.[27] Significantly, along with the word '*gei*' emerged the label '*gei-lo*', commonly used by the media as a derogatory label for gay men, as '*lo*' is a suffix generally attached to vulgar men of lower classes. Nevertheless, the word '*gei-lo*' is sometimes used by gay men themselves as a fashionable and subversive self-label.

The word '*gei*' was also used as a collective noun. Within the religious domain, which at one point was dominated by intolerant voices, lesbigay individuals have been successful in building enclaves called the *Gei-yan-ji-ka*. *Gei-yan-ji-ka*, which has the double meaning of 'the family of the grace of being gay' as well as 'the family of the grace of Christ', was set up in 1992 as a splinter of the Ten Percent Club Religion Group.[28] As a way to negotiate between the two major language systems of English and Chinese/Cantonese, people in Hong Kong freely use English words in their native Cantonese speech. Some people have referred to this hybrid language as 'Chinglish'. The invention of the word '*gei*' and the naming of organisations like *Gei-yan-ji-ka* illustrate how the identity construction of lesbigay individuals in Hong Kong is related to the mediation of the Chinese and Western elements in the local context.[29]

Gei-poh, tung-ji, nui tung-ji: the emergence of lesbigay communities

Like gay men, lesbians struggled to establish their own separate community. Given the lack of reference in government reports to lesbian women, their struggle was an even more complex one. It should be noted that the colonial legal system was only concerned with male homosexual conduct, not sexual orientation itself. Lesbianism was not implicated. The lack of representation of women in general, and lesbians in particular, in an ostensibly male-centred debate might further marginalise women and their voices in colonial sexual politics.[30]

Initially, lesbians were literally called '*nui tung-sing-lyun-je*' (female same-sex-love person) and were later being reinvented as '*gei-pau*' (gay women), '*dau-foo-pau*' (beancurd women), '*nui tun-ji*' (female comrade) or '*jimooi tungji*' (sister-comrade). Along with the term '*gei-lo*' came the term '*gei-poh*' for lesbians, where '*poh*' is also a negative suffix with lower-class connotation. In this particular application, the gender specific word '*gei*' or gay is neutralised. '*Dau-foo poh*' (beancurd women), though more rarely used, is a more pejorative term applied to lesbians. The term is derived from the colloquial reference to genital rubbing between two women as '*muo dau-foo*' (rubbing action between two components of the grind in the process of making '*dau-foo*'). This more explicit reference to a sexual act, though conveying a sense of disgust, reflects a recognition of lesbian sexuality which is not a regular part of everyday discourse.

The label '*tung-ji*' (comrade) is now popularly used to refer to gay men and lesbians are then called '*nui tun-ji*'. The word '*tung-ji*' was originally used by the nationalist revolutionaries who overthrew the Qing dynasty. The communists adopted the term later and used it to refer to all citizens of the Peoples Republic of China during the Cultural Revolution. In Hong Kong, the term first entered into popular usage as a cynical reference to Mainland communists, who were stereotypically represented as less civilised or less sophisticated. After the Sino-British Joint Declaration of 1984, which confirmed the termination of British colonial rule and the return of Hong Kong to Chinese sovereignty, an insidious shift in the meanings attached to colonial and Chinese icons ensued, and the derogatory usage of the word '*tung-ji*' gradually faded out. The word '*tung-ji*' was first associated with the Hong Kong lesbigay community in 1991, with the naming of the First Gay and Lesbian Festival as 'Tung-ji Film Festival' in Chinese. The popularity of the '*tung-ji*' label, the use of which has now been extended beyond Hong Kong into Taiwan and Mainland China, can be attributed to the work of scholars such as Chow and Chiu, who document the Hong Kong lesbigay experience.[31] Chow even uses a new category of '*jik-tung-ji*' (straight-comrades) to refer to straight men who 'support' the lesbigay agenda to the extent of being taken as spokespersons for them.[32]

It is of interest to note that while the lesbigay community has become more sensitive to sexist and non-sexist language practices, '*tung-ji*' is actually a label whose local application can be sexist at times. '*Tung-ji*' refers either to gay men or the collective community of lesbigay individuals. Lesbians are qualified as '*nui tung-ji*' (woman comrades). Like other presumably gender-free terms, the word '*tung-ji*' in fact privileges the masculine. The critical point, however, is that the term '*tung-ji*' is consistently used without being challenged in the mainstream discourse, including the media.

Even though mens voices were generally privileged both by the media and public documentation, many women participants were found in most groups involved in the debate. Womens voices, like those of men, were initially dominated by political and professional elites. The diversity of voices of different constituencies only became more audible in the later stages of the process. *Jimooi Tungji* (Queer Sisters), for example, was formed four years after decriminalisation of homosexuality to assert lesbians' distinctive identity beyond the confines of the male-centred gay paradigm.

With a strong distaste for discrete boundaries, the Queer Sisters, or *Ji-mooi Tung-ji* in Chinese (Sister Comrades), toyed with calling themselves *Fei Kwaang Kwaang Tung-ji Ji-mooi*. The phrase '*Fei Kwaang Kwaang*' means negating the boundaries (of what it means to be lesbian, women, and so on). The word 'queer' has no exact equivalent in Chinese and is seldom used by lesbigay people in Hong Kong. The Chinese name of the group was later revised to the current *Ji-mooi Tung-ji* to focus more on mobilising sisters or women willing to identify themselves as queer instead of gay, lesbian or bisexual, and adopt a political stand, a common vision related to the idea of being queer and different. Attempts are being made to expand the definition of *'tung-ji'*, which has been claimed primarily by gay men, and to mobilise those who are being neglected or marginalised by the gay community in a joint effort to promote equal opportunities for all. The existence of this new group and other lesbian organisations[33] shows that there is a movement (at least by a few members) within and beyond the lesbigay community towards a more thorough resistance to the regimes of the normal.

'Tung-ji' can also be used as a collective term by people who are not lesbigay to refer to people who are. Some lesbigay individuals, however, do not like to call themselves *'tung-ji'*. It has been argued that the term actually distracts from the central issue of sexual orientation,[34] and its seriousness and political connotation make it difficult for some lesbigay individuals to identify with the term.[35] The occasional adoption of such products of dominant discourse can be juxtaposed with a corresponding proliferation of literature, performing arts, organisations, and self-narration by lesbigay individuals and groups who are constantly reinventing their own realities and critically examining them.

In a similar vein as the term *'gei'*, *'tung-ji'* became sedimented in organisational forms. The 97 Tung-ji Forum, whose English name is 97 Lesbigay Forum, was formed at the end of 1992 to provide a platform for discussing issues in light of Hong Kongs 1997 change of sovereignty. This represented another strategic move by the lesbigay community to assert its voice over a serious mainstream political agenda while at the same time fostering alliances under its own control.

Satsanga (Tung-gin) was formed in 1993. The Sanskrit word of *'Satsanga'* refers to people who practice perfecting themselves together. The Chinese name means 'Hong Kong Tung-ji Health Promotion Association'. The organisers are both heterosexual and lesbigay individuals, including social workers, psychologists, writers, academics and volunteers from different sectors who want to serve the lesbigay community by offering professional counselling and courses on issues such as sexual identity, relationships, family and job stress. This organisation utilises professional knowledge from the disciplines of psychology and mental health for the benefit of the lesbigay community and thus turns around the once oppressive, diagnosing and homophobic practices associated with these professions. The alliance developed with heterosexual mental health professionals creates a new set of dynamics in the definition and management of lesbigay issues.

Siu Yiu Paai and *Ji Joi Se*: the politics of anti-political gayness

Against the backdrop of all these movements, most of which have a serious sense of mission, a gay organisation dedicated to the pursuit of sensual pleasure and fun was founded in 1996. *Siu Yiu Paai* (Freemen) is an all-male group with both Western and Chinese members, who get together not to talk about religion or politics, but to meet other gay men, enjoy themselves and participate in some charitable work for the community at leisure. For them, to demand of lesbigay individuals to make an extra effort to define who they are and assert their existence as social beings are both unfair and annoying. The emphasis on '*siu yiu*', which means a state of freedom and roaming around at leisure, can be read as a protest against the difficult and tiring lesbigay politics, and an assertion of the right to enjoy gay life as it is, free from harassment, burden and duty. It can also be seen as a response to the lesbigay organisations' mobilisation efforts by individuals who resent the increasing politicisation of the issue.

Another gay organisation worth noting is *Isvara*. *Isvara* is a Sanskrit word meaning 'at ease'. Also known as the Buddhist Gay Association in English, the group bears the Chinese name of *Ji Joi Se*, '*Ji-joi*' being the translation of *Isvara* with a clearly Buddhist tone. Founded in 1994, the organisation projects an image of Buddhist lesbigay individuals both at ease with their own sexual orientation and interested in the spiritual pursuits of Buddhism. Such an organisation effectively subverts the dominant pattern of religious discourses that are intolerant of homosexuality, and they articulate the claim to religiosity by lesbigay individuals.

Members of these organisations do not want to become political beings in the sense that their desire has to be conditioned and rearticulated in political terms. Their practices, however, constitute a distinct political intervention in the overall lesbigay movement for what they are advocating is, again, the creation and maintenance of a social space for the pursuit of what they desire, and to defend that space from the more dominant organisational culture shared by most lesbigay communities. They are also asserting a fundamental claim that being gay is about having pleasure and enjoying life with ease. If one does not assume a single objective scale for assessing the political significance or subversive potential of any given movement or act, then it can be argued that these groups actually expand the range of options open to lesbigay individuals by articulating a claim to pleasure and the option to refuse formal and institutionalised politics.

Conclusion

The above dossier of the various self-narration and strategies of identification amongst lesbigay individuals in Hong Kong shows the intersecting discourses and their differences in origin, form, organisation and function. Tracing the movements across multiple sites, the dossier traces how Hong Kong gay men, and subsequently lesbian and bisexual women, started off by negotiating their identity in relation to the label of 'homosexual' constructed under dominant discourses, and later emerged as many self-identifying groups and generated multiple references to themselves such as '*tungsing-oi-je*', gay, '*gei*', '*gei-lo*' and '*tung-ji*', lesbian '*dau-foo poh*', '*gei-poh*', '*nui tung-ji*', and so on.

This reveals the multiplication of positions occupied by the emerging groups of Hong Kong lesbigay individuals and the frontiers they advance.

Apart from the production of names, lesbigay individuals create organisations which offer yet another site of resistance. It is impossible in the context of the present chapter to give a detailed analysis of the development of these organisations and the issues that they have dealt with since their formation. What we want to highlight here is the rapid increase in the number of gay groups in the past few years and how each one of them has helped to expand the scope of concern of the lesbigay community with the inclusion of new elements which initially may have looked incompatible (for example, Christianity, Buddhism, bisexuality, queerness). The same movement has also created sites of identification with exclusionary boundaries where the aims of each group are so specific that only people who identify with those aims were included. It is around these movements of inclusion and exclusion, battles against each other and the self, that lesbigay identities and communities of interest evolved.

In the light of this approach to analysis, the notions of identity as a consolidated unit, and homosexual identity as a homogeneous category, both become problematic. The dossier of Hong Kong lesbigay individuals is used to show how the creation of new subjectivities is a way of participating in an ongoing movement of power relations in its context. These groups of people are no longer a social category of 'homosexuals' who are being talked about. They have invented ways of defining and redefining themselves. This analysis captures the moments of lesbigay individuals engaging with, and at the same time transforming, dominant discourses in the constitution of their identities.

Sexual identity is power. When an individual identity is constructed, it involves a process in which values are created anew and previous categories are redefined. Many lesbigay individuals did not see legislative change as their central political interest. Instead, they have tried to transform the conditions of their lives by actively challenging the dominant social codes, exposing the power of domination, and informing society as to how it should relate to people who are different. These tactics, employed at less visible sites of resistance involving choices and actions of individuals or small groups, though often unnoticed, are not meaningless, less subversive or ineffective even though they may not be part of a planned strategy in major sites. Thus, these discursive practices should not be eliminated from the discourse analysis of political participation even though it may be difficult to determine their social significance and effectiveness.

This approach to identity has implications for the lesbigay movements in Hong Kong. Political projects do not necessarily take the forms of organised opposition or institutional reforms. Those who do not vote, are not registered voters, have not participated formally in any organisation or articulated their ideas in a public forum can also be political actors. They can even include people who are explicitly not interested in politics. The political space for direct electoral participation is restricted in Hong Kong after its change of sovereignty. Popularly elected politicians are now replaced by state-selected legislators and prospective elections are going to be much more circumscribed. Under such circumstances, it becomes even more relevant to articulate alternative political practices by people who are being marginalised or displaced. These people can engage in the terrain of the political through the translation of cultural representations, promotion of new subjectivities, alternative forms of relationships and communities. By insisting on an unconventional way of life or on multiple identities/loyalties which are now more actively contested with the moving in of the new masters from Beijing, individuals can make problematic what is presumed to be the 'normal' way of life for everyone. In so doing, they can weaken the power of a monolithic government structure on the life of ordinary people and undermine the authority derived from ordained necessity. Such bottom-up movements can be a social force for change in executive-led politics and for democratic reforms in other arenas of social life. This can lead to the diffusion of political sites, proliferation of political spaces, expansion of range of strategies of contestation and widening the arena for democratic movement.

Notes

1 See for example M. McIntosh, 'The homosexual role', *Social Problems*, 16 (1968), 182–92; K. Plummer (ed.), *The Making of the Modern Homosexual* (London, Hutchinson, 1981); T. S. Weinberg, *Gay Men, Gay Selves: The Social Construction of Homosexual Identities* (New York, Irvington, 1983); J. P. De Cecco and M. G. Shiverly, 'From sexual identity to sexual relationships: a contextual shift', *Journal of Homosexuality*, 9:2/3 (1984), 1–26; P. S. Y. Ho, 'Male homosexual identity in Hong Kong: a social construction', *Journal of Homosexuality*, 29:1 (1995), 71–88.

2 C. Y. Costello, 'Conceiving identity: bisexual, lesbian and gay parents consider their children's sexual orientations', *Journal of Sociology and Social Welfare*, 24:3 (1997), 63–89.

3 T. B. Burke, 'Assessing homosexual stress', *Journal of Homosexuality*, 33:2 (1997), 83–99.

4 E. Laclau, *New Reflections on the Revolution of Our Time* (London, Verso, 1990), p. 31.

5 J. Derrida, 'Signature event context', in P. Camuf (ed.), *A Derrida Reader: Between the Blinds* (New York, Columbia University Press, 1991).

6 Many commentators have given much theoretical and empirical support to the assertions of Hong Kong peoples political apathy. Shivley and Miners, for example, characterise the local people as politically apathetic, while Hoadley argues that Hong Kong people have a 'subject and parochial' political culture. For details, see S. Shivley, 'Political Orientations in Hong Kong: A Social-psychological Approach' (Hong Kong, Social Research Centre, Chinese University of Hong

Kong, 1972); N. J. Miners, *The Government and Politics of Hong Kong* (Hong Kong, Oxford University Press, 1986); J. S. Hoadley, 'Political participation of Hong Kong Chinese: patterns and trends', *Asian Survey*, 13:6 (1973). King also adds his empirical evidence that 23.9 per cent of his respondents perceived themselves as passive subjects in the political system while 63.4 per cent showed no interest in or had no knowledge about exerting influence in the system. See A. King, 'The Political Culture of Kwun Tong: A Chinese Community in Hong Kong' (Hong Kong, Occasional Paper, Social Research Centre, Chinese University of Hong Kong, 1972). Laus 1977 survey also found that 96.7 per cent of his respondents opined that they had no power to change government policies. Even today, when opportunities for political participation has increased, these studies of the 1970s and 1980s are still often quoted and believed to be influential in describing and shaping the perception of Hong Kong people today. See S. K. Lau, *Society and Politics in Hong Kong* (Hong Kong, Chinese University of Hong Kong Press, 1982).

7   Section 118C Crimes Ordinance Law of Hong Kong Cap. 200.

8   M. Foucault, *I, Pierre Rivière: Having Slaughtered My Mother, My Sister, My Brother ... A Case of Parricide in the 19th Century* (Lincoln and London, University of Nebraska Press, 1975).

9   N. Fairclough, *Discourse and Social Change* (Oxford, Polity Press, 1994).

10   The importance of naming in identity constitution is discussed in S. Žižek, *The Sublime Object of Ideology* (London, Verso, 1992), pp. 94–5. Žižek argues that it is naming itself which retroactively constitutes or supports the identity of the subject. In the context of the present discussion, it is important to note how an individual finds himself/herself being constantly transformed by the very act of adopting new names.

11   Hong Kong Government, 'Report of the Commission of Inquiry into Inspector MacLennan's Case' (Hong Kong, Government Printer, 1981).

12   *Ibid.*

13   Hong Kong Government, 'Law Reform Commission of Hong Kong, Homosexual Offenses: Should the Law be Changed? A Consultation Paper' (Hong Kong, Government Printer, 1988).

14   Hong Kong Government, 'Equal Opportunities: A Study of Discrimination on the Grounds of Sexual Orientation. A Consultation Paper' (Hong Kong, Government Printer, 1996).

15   In 1981, Pink Triangle Press published Samshasha's *25 Questions about Homosexuality* (Hong Kong, 1982), a Chinese translation of Western gay liberation material, with the support of an international gay association. Samshasha argues in this work that the word 'homosexual' should not be translated as '*tung-sing-lyun-je*' for the word '*lyun*' carries a connotation that the relationship between people with the same sex is more of an infatuation, sexual desire rather than love. The word '*oi*', he thinks, is more appropriate for it means love which gives the due respect to the relationship between two persons of the same sex.

16   J. Weeks, *Invented Moralities: Sexual Values in an Age of Uncertainty* (Cambridge, Polity, 1995), p.104.

17   M. Foucault, *History of Sexuality. An Introduction* Vol. 1 (Harmondsworth, Penguin, 1978).

18   For the meaning of this concept, see H. Dreyfus and P. Rabinow, *Michel*

Foucault: Beyond Structuralism and Hermeneutics (Chicago, University of Chicago Press, 1983), pp. 175, 235.

19 H. Bhabha, *The Location of Culture* (London, Routledge, 1994), p. 15.

20 P. S. Y. Ho, 'Politicising identity: decriminalisation of homosexuality and the emergence of gay identity in Hong Kong' (Ph.D. thesis, University of Essex, 1997), p. 201.

21 See S. Lash and J. Urry, *The End of Organised Capitalism* (Cambridge, Polity, 1987), p. 300; E. Laclau, *Hegemony and Socialist Strategy* (London, Verso, 1985), p. 181; C. Mouffe, 'Democratic citizenship and the political community', in C. Mouffe (ed.), *Dimensions of Radical Democracy* (London, Verso, 1992), p. 237; C. McClure, 'On the subject of rights: pluralism, plurality and political identity', in Mouffe (ed.), *Dimensions of Radical Democracy*, p. 124.

22 Hong Kong Government, 1996.

23 Hong Kong Government, 'Education Department. Guidelines on Sex Education in Schools' (Hong Kong, Government Printer, 1997).

24 C. T. Monhanty, A. Russo and L. Torres, *Third World Women and the Politics of Feminism* (Bloomington and Indianapolis, Indiana University Press, 1991), p. 21.

25 Hong Kong Government, 1981, pp. 4–17; Y. H. Li, *Homosexual Subculture* (Beijing, Beijing Jinri Zhungban, 1998) (in Chinese), pp. 19–22.

26 It should be noted that it is not an uncommon practice for Hong Kong people to borrow similar sounding Chinese characters to integrate Western words into their own language. For instance, the new import bus', which did not have a equivalent in the Chinese context, became *ba-shi*, made up of two existing Chinese words having no particular relationship to each other.

27 For those not familiar with the language environment of Hong Kong, the local people, generally speaking, write in Chinese, but speak in Cantonese, a southern dialect in China, which sounds different from the official Chinese, that is, *putonghua*.

28 The Ten Percent Club is one of the more visible lesbigay organisations in Hong Kong. It was founded by Alan Lee in 1986 when he returned to Hong Kong after completing his medical training in Canada. The name 'ten percent', referring to the famous research by Alfred Kinsey which found that 10 per cent of the population were gay, reflects the respect of the organisation for scientific knowledge and implies that lesbigay people are not a negligible minority in society. That the founder of Ten Percent Club was someone from abroad and heavily influenced by Western culture speaks to the colonial realities conditioning lesbigay identity creation in Hong Kong.

29 Another interesting example is 'Horizons', which was also initially dominated by young middle-class Chinese gay men schooled in the Western system. Horizons is an English language organisation, which again reflects the special position occupied by its members within the colonial context. It was founded by Barry Brandon in 1991 after he had organised a telephone hotline to provide guidance and advice, primarily to gay men. Brandon used to work with the Switchboard, a similar telephone service in London. The idea of the horizon, the line at which the earth or sea and sky meet, shows a vision to extend, to see beyond, to open to a wider terrain. When asked if it has a Chinese name, the group says there is no direct translation of the nameof the group. The Chinese name, Hong Kong

Tung-ji Counselling Hotline, was only developed at a much later stage. It shows how this group positions itself and appeals more to those who have knowledge of English and can identify with such a name. This is another example of the hybridisation of Chinese and English in the construction of identities in Hong Kong.

30 For details of the argument, see W. S. Chow and M. C. Chiu, *The Closet Sex History* (Hong Kong, Comrade Research Centre, 1995) (in Chinese), p. 173; and W. S. Chow, *Postcolonial Tongzhi* (Hong Kong, Hong Kong Comrade Research Institute, 1997) (in Chinese), pp. 364–6.

31 Chow and Chiu, *Closet Sex History*.

32 Chow, *Postcolonial Tongzhi*, p. 42.

33 In the 1990s, lesbian and bisexual women became more active once multiple spaces had been opened up in the complex contestations over sexual orientation and identities. The XX Meeting, for example, is an interesting case of the mobilisation of lesbian and bisexual women. The group started with a number of women who met on a more or less regular basis at one of the bars in Lan Kwai Fong, a downtown enclave frequented by lesbigay people. The XX reference spells out the ambiguity and fluidity they wish to present with their identity. Whereas XX may be interpreted as a genetic label for women, it could also be taken to represent an algebraic unknown. Another lesbian phenomenon is the newsletter *Tung-ji Hau Long* (Comrades Succeeding Wave), which was started and operated single-handedly by a lesbian and circulated among a small circle of friends. It stood out as a distinct, albeit restricted, lesbian voice before the more popular women groups came into existence. It is difficult to assess the contribution of this newsletter but it is definitely an example of womens' contestation in the face of dominating and overbearing voices.

34 The issue was discussed in X. S. Lin, 'It's Too Heavy to Call Homosexual, Special Issue: Its a Queer World 1997 – An A to Z Guide to Gender Sexuality and Youth Culture', *Chun Pao* (Hong Kong, Zuni Icosahedron, July 1997) (in Chinese).

35 In the interviews with gay men, it is found that there is still some reluctance on the part of many gay men to adopt the label '*tung-ji*'. Some interviewees felt that this word was too heavy for those who simply wanted a gay life rather than become a revolutionary for a cause that they could not identify with. Some interviewees even preferred the pejorative label as '*gei-lo*', saying it was more honest than '*tung-ji*' when they in fact found communism alien or did not want to be associated with China at all. This shows how an individual gay identity, under the broad category of gay identity, is constructed by searching for similarities with others who identify with the same social category but at the same time trying to be different from them, thus giving rise to a multiplicity of identities.

The secret and the promise: women's struggles in Chiapas

On 1 January 1994 over three thousand Mayan Indians belonging to the *Ejército Zapatista de Liberación Nacional* (Zapatista Army of National Liberation, EZLN) rose up in arms against the Mexican government. They briefly occupied six towns in central and eastern Chiapas and, denouncing a long history of discrimination and exploitation by local and national elites, presented their programme of eleven demands for work, land, housing, food, health care, education, independence, liberty, democracy, justice and peace. Following several days of armed combat with federal troops, the Zapatistas retreated to their base communities in the mountains of the Lacandón jungle. Mass demonstrations in favour of a peaceful solution were held in Mexico City, forcing the government to declare a ceasefire on 12 January, while opening the way for peace talks six weeks later. However, talks did not result in any definitive solution to the conflict. The 'San Andrés' Accords on indigenous rights were reached in February 1996 but the government failed to implement them, leading to a deterioration of the entire peace process and the decision by the EZLN in September of that year to suspend talks until the San Andrés accords were carried out.

The uprising was at first represented as a novel form of resistance to the pressures of neoliberal or 'free-market' economics. By timing the uprising to coincide with the start of the North American Free Trade Agreement (NAFTA), the Zapatistas drew attention to the fact that the majority of Mexico's rural poor were dispensable to the neoliberal model. Their rebellion also renewed hope among the left in the future of anti-capitalist struggles in Mexico and internationally. In addition, the Zapatistas raised questions concerning the future of indigenous peoples in the face of cultural and economic globalisation.[1]

The discourse of the EZLN also differed from that of earlier national liberation movements in Latin America. Instead of seeking to 'seize power', the EZLN sought to 'democratise power'. Its discourse did not identify one single central authority that it sought to replace with its own programme. Rather, it called for all Mexicans to mobilise in their own ways to democratise all spheres of social, economic, political and cultural life. The Zapatistas were protesting not only the effects of the economic model, but also the denial or violation of civil, political and social rights, particularly agrarian, indigenous and human rights. The rebellion could therefore be seen as part of an increasingly pronounced struggle between a democratic 'civil society' and an authoritarian state. In sum, this was a struggle for citizenship and democracy.[2]

The rebellion has also been seen as creating new spaces for women's participation in the transformation of oppressive gender relations. Observers noted the large female composition of the EZLN (estimated at one-third of total combatants) and welcomed the gender-specific proposals contained in the Zapatistas' Revolutionary Women's Law. Feminists argued that women in Chiapas suffer from a triple oppression, as poor, as indigenous and as women. The fact that women's demands were included in early Zapatista communiqués created a sense of hope that the rebellion would not solely reflect a male-dominated agenda.[3]

During the five years following the rebellion the EZLN was indeed able to make important advances in each of the above areas. It helped consolidate an international network of social movements committed to resisting neoliberalism. It developed a strong set of alliances with groups and citizens in Mexican civil society. It also provided new opportunities for linking the struggles of indigenous and non-indigenous women across the country. However, by 1998, without significant success in the arena of political reform, and faced with increasing violence against its supporters, the EZLN appeared to have been pushed into a defensive position. Several observers who remained sympathetic to the Zapatistas commented on the lack of direction that they claim has marked the EZLN and its supporters since late 1996.[4] The long period of silence on the part of the Zapatista leadership during 1997, mostly notably that of subcomandante Marcos, perplexed many pro-Zapatista intellectuals in the rest of Mexico.

While such silence could be seen as an understandable reaction to the government's lack of interest in resolving the conflict, it was less clear why the EZLN appeared to distance itself from other actors, particularly the centre-left *Partido de la Revolución Democrática* (Party of the Democratic Revolution, PRD). Some concluded that the Zapatistas had lost their sense of connection to the broader struggles for democracy in Mexico, precisely those connections that provided them with their strongest appeal in 1994. Others commented that the political conjuncture shifted decisively in 1997, when the centre stage was occupied no longer by the EZLN but by the political parties.[5] The victories obtained by opposition parties, particularly the election of a PRD government in Mexico City, caused attention to become firmly fixed on the electoral process and the race for the presidency in the year 2000. Although the Zapatistas were able to retake the political initiative in the spring of 1999, organising a successful citizens' referendum on indigenous rights, they would still be faced with the prospect of political marginalisation if they did not define a clear position with regard to the presidential elections.

Although the above concerns need to be addressed, we believe that they should not divert attention from more local processes. We refer specifically to the variety of efforts to establish alternative spaces for distinctive forms of political participation in Chiapas, including the creation of autonomous municipalities, as well as the emergence of a national movement for indigenous rights. In this respect, we consider that local and ethnically distinctive experiences of the rebellion add new meanings to the concepts of citizenship, democracy and feminism. In order to illustrate this point, we focus on some of the different forms of women's participation in support of the Zapatistas in Chiapas. By choosing women's struggles for our analysis, we hope to highlight the importance of singular experiences for developing more inclusive and open forms of political discourse. By 'women's struggles' we mean the multiple ways in which women have identified and challenged relations of subordination within their families, communities, organisations and nation.[6] We argue that a recognition of the specificity of these struggles can help deconstruct conceptual dichotomies that have traditionally privileged the 'universal' over the 'particular', thereby expanding the field of political participation as well as the potential scope of democratic change.

The chapter is organised into three sections. The first attempts to deconstruct the opposition between the universal and the particular following, among others, the argument put forward by Laclau's discourse theory. We believe that this is a necessary first step towards recognising difference as constitutive of identities, rather than simply 'examples' of universal rules. In this section we also show how recent feminist writings have been concerned with deconstructing this binary opposition and promoting a politics of difference. By affirming the irreducibility of difference we face the challenge of conceptualising the political significance of experience. In the second section we therefore describe how Derrida's recent work on 'the secret' can help direct our attention to the singularity of experience and otherness. This recognition of otherness is also necessary for rethinking democracy in terms of its 'promise' in the here-and-now, rather than its abstract appeal as some future utopia. By establishing the conceptual basis for rethinking women's experiences in these terms, we are able to analyse their political articulation through collective identities. The third section takes up this task, focusing on how women in Chiapas have contributed to Zapatista discourse on the basis of their own lived experience, including their current participation in autonomous municipalities. The chapter concludes by reflecting on the dilemmas facing women's struggles in Chiapas today and the need to open up familiar concepts of citizenship, democracy and feminism to new meanings.

Deconstructing the universal/particular distinction

The universal is impossible. There are no pre-given identities or interests. All attempts at locating a centre, of creating a 'logos', or finding an origin, have failed. Why have these attempts failed? The answer to this question lies in how the 'universal' is constructed. Any attempt to create a universal, to define what a category 'is', to endow it with a 'presence', necessarily excludes that which it is not. In other words, any attempt at creating a universal entails the formation of a binary opposition that delineates an 'other.' But, as Derrida has shown (with reference to the speech/writing opposition in Western philosophy), the excluded or marginalised 'other' (writing) is always already subverting such universalising, totalising attempts to comprehend the world (speech).[7]

Similarly, Laclau has questioned the possibility of society ever fully constituting itself as a rational whole. In his discussion of the universal and the particular, Laclau argues that any universal 'needs – for its expression – to be incarnated in something essentially incommensurable with it: a particularity'.[8] The universal exists in relation to the particular. However, this relation is by no means stable. Laclau and Mouffe point to the dislocated nature of all structures, denying the possibility of simply replacing one pole of a binary opposition with its opposite.[9] The emancipation of the female subject, for example, does not create a unified space from which gender oppression can be understood and transformed. Instead, Laclau demands that we recognise the instability and unfixity of all spaces, leading to a politics of difference rather than universality.

These considerations are useful in trying to overcome some of the problems in feminist writings. These problems arise from various binary oppositions that require deconstruction. For example, Molyneux creates an opposition between strategic and practical gender interests in which strategic gender interests challenge underlying structures of patriarchy, whereas practical gender interests are expressed within traditional gender roles.[10] This dichotomy has been exceptionally problematic in discussions of feminism in Latin America, where women's demands for basic needs would automatically be relegated to the realm of practical gender interests and a priori made subordinate to the 'real' interests of challenging the male-dominated structures of power. However, many scholars have pointed out that this dichotomy is problematic. Lynn Stephen, for example, points out that the claims made by many Latin American women may fall into both strategic and practical gender-interest categories.[11] By petitioning for basic needs, these women are also frequently participating in larger arenas in which the male dominated structures of power are questioned. Thus, the individual experiences of women cannot be so readily limited to the practical/particular sphere as they influence and challenge the strategic/universal sphere simultaneously.

A second binary opposition that requires deconstruction is that between epistemology and experience. Some feminist writers have sought to contest male-centred theories on the same ground as Enlightenment epistemology. Believing in the possibility of achieving more firmly grounded arguments, feminists such as Sandra Harding and Nancy Hartsock have tried to show how we can come up with 'objective' knowledge about the status of women and their rights. In their view, feminism does indeed require secure foundations from which to expose and challenge women's oppression. Those foundations cannot exist without privileging epistemology over what are seen as the destabilising effects of contingency, particularity and difference. It is not that particularity is ignored. Rather, it is seen as a necessary expression of a more general rule, one that 'proves' the validity of feminism as a universal discourse and set of practices. Difference and particularism are tolerated as long as they uphold the epistemological rationality of a universal feminism. In effect, such a foundationalism denies difference a constitutive role in women's struggles, consigning it instead to the subordinate position of that which threatens universal reason, and hence an effective feminist politics.[12]

If the universal is impossible, so too is the purely particular. All attempts to completely separate out a particular identity, to construct a completely differentiated and autonomous 'other', will also fail. Just as any attempt to realise a universal results in the construction of a binary opposition, so too does the attempt to bring about the pure particular. Once again, one cannot simply switch one polar extreme for another. Laclau states that: 'to assert one's own *differential* identity involves ... the inclusion in that identity of the other, as that from whom one delimits oneself'.[13]

We are thus faced with a situation in which the universal is impossible, but so too is the particular. What implications does this dual impossibility have for our conception of a feminist identity and its project(s) of emancipation? Laclau points towards two 'symmetrical dangers' that the assertion of a collective identity, such as being a 'woman', might entail. First, if this group attempts to assert its identity based upon its particular (purely context specific) position, it faces the danger of being marginalised by a larger, exclusionary system. However, if that same group attempts to transcend its particular position by making 'universal' claims, it faces a struggle in which it may lose all of its particular character and be subsumed under a larger discourse. If we cannot make identity claims based upon some appeal to the universal, nor to some purely particular position, we are left with the task of establishing points of articulation between the two polar extremes. These points of articulation emerge from the continually contested negotiation of multiple experiences and are manifested performatively as collective identities.

There are a number of feminists who recognise the need to bridge the gap between the universal and the particular as well as celebrate difference and identity, particularly with regard to the position of women of colour and women outside the rich, industrial countries. These feminists recognise the irreducibility of experience in the formation of collective identities. Experience here is not understood in an empiricist fashion, whereby women's narratives of experience would be seen as somehow independent of discourse.[14] Rather, it gives weight to the particular ways in which differentially situated women experience relations of gender subordination. Although it is entirely possible that women create a collective identity in response to such subordination, we do not believe that their entire experience can be articulated within such an identity. Instead, we recognise that there will always be a remainder, some element that cannot be brought into a common language. Note that we are not affirming the impossibility of collective identities. Nor are we stating that each individual has a private experience that is incommensurable with those of others. Both of these claims would lead us back to the logocentric reason that is based on the binary oppositions between universal and particular or between public and private. Instead, we are affirming the need to conceptualise this 'remainder' in terms of its political significance for women's struggles against multiple forms of subordination.

The 'secret' of lived experience: conceptualising the remainder

How are we to conceptualise this 'remainder'? What discourses can we draw on to describe the importance of the singular experience of living without relegating that experience to either some universal or particular terrain? In order to answer these two questions we draw on the works of Jacques Derrida, a noted post-structuralist who, by nature of his own singular experience, has postulated ways of describing this 'remainder.' Bernstein's description of Derrida illuminates this concept of the remainder:

> He [Derrida] was and was not a Jew. He was and was not an Algerian. As an Algerian Jew he was and was not a Frenchman. By his own testimony his primary experience was a 'feeling of non-belonging' – of 'otherness'.[15]

We can see the notion of 'remainder' in this description of Derrida. His singular experience of living did not allow him to wholly identify with the categories of Jew, Algerian, or Frenchman. But neither did it allow him to wholly escape those categories. In this sense, the most accurate description may be that he 'was and was not' a Jew, Algerian, and Frenchman. This sense of in-betweenness, of 'otherness' that comes from living within a multiplicity of discourses is the 'remainder', or in the words of Derrida, the 'secret.'

The 'secret' is, therefore, the portion of lived experience that escapes being categorised into universal narratives of identity and at the same time cannot be purely limited to the individual. Derrida argues:

> The secret is irreducible to the public realm – although I do not call it private – and irreducible to publicity and politicisation, but at the same time, this secret

is that on the basis of which the public realm and the realm of the political can be and remain open.[16]

Thus, the 'secret' is neither purely public nor is it private. However, why is it that this secret becomes the basis for the political remaining open? How is it that this secret becomes the very possibility for the political?

The secret becomes the possibility for politics as it removes the privileged positions of the purely universal and the purely particular as possibilities from which political decisions can be made. Instead, the acknowledgement of the secret means that all decisions must be made from a condition of undecidability, in which there are neither absolutes nor secure foundations.[17] This has profound implications for such grand concepts as citizenship, democracy and feminism. The recognition of the secret, of the remainder that denies the possibility of both the universal and the particular, also means that there can be no single way of defining citizenship, democracy and feminism. Instead, the definition of each term is contingent upon the negotiations that occur between a multiplicity of singular experiences.

This tension between the experience and discourse has been recognised by a number of feminist theorists. Kensinger, for example, critiques traditional categories of liberal feminism as being problematic when viewed against the individual experiences of those women that feminism attempts to assimilate.[18] She recognises that the categories of radical, liberal, and socialist feminism were incapable of incorporating all experiences – 'something spilled out'. Specifically, Kensinger points to the experiences of women of colour. Their singular experiences of subordination, which were based not only on gender, but also on class, race and ethnicity, were often ignored or marginalised by liberal feminism in which 'white voices' are privileged.[19] Therefore, Kensinger calls for a rethinking of how experience is incorporated into feminist theory by advocating non-essentialist notions of 'women' and also for a rethinking of the traditional categories of feminism. She argues:

> What seems necessary today are works that address each viewer in her unique (but) social self, that speak to her personally, inviting her to perceive them according to her own experience and background while soliciting at the same time her ability to reflect on her social conditioning or on the ties that bind her to other social selves in the very process of perceiving.[20]

A second feminist who has recognised this tension between feminist discourse and lived experience is Shari Stone-Mediatore. Like Kensinger, Stone-Mediatore wishes to rethink the way that experience is used in the process of theorising and practising feminism. Specifically, she rejects empiricist narratives of experience as well as those accounts that seek to reduce experience to a simple reflection of fixed discourses. Instead, she wishes to advance a conception of experience that 'does not treat experience as indubitable evidence but nevertheless recognises experience to be a resource for critical reflection'.[21] In so doing, she emphasises the work of Chandra Mohanty.[22]

Mohanty, who has stressed the importance of feminist writings that come from the 'Third World', advocates a view of experience that is both pluralistic and empowering. This view does not regard differences among women in an abstract sense of plurality, nor does it assume that patriarchy means the same for all women. Stone-Mediatore concludes:

> I propose a Mohanty-inspired notion of experience. The experience that facilitates oppositional discourses consists of tensions between experience and language, tensions that are endured subjectively as contradictions within experience-contradictions between ideologically constituted perceptions of the world and reactions to these images endured on multiple psychological and bodily levels.[23]

While Stone-Mediatore levelled criticism at post-structuralist as well as empiricist approaches, it is clear that her call for an alternative understanding of experience is not incommensurable with the ideas of Derrida. In fact, Kensinger and Stone-Mediatore appear to be discussing the same phenomenon of otherness and plurality. Each of these authors, in their own vocabularies, recognises the 'secret' and the importance that lived experience has in any project of feminism or emancipation. However, the recognition of the 'secret' is only the first step in reconceptualising the 'remainder' and gaining an understanding of how collective identities are formed outside the universal/particular dichotomy. In order to understand how collective identities become possible while still affirming the irreducibility of individual experiences we must introduce the concept of the 'promise'.

The 'promise' is also to be found in the works of Derrida. When most Western philosophers describe the 'promise' of 'democracy', they are in fact describing the necessary steps that need to be taken in order to achieve a 'democracy' that has been defined a priori. This is not the 'promise' of Derrida, who instead writes of the 'promise' of 'democracy to come' (*la démocratie à venir*).[24] By this he means that the definition of democracy should be left open and incomplete so that argumentation and discussion can continue.[25] If we recognise the irreducibility of singular experiences, the 'promise' of openness becomes a necessity in any discourse of democracy, citizenship, or feminism. As soon as a discourse attempts to proclaim its own closure, those singular experiences are no longer valued and the 'promise' is effaced. Thus, in opposition to all forms of logocentric reason, in which experiences would simply confirm pre-given definitions of democracy, citizenship, or feminism, the notion of the 'promise' invites a deeper recognition of how the meanings of these terms are shaped in everyday contexts, while understanding that these meanings will never be fixed or closed.

The recognition of the 'promise' also opens the possibility for the creation of collective identities. If the 'promise' allows us to conceive of struggles that, ultimately, remain open, then there is no need to abandon our 'secret' in order to participate. Rather, what becomes necessary is that we articulate our lived experience of citizenship, democracy, or gender with others, not with the intention of defining the 'true' experience of each of these, but with an eye towards opening the possibilities of what is to come. Collective identities are thus created through the articulation and negotiation of our particular experiences in historically specific contexts.

If we accept this point, then the reality of citizenship, democracy, or feminism is transformed from a 'transcendental signifier' (which only has to be realised through political reforms), into a 'floating signifier' whose content is shaped by the political choices of social agents. We are thereby forced to analyse the processes through which collective identities emerge and are transformed. Women's struggles in Chiapas reveal how such processes involve the articulation of multiple experiences of subordination amid competing discourses of citizenship, democracy and feminism.

Women's struggles in Chiapas: articulating citizenship and autonomy

The Zapatista uprising provided a new opportunity for indigenous women to demand equal participation in their homes, communities, organisations and nation. Although grassroots organising in Chiapas prior to 1994 was marked by a predominantly male leadership, the participation of women in community life did create the conditions for a reappraisal of gender relations in the wake of the rebellion. At first, this was most evident in the Lacandón forest where three interrelated processes helped indigenous women in asserting their own demands during 1994–96. The first of these was the very process of migration and colonisation of the forest, which required women to adopt non-traditional roles in the new lowland communities. Women carried out as much of this work as the men, as well as caring for children and the elderly. The second process was the incorporation of women into grassroots agricultural co-operatives, health and education programmes run by the Catholic Diocese of San Cristóbal de Las Casas and a number of nongovernmental organisations. These programmes began when the Diocese adopted its 'preferential option for the poor' in the 1970s. They were extended in the 1980s by new projects initiated by NGOs, university researchers, students and craft co-operatives. The third process was the creation of the EZLN itself. Male-dominated community assemblies were transformed by women's demands for equal participation in the struggle. This was reflected in the Zapatistas' Revolutionary Women's Law, which states that all women should have the right to a life free of sexual and domestic violence, the right to choose one's partner and number of children, and the right to political participation on an equal footing with men.[26]

During the first quarter of 1994, indigenous and *mestiza* women from independent organisations began to construct a common platform in support of the Zapatistas. In preparing their proposals for a National Democratic Convention, they met in San Cristóbal in late July 1994, where they formed the Chiapas Women's State Convention. The meeting issued a list of demands that reflected the spirit of the Zapatistas' Revolutionary Women's Law. They also addressed gender discrimination within indigenous communities by demanding an end to the practice of exchanging girls for money, animals or objects and the right to choose marriage partners.

The Chiapas Women's State Convention gradually became embroiled in political rivalries during 1995 and lost its earlier independence from parties and other social organisations. It also had to deal with divisions over the meaning of feminism and women's goals. Against the universalism of some feminists, the indigenous women appeared to be demonstrating the validity of their own particular struggles as women within a patriarchal society. As noted earlier, analytical distinctions between the 'practical' and 'strategic' gender interests of women were seen by some observers as reflecting the ethnocentric views of feminists in North America and Europe. Women's struggles in Chiapas, whether in the EZLN or the state-level convention, were considered to be simultaneously practical and strategic in that they sought solutions to material problems and, in doing so, challenged the gendered power relations which had traditionally subordinated women to men.[27]

Indigenous women became active participants in organising acts of civil resistance against the imposition of mayors belonging to the ruling *Partido Revolucionario Institucional* (Institutional Revolutionary Party, PRI) during the fall of 1994. They also participated in protecting the Zapatista delegates at the peace talks and in building the EZLN's bases of support throughout the highlands and Lacandón forest. Women also drew attention to the use of sexual violence against indigenous women. Although a large number of cases of rape and other abuses by soldiers and police were denounced by human rights groups in the national and international media, the majority of abuses were covered in a blanket of silence. By 1996, many grassroots activists were perplexed by the weakness of the Zapatistas' own response to this issue. Despite the opening created by the Revolutionary Women's Law, indigenous women still felt alone in their struggle for respect and dignity. Many women who made frequent trips outside their home communities to attend meetings or take part in demonstrations aroused jealousy and suspicion from their husbands. In several cases women were beaten and even killed for being 'too independent'. Mistreatment occurred within families who participated in the same pro-Zapatista organisations or communities, revealing the great distance still to be travelled between the Revolutionary Women's Law and daily practices.[28]

Similarly, women have had to fight to have their demands included in male-dominated agendas for democracy and autonomy. For example, the formal organisation of the *Convención Nacional Democrática* (National Democratic Convention, CND) in August 1994 was marked by a gender bias. The EZLN had called this meeting to address the main national problems facing Mexico on the eve of the presidential elections. Although many women's organisations sent delegates to the meeting, feminist writers criticised the lack of reference to patriarchy as one of Mexico's main 'national problems'.[29] They also criticised the composition of the directorate of the CND. Of the 100 members of this directorate, twenty-one were women (thirteen state delegates and eight public figures). Feminists also noted that the various discussion tables were also run by men, with women responsible for typing up summaries and carrying out other secretarial tasks.[30] Similar criticisms were made concerning the apparent lack of representation of indigenous women in the first Regiones Autónomas Pluriétnicas (Pluriethnic Autonomous Regions, RAP) which were established in October 1994. For example, women's committees were present in only two of the thirty communities that made up one of the RAP in the municipality of Las Margaritas. In addition, women were not given formal land rights or the opportunity to participate in decision-making structures.[31] While each of these criticisms need to be addressed, an exclusive focus on formal, observable and numerical representation obscures the multiplicity of other types of activism at the grassroots level.

Consider, for example, the conclusions to the discussion group on 'Women and the Excluded Civil Society' at the first Intercontinental Encounter Against Neoliberalism and For Humanity, organised by the EZLN and held in Chiapas in July 1996. The mainly non-indigenous participants stated that the structures of neoliberalism are grounded upon patriarchy. The patriarchal family prevents the construction of more plural forms of social structure, encompassing all in a nationalist ideology as members of one single family, based on the rule of money, armaments and sexual violence. While the indigenous Zapatista women who participated in the discussions could agree with these very general arguments, for them the main issue was how to overcome exclusion, not only by the government, but also by their own social organisations. To be listened to, to be taken into account, and to have a voice in collective decision-making were their central demands.[32]

However, the spaces in which indigenous women's voices are being raised are not reducible to the formal, institutionalised realm of mass organisations, parties, churches or social movements. Instead, we need to recognise how women are creating new spaces for political participation in Chiapas. This process is a slow one which, among the Zapatistas, involves a constant struggle to redefine gender relations in accordance with their stated goals of democracy, justice and liberty. Since 1996 such struggles have increasingly taken place within the context of autonomous municipal governments which have broken with the structures of local power controlled by the PRI. The failure of the Mexican government to implement the San Andrés accords on indigenous rights has not prevented indigenous people from pursuing the goal of autonomous representation. By 1998 the EZLN claimed the existence of thirty-eight autonomous municipalities which were governed by Zapatista bases.[33] Women have played a key role in this process, drawing upon their prior experience in community leadership positions and demanding equal rights of participation in the new decision-making structures. In this regard, indigenous women have expanded the meaning of autonomy by inserting a gender perspective. This was made clear by women's participation in the first *Congreso Nacional Indígena* (National Indigenous Congress, CNI), held in Mexico City in October 1996. Women proposed (and achieved) the incorporation of language in the CNI resolutions on indigenous autonomy that reflected their demands. These included a concept of economic autonomy, understood as equal access for women to land and other means of production; political autonomy, including the defence and protection of women's rights; physical autonomy in terms of women's control over their own bodies and sexuality; and cultural autonomy, understood as the right to affirm their specific identities as indigenous women.[34]

How have women themselves seen their participation in these struggles? Recent work by anthropologist Christine Eber has provided us with women's narratives of the conflicts in Chiapas.[35] Eber's work shows how women in the municipality of San Pedro Chenalhó (or *Pedranas*) are reworking ideas and practices in their struggles against all forms of domination. Rather than invoking a single, homogenous Zapatista or feminist discourse capable of giving expression to the variety of ways in which indigenous women are subordinated, Eber demonstrates the differences between women's struggles, while simultaneously upholding the potential for the remaking of collective identities.

For example, since the early 1970s, Pedranas have participated in a variety of religious, co-operative and political associations, responding to problems ranging from alcohol abuse to economic survival. In fact, many women who currently occupy leadership positions in the Zapatista support bases made their first public statements regarding oppression in meetings to discuss the need to control alcohol sales in their communities. Although alcohol consumption was tied to the celebration of religious festivals, women were particularly affected by its abuse as it led to domestic violence, a lack of respect and the depletion of already scarce income. However, in publicly addressing alcohol abuse, women inevitably found themselves challenging the authority of traditionalist religious authorities, for whom alcohol sales were an important element of political control and economic privilege. Women found alternative spaces from which to resist alcohol abuse through groups organised by Protestant churches or by priests and catechists associated with the Catholic Church's 'preferential option for the poor'.

Similarly, in response to the economic crisis of the 1980s, women found themselves contributing ever larger shares of household income. In many cases this income derived from the sale of crafts through membership in new, decentralised co-operatives. Unlike government-run co-operatives or NGOs, where decisions tended to be taken out of the hands of women artisans, the new independent co-operatives allowed Pedranas to work at home and maintain more decentralised networks among their members. As Eber notes, this did not translate into a conservative position condemning women to the 'private' sphere. Instead, women were able to rework their own culturally specific ideas of work and respect within a new discourse of co-operation and solidarity.[36]

In both instances, women have sought to create new spaces for resistance, not by appealing to universal notions of gender consciousness, but by actively challenging particular forms of subordination. These and other struggles have also contributed to the revitalisation of ethnic identities in the wake of the Zapatista uprising, drawing attention to the obstacles to liberation within their own communities, including alcohol abuse, adultery, denial of women's inheritance, lack of family planning, and restrictions on girls' education. These are not seen as 'community traditions', but rather as the result of the political alliances between male, traditionalist authorities and outside *ladino* elites tied to the PRI. On the other hand, women have sought to reinvigorate other traditions which are important in their efforts to overcome subordination. These include religious practices associated with the Day of the Dead celebrations, the preparation of certain foods, weaving traditional clothing and marriage rituals that promote principles of complementarity. Common to these struggles is the effort to regain balance within gender relations, within communities as well as with the natural and spiritual worlds.[37]

These struggles serve to underline the importance of respect for difference, or what we have been calling 'the secret' of singular experience. It is neither feasible nor desirable that each of these experiences be brought within a permanently unified space, language or politics. This does not rule out the possibility of forming collective identities that transcend particularity. However, there is always a gap between experience and discourse which cannot be filled, even by (especially by) the most radically democratic discourse. In fact, it is this gap which makes possible the promise of alternative political identities and forms of participation. The danger of uncritically celebrating Zapatista discourse from the outside is that we end up effacing this gap and choking off the promise of its own democracy to come.

At the local level, then, the significance of Zapatista discourse is given not only by its radical anti-government rhetoric, but rather by the numerous ways in which indigenous men, women and children are able to appropriate it for their particular and shared struggles against injustice. These include not only efforts to resist 'outside' authorities in Tuxtla or Mexico City, as well as paramilitary groups, but also struggles against exclusionary practices within their own communities and organisations. Women's struggles cannot be seen as separate from the broader, national goals of Zapatismo. In fact, the success of the latter may be contingent on the spaces opened up by the former.

Conclusions

Women are today bearing the brunt of paramilitary violence in Chiapas. On 22 December 1997, twenty-one women, nine men and fifteen children were massacred while praying in the hamlet of Acteal in the municipality of San Pedro Chenalhó. Their killers belonged to the *Máscara Roja* (Red Mask), a paramilitary organisation funded, armed and trained by government officials to terrorise anyone suspected of sympathising with the EZLN. Although those killed in Acteal supported the goals of the EZLN, they did not belong to its local support base. Instead, they were members of an economic co-operative known as *Las Abejas* (The Bees). However, they had refused to give money or join *Máscara Roja* in its actions against the autonomous municipality located in the nearby community of Polhó. The paramilitaries acted with impunity. The commander of the state police unit was stationed just two hundred yards from the site of the massacre, in which men with AK-47 assault rifles slaughtered the forty-five unarmed victims, over a period of several hours. Women were again brutalised in this act, with one pregnant woman having her womb cut open and the foetus pulled out. Over ten thousand indigenous people have been forced out of their homes and communities by the continual threat of paramilitary violence. Most of these live in conditions of poor sanitation where sickness and hunger are daily realities, claiming the lives of young children. Indigenous women are now faced with new and ever more difficult struggles to survive and rebuild their communities.

During 1998 the state government also attempted to dismantle the Zapatistas' autonomous municipalities located in the Lacandón forest. Women were again targeted by soldiers and police, as well as by another paramilitary group, known as the *Movimiento Indígena Revolucionario Anti-Zapatista* (Anti-Zapatista Indigenous Revolutionary Movement, MIRA). When Zapatista men were forced to flee their communities and hide in the nearby mountains, women were threatened with rape if they went out to gather firewood or fetch water. Despite these pressures, women have remained firm in their conviction to defend the autonomous municipalities, refusing to ally with the PRI or accept 'aid' from the state government.

This chapter has attempted to draw attention to the political articulation of the universal and the particular, specifically the need to recognise difference and 'the secret' of singular experience in women's struggles. In 1999 such experiences are marked by the pain of war and brutality. Women have become key targets in a counter-insurgency campaign that recognises both their vulnerability but also their centrality to the future of the EZLN and the autonomous municipalities. Their resistance is a powerful lesson in the strength of conviction, but is also a call for recognition of their role in building and protecting a much broader set of demands for gender equality and democracy in Mexico.

In responding to this call, the overriding task for democratic movements in Mexico is to effectively oppose the government's counter-insurgency operation and create new conditions for achieving peaceful solutions in Chiapas. However, this response can only succeed if it continually strives to open up new spaces for participation in the peace process. If it is the case that women's experiences of the rebellion cannot be fully incorporated by universal discourses of citizenship, democracy and feminism, we are obliged to support their efforts in defining the terms by which peace and justice can be brought to their communities.

The gains made by women in Chiapas are not guaranteed. Rather, the extent to which they have been able to overcome subordination remains an open question. However, in addressing this question, future research should be careful not to assimilate women's struggles into pre-existing discourses of citizenship, democracy and feminism. Instead it should focus on how women's singular experiences of the rebellion continue to create new meanings and possibilities for each of these terms. In this way, the content of Zapatista discourse can be seen as dynamic and changing, keeping alive the 'promise' of 'democracy to come'.

Notes

We would like to thank Aletta Norval and Tony Lucero for their valuable observations and comments on an earlier version of this chapter.

1 See R. Burbach, 'Roots of postmodern rebellion in Chiapas', *New Left Review*, 205 (1994), 113–24; G. Collier and E. Quaratiello, *Basta! – Land and the Zapatista Rebellion in Chiapas* (Oakland, Ca., Food First Books, Institute for Food and Development Policy, 1994); and J. Ross, *Rebellion from the Roots: Indian Uprising in Chiapas* (Monroe, Common Courage Press, 1995).

2 See the analyses by N. Harvey in *The Chiapas Rebellion: The Struggle for Land and Democracy* (Durham, NC, Duke University Press, 1998), and 'The Zapatistas, radical democratic citizenship and women's struggles', *Social Politics*, 5:2 (1998), 158–87.

3 See R. Rojas (ed.), *Chiapas: ¿y las mujeres qué?* (Mexico D.F., Centro de Investigación y Capacitación de la Mujer, A.C., Colección del Dicho al Hecho, vol. 1, 1994 and vol. 2, 1995) and G. Rovira, *Mujeres de Maíz* (Mexico D.F., Editores Era, 1997).

4 For example, see A. García de León, 'Prólogo; La historia, si acaso tiene un sentido', in A. García de León (ed.), *EZLN: Documentos y Comunicados*, Vol. 3 (Mexico D.F., Editores Era, 1998), pp. 17–20.

5 A. Bartra *et al.*, 'Debate sobre los Acuerdos de San Andrés y los proyectos de autonomía', *Chiapas*, 6 (1998), 151–209.

6 This non-essentialist position has been expressed by Chantal Mouffe in the following terms: 'Feminism, for me, is the struggle for the equality of women. But this should not be understood as a struggle to realize the equality of a definable empirical group with a common essence and identity – that is, women – but rather as a struggle against *the multiple forms in which the category "woman" is*

constructed in subordination' (emphasis added). C. Mouffe, *The Return of the Political* (London,Verso, 1993), p. 88.

7   J. Derrida, *Of Grammatology*, trans. by G. Chakravorty Spivak (Baltimore and London, Johns Hopkins University Press, 1976).

8   E. Laclau, *Emancipation(s)* (London, Verso, 1996), p. 57.

9   E. Laclau and C. Mouffe, *Hegemony and Socialist Strategy: Towards a Radical Democratic Politics* (London, Verso, 1985), p. 128.

10 M. Molyneux, 'Mobilization without emancipation? Women's interests, the state and revolution in Nicaragua', *Feminist Studies*, 11:2 (1985), 227–54.

11 L. Stephen, 'Democracy for whom? Women's grassroots political activism in the 1990's, Mexico City and Chiapas', in G. Otero (ed.), *Neoliberalism Revisited: Economic Restructuring and Mexico's Political Future* (Boulder, CO, Westview Press, 1996), pp. 167–85, at p. 169.

12 J. Flax, 'The end of innocence', in J. Butler and J. Scott (eds), *Feminists Theorize the Political* (New York, Routledge, 1992), pp. 445–63.

13 Laclau, *Emancipation(s)*, p. 48.

14 S. Stone-Mediatore, 'Chandra Mohanty and the revaluing of "experience"', *Hypatia* [online], 13:2 (1998), Available: UMI/Proquest Direct. [1999, Jan. 13].

15 R. Bernstein, 'An allegory of modernity/postmodernity: Habermas and Derrida', in G. Madison (ed.), *Working Through Derrida* (Evanston, Ill., Northwestern University Press, 1993), pp. 204–29, at p. 214.

16 J. Derrida, 'Remarks on deconstruction and pragmatism', in C. Mouffe (ed.), *Deconstruction and Pragmatism* (London and New York, Routledge, 1996), pp. 77–88, at p. 80.

17 J. Derrida, 'Force of law: the "mystical foundation of authority"', in D. Cornell, M. Rosenfeld and D. Gray Carlson (eds), *Deconstruction and the Possibility of Justice* (New York: Routledge, 1992), pp. 3–67, at p. 24.

18 L. Kensinger, '(In)quest of liberal feminism', *Hypatia* [online], 12:4 (1997). Available: UMI/Proquest Direct [1999, Jan. 13].

19 See also N. Caraway, *Segregated Sisterhood: Racism and the Politics of American Feminism* (Knoxville, University of Tennessee Press, 1991).

20 Kensinger,'(In)quest of liberal feminism'.

21 Stone-Mediatore, 'Chandra Mohanty and the revaluing of "experience"'.

22 See C. T. Mohanty, A. Russo and L. Torres (eds), *Third World Women and the Politics of Feminism* (Bloomington: Indiana University Press, 1991); and C. T. Mohanty and M. J. Alexander (eds), *Feminist Genealogies, Colonial Legacies, Democratic Futures* (New York: Routledge, 1996).

23 Stone-Mediatore, 'Chandra Mohanty and the revaluing of "experience"'.

24 Derrida, 'Remarks on deconstruction and pragmatism', p. 83.

25 J. Derrida, *The Other Heading: Reflections on Today's Europe*, trans. P. A. Brault and M. Naas (Bloomington: Indiana University Press, 1992), pp. 76–9.

26 R. A. Hernández Castillo, 'Reinventing tradition: the revolutionary women's law', *Akwekon. A Journal of Indigenous Issues*, Summer (1994), 67–70.

27 L. Stephen, 'Democracy for whom?'.

28 R. A. Hernández Castillo, 'Construyendo la utopía: esperanzas y desafíos de las mujeres chiapanecas de frente al siglo XXI', in R. A. Hernández Castillo (ed.), *La Otra Palabra: Mujeres y Violencia en Chiapas, Antes y Después de Acteal* (Mexico D.F., CIESAS, 1998), pp. 125–42.

29 M. Lagarde, 'Hacia una nueva constituyente desde las mujeres', in Rojas (ed.), *Chiapas: ¿y las mujeres qué?*, pp. 170–4.
30 Rojas (ed.), *Chiapas: ¿y las mujeres qué?*, vol. 1, pp. 167–9.
31 *Ibid.*, vol. 1, pp. 209–26.
32 Ejército Zapatista de Liberación Nacional, *Crónicas Intergalácticas: Primer Encuentro Intercontinental por la Humanidad y contra el Neoliberalismo* (Chiapas, Planeta Tierra, 1996).
33 Frente Zapatista de Liberación Nacional, *Fuerte es su Corazón: Los Municipios Rebeldes Zapatistas* (Mexico D.F., FZLN, 1998).
34 Hernández Castillo, 'Construyendo la utopía', p. 135.
35 C. Eber, 'Las mujeres y el movimiento por la democracia en San Pedro Chenalhó', in Hernández Castillo, *La Otra Palabra*, pp. 84–105; '"Buscando una nueva vida": liberation through autonomy in San Pedro Chenalhó, 1970–1998', in J. Rus, S. Mattiace and R. A. Hernández Castillo (eds), *Taking the Future into Our Own Hands: The Impact of the Zapatista Uprising Four Years After*, (1999); and, '"Seeking our own food": indigenous women's power and autonomy in San Pedro Chenalhó, Chiapas (1980–1998)', *Latin American Perspectives*, 26:3 (1999), 6–36.
36 Eber, 'Buscando una nueva vida'.
37 *Ibid.*

The difficult emergence of a democratic imaginary: Black Consciousness and non-racial democracy in South Africa

At first glance, the picture of South African politics between the Soweto uprisings of June 1976 and the declaration of a national state of emergency in 1986 suggests a chaotic set of ideological and organisational realignments, accompanied by significant shifts in strategy and personal ideological affiliation.[1] On a deeper level, a more coherent pattern of events and logics emerges. The disintegration of the Black Consciousness Movement (BCM) as a leading political force both inside the country and in exile is inversely proportional to the growing importance and power of a series of movements that came to adopt the ANC's Freedom Charter as their guiding ideological document and political programme. This failure of Black Consciousness discourse to transform its myth of Black Solidarity and Black Communalism into a fully-fledged social imaginary, coupled with the consolidation of Charterism as the leading internal opposition discourse, raises four basic questions. Why did Black Consciousness fail? What was the character of Charterism, and how did it become hegemonic? How can we account for the transition between the two discourses?

This chapter addresses these questions from a discourse-theory perspective. I argue that to understand and explain the transition in non-essentialist terms requires us to rethink the Soweto uprising as a dislocatory experience. Given this, it is possible to begin to account for the National Party's (NP) failed restructuring of the context of apartheid domination in the post-Soweto period, and it is also possible to explain the failure of Black Consciousness discourse to reinscribe the dislocatory experience of Soweto in a new series of antagonistic relations. Moreover, I show how Charterist discourse, which was articulated around the reactivation of the ANC's 'Freedom Charter' and organised in the form of the United Democratic Front (UDF), was successful in both challenging the NP's reform programme and instituting a new popular democratic discourse. Subsequently, it was this new discourse that formed the basis of a proto-democratic imaginary, which could represent the various grievances and demands of those opposed to the apartheid regime, and serve as the basis for a new post-apartheid order.

In order to justify these arguments, I begin by examining the significantly different material context of domination that emerged after the Soweto events of June 1976. This context is heavily marked by the organic crisis of the apartheid regime, and its efforts to articulate a comprehensive reform programme designed to overcome the crisis. After briefly discussing this dialectic of crisis and reform, I then examine the failure of Black Consciousness to impose its vision of society by constituting itself as a viable social imaginary. Finally, I turn to those resistance currents that did occupy the new political spaces opened up by the reformist discourse of the period. Here I examine the emergence and formation of the UDF, and the logics through which it gradually became hegemonic within the field of opposition politics during the 1980s.

'Soweto' and the new context of Apartheid domination

Beginning on 16 June 1976, when white police shot down black high-school students protesting against the imposition of Afrikaans as a language of instruction, the Soweto uprising changed the contours of South African politics. Not only did it trigger off the long wave of mass, popular resistance to the apartheid state, which would only be temporarily curbed by the declaration of the national state of emergency in 1986; it also stimulated a major restructuring of the apartheid project.[2] From a discourse-theory perspective, 'Soweto' is best understood as a dislocation of the social. In other words, it was an event that could not be symbolised in the apartheid symbolic order and in the existing resistance discourses.[3] Thus the crucial questions raised by 'Soweto' concern the way in which this dislocatory event would be inscribed by different discursive practices. In other words, which forces would hegemonise its destabilising effects? Would its resolution resemble that of the Sharpeville crisis sixteen years previously, in which the NP government managed to unify the power bloc and the state around the 'total apartheid' project of 'separate development'? Or would it result in a significantly changed context of domination?

The organic crisis of the state

In fact, the main effect of 'Soweto' was to engender an organic crisis of the apartheid state.[4] It was 'organic' in the Gramscian sense that it could not be repaired within the confines of the existing system, but required a more fundamental restructuring of the state.[5] For purposes of analysis, five sets of contradictions were fused together by the Soweto events. First, the 1970s had brought a major transformation in the geopolitical context of the Southern African region. The collapse of Portuguese colonialism and the rapid installation of Marxist-oriented regimes in Mozambique and Angola, coupled with an intensification of the Zimbabwean war of liberation and the growing struggle for Namibian independence, shattered the confidence of the South

African state and renewed optimism about the possible overthrow of the apartheid state.[6] Secondly, a series of economic difficulties became more prominent during the period, as the previously dynamic regime of accumulation that can be characterised as 'racial Fordism' began to break down.[7] Here the central problem concerned the contradiction between the dominant growth model, which was based around capitalist accumulation, and the apartheid mode of regulation.[8] This was exacerbated by the dependent form of capitalism that had developed in the South African context and the inbuilt structural rigidities (restrictions on labour mobility, limited consumer markets, and so forth), consequent upon the racial division of labour.[9]

Thirdly, one of the most important effects of this growing economic crisis was the intensifying disintegration of the key barriers separating blacks into a group of permanent 'urban insiders', on the one hand, and a set of 'rural outsiders' living in the 'independent homelands' and Bantustans on the other.[10] This blurring of the division that effectively separated 'white' South Africa from its racial and ethnic 'others' was manifest in an increasing political and ideological crisis of the state, as it cast around for a solution to the growing numbers of urbanised blacks in South Africa who were totally without representation and rights. The exposure of this absence of a ready-to-hand solution, coupled with the deepening illegitimacy of those apartheid structures that were in place, constitutes the third dimension of crisis.

The reliance on increasing doses of state coercion and repression, rather than the more normalised forms of maintaining domination, constituted the fourth contradictory dynamic of apartheid rule during the period. As the institutional boundaries of apartheid rule began to crumble, and as resistances intensified, so the direct policing of the subjugated was stepped up. This was to culminate in the massive deployment of state force during 1976 and 1977, and the growing militarisation of the state as it faced the changing geopolitical situation.[11] The spiralling relation of repression and resistance in a context marked by the collapse of social control greatly contributed to the growing disorganisation and crisis of the state.[12] Finally, all these logics were exacerbated by the growing popular and working-class struggles of the time. The sporadic strikes in Natal during late 1972 and 1973, following working-class struggles in Namibia the previous year, spread haphazardly and unevenly to other parts of the country later in the year, and stimulated the formation of trade unions in various sectors of the economy.[13] Moreover, the struggles of students at black universities and colleges under the aegis of Black Consciousness, and the growing resistance of black schoolchildren toward the imposition of apartheid education, contributed to the rebirth of popular struggles in the 1970s.[14]

The 'Total Strategy'

As the political rhetoric suggests, the formative set of reforms named the 'Total Strategy', designed to counter a perceived 'Total Onslaught' in the

Southern African region, endeavoured to address the complete array of contradictions condensed together by the Soweto uprising.[15] The reform programme aimed at an intensive restructuring of the state and the apartheid order, so as to deflect the groundswell of popular protest, and to broaden the apartheid state's basis of consent.[16] Without developing a comprehensive analysis of this project, it is necessary to touch on the three-pronged strategy which was put forward by the NP.

In the first place, following in the wake of the 1978 Riekert Commission report into the regulation of black labour, the three so-called 'Koornhof Bills' aimed to draw a sharper distinction between 'permanent urban residents' and 'temporary' Africans residing in the urban areas, and by extension between those in the existing urban and rural areas.[17] They also aimed to rationalise and augment the powers of African local government in 'white' South Africa.[18] The principal objective of this first plank of the reform programme was to strengthen the position of the relatively privileged section of the urban African populace by granting certain political and economic privileges, thus stabilising a permanent African working class of manageable dimensions, while displacing and relocating mass unemployment and poverty to 'black spaces'.[19]

In addition to these measures designed to tighten up 'influx control', the Wiehahn Commission sought to restructure the existing industrial relations machinery by substantially amending the antiquated 1926 Industrial Conciliation Act, which differentially regulated white and black labour.[20] In order to create a 'structured and orderly situation' in the field of labour relations, Wiehahn proposed to 'normalise' the handling of labour disputes (which were steadily escalating during the period), while 'regulating' wage rates and working conditions, by formally recognising the expanding set of African trade unions.[21] In advocating the dismantling of the existing dual system of industrial relations, the Commission envisaged, as Murray suggests, 'the formal registration of the African trade unions into the officially-sanctioned industrial conciliation machinery instead of their relegation to non-voting observer status'.[22] This strategy of co-optation would, it was hoped, make the emergent unions subject to the 'protective and stabilizing elements' of the new system, with 'its essential discipline and control'.[23]

Finally, there was the restructuring of the national political system. The constitutional reforms, which had first been mooted in the National Party's 1977 constitutional proposals, endeavoured to incorporate Indians and Coloureds into the representative apparatuses of the South African state. The so-called 'New Deal' sought to entrench overall white political domination, while simultaneously articulating a new set of roles that 'Coloureds and Indians should play within the order of domination.'[24] To simplify another baroque set of neo-apartheid structures, this set of political changes comprised the establishment of a separately elected 'tricameral parliament' for whites, coloureds and Indians; the abolition of the previous, racially defined

Westminster parliament; and the creation of a powerful executive President, with a so-called President's Council – heavily dominated by white members of parliament, or those appointed by the Presidency (in turn mainly by the 'white' chamber of parliament) – to formulate and implement policy.[25] It should be noted that this attempted expansion of the state's basis of political consent was accompanied by a growing centralisation and militarisation of the state structures.[26]

The failure of Black Consciousness in South Africa

Having sketched out the changed context of domination, we need now to account for the fact that the BCM, which was the leading political force at the time, was unable to reinscribe the Soweto dislocation in its own terms, thus failing to become the major opponent of the new order of domination. Apart from those Marxist accounts that stress the BCM's inability to incorporate working-class interests and demands into their discourse,[27] most interpretations of the decline and transformation of Black Consciousness do not adequately explain the historical context and conditions in which this transformation took place. At most, their analyses provide detailed political histories or tend to focus on those activists whose political and ideological positions underwent change in the period.[28] However, this begs the question as to how and why these positions changed, and why these changes took the particular form they did.

At the conjunctural level, the failure of Black Consciousness can be explained by the state's response to the Soweto uprising. The massive deployment of state power, followed by the bannings of Black Consciousness organisations in September 1977, made the continued functioning of the BCM in its original form impossible. State repression also resulted in a flood of young black refugees into political exile. The inability, and at times unwillingness, of those Black Consciousness activists and supporters to consolidate viable organisational structures made them ill-equipped to interpellate the radicalised generation of black youth seeking alternative ways to prosecute the anti-apartheid struggle. Hence it was the older, more established liberation movements such as the African National Congress, and to a lesser extent the Pan-African Congress, which benefited immediately from the influx of militant and politicised youth.[29] For the ANC in particular, the greater experience of conducting exile politics had furnished them with a more sophisticated array of international connections and a greater degree of international legitimacy, as well as a remarkable capacity to remain relatively united organisationally and ideologically.

However, these conjunctural factors point to a deeper set of structural logics that ultimately account for the incapacity of the BCM to transform itself from a purely oppositional movement into a force for the construction of a new social and political order.[30] Of obvious importance in this regard were the organisational and leadership deficiencies that were cruelly exposed during the Soweto uprisings and the post-Soweto clampdown.[31] While the student uprising was to some extent made possible by the availability and dissemination of Black Consciousness discourse,[32] BCM activists and leaders failed to take advantage of an undoubtedly favourable political situation. This was a consequence of the weakening of organisations through state repression immediately prior to the uprising, the slowness of leaders to react to events, and their strangely conservative responses to the opportunities that manifested themselves.

These failures were rooted in deeper and longer-term weaknesses. It is possible to pinpoint at least three major structural weaknesses in the BCM's organisational infrastructure. First, it exhibited a limited scope of operation, that is, the BCM found it difficult to extend its influence into those sectors of black society such as the townships, workplaces and rural areas, which could provide a mass base of support in moments of crisis and/or political opportunity. Secondly, the scale of organisation was limited, which is to say that even in those areas where Black Consciousness discourse had become relatively well rooted – in the universities, colleges, churches, African schools, and amongst the black intelligentsia and cultural producers – there did not emerge mass organisations which could easily and efficiently mobilise large-scale popular support around particular issues and causes. Finally, and closely connected to the foregoing, there did not emerge organisations of great quality and depth, that is to say, organisational forms which could easily reproduce themselves in the face of state repression.

This structural explanation advanced so far has focused on the visible difficulties of Black Consciousness organisation and leadership from the moment of its inception to the Soweto events. However, at a deeper archaeological level, we need to uncover more basic reasons for the movement's failure to become a surface of inscription able to register a series of demands and interests much broader than its initial form of articulation.[33] Comparatively speaking, there is nothing particularly exceptional about the fact that radicalised and relatively disconnected students and intellectuals dominated the BCM; many collective social imaginaries are established from these ignoble origins. What calls for analysis in the case of Black Consciousness is why this discourse did not manage to transcend the limitations of its own origins.

Myths and social imaginaries

This question centres on the failure of Black Consciousness to move beyond its status of being a mythical space to become a collective social imaginary. The discourse of Black Consciousness clearly functioned as a mythical space in the late 1960s and early 1970s. Black Consciousness activists successfully constructed a mythical image of black unity and identity that was rooted in a retrospective construction of a black historical past unsullied by the arrival of white settlers with their dominating logics of colonialism and imperialism.[34] Thus the fullness of pre-existing African social relations and forms of consciousness countered the evils of European domination. Moreover, by employing the discursive logics of equivalence and iterability they were able to present a series of positive inversions of 'Europeanness' and 'whiteness'.[35] For example, in a paper entitled 'Some African Cultural Concepts', which was presented to a conference culminating in the formation of the Black Peoples' Convention in 1971, Steve Biko emphasises the 'authentic cultural concepts of the African people by Africans themselves'.[36] He goes on to articulate a conception of 'modern African culture' by a discursive strategy of excluding elements deemed to be symptomatic of Western or 'Anglo-Boer' culture. Thus, the positive elements of 'African' and 'black' culture are constituted through an inversion of the existing white/'non-white' opposition. Whereas white racism had relegated 'non-white' values to an inferior (or secondary) position, Biko's recuperation of a distinctive black tradition is achieved through opposing them to the dominant white values. Central to this operation is the idea of black society as being 'man-centred', a fact that is posited against the inherent competitiveness, instrumentality and generalised anomie of Western or white society. This man-centredness is manifest in an emphasis on the values of collectivism, friendship, sharing and group solidarity, which are purportedly absent in the reason-centred, materialistic and individualistic other. As Biko puts it:

> One of the most fundamental aspects of our [African or black] culture is the importance we attach to man. *Ours has always been a man-centred society.* Westerners have on many occasions been surprised at the capacity we have for talking to each other – not for the sake of arriving at particular conclusions but merely to enjoy the communication for its own sake. Intimacy is a term not exclusive for particular friends but applying to a whole group of people ... .
>
> These things are never done in the Westerner's culture ... . We are not a suspicious race. We believe in the inherent goodness of man. We enjoy man for himself ... . Hence in all we do we always place man first and hence all our action is usually joint community-oriented action rather than the individualism which is the hallmark of the capitalist approach. We always refrain from using people as stepping-stones.[37]

This passage crystallises an important dimension of Black Consciousness discourse, namely, the way in which a specifically black culture and identity is constituted by drawing contrasts, and ultimately through excluding, white 'Anglo-Boer' culture. Against the 'suspiciousness', 'endless competition', 'individualism' and instrumentality of Western capitalism and modernity, Biko advocates the reactivation of African societal values which are 'man-centred' and based on the 'inherent goodness of man', in which there is 'a community of brothers and sisters jointly involved in the quest for ... composite answers to the varied problems of life'. This distinctive African tradition is presented as diametrically opposed to Western values.[38]

In this way, Black Consciousness intellectuals were able to resist the apartheid system, while presenting an alternative vision of society predicated on an authentic black human nature and community. In short, the signifier 'black' became a central means for representing and registering opposition to the apartheid order, and the mobilisation of 'blackness' became a condition of possibility for voicing protest irrespective of the particular enunciative position from which protest emanated. This is evident in the fact that a variety of political movements and forces employed the language of Black Consciousness to advance their interests. Thus, the discourses of Bantustan leaders, members of the Natal Indian Congress, the independent trade union movement, liberal commentators, and even state officials, were marked and mediated by this central category, and what it represented.[39]

The limits of 'blackness' as an empty signifier
However, there were two substantial limitations that prevented the stabilisation of blackness as a universal point of identification and precluded its full evolution into a collective social imaginary. In the first place, the transformation of blackness from a floating signifier into a relatively fixed empty signifier was never fully accomplished. This was a product of tendencies both within and outside the ranks of the BCM. One difficulty was that the signifier of blackness in the philosophy and discourse of Black Consciousness could not conceal its manifest ambiguities. It was not clear whether blackness referred to a common experience of racial oppression under white domination,[40] or whether it designated a peculiarly African consciousness and sensibility, as is sometimes the case in the writings and speeches of sophisticated Black Consciousness intellectuals such as Steve Biko,[41] or whether it signified a more general Third-Worldist rejection of Western imperialism and colonialism.[42] This posed difficulties for the coexistence of racial, ethnic and cultural differences within Black Consciousness discourse. For instance, even those Black Consciousness supporters, such as the Coloured activist Jakes Gerwel, who were intent on rescuing and defending the forcefulness of Black Consciousness against the divisive ethnic particularism of apartheid, recognised the ambiguities of the new discursive configuration for certain categories of black people:

> Black Consciousness was the one movement which provided a concrete point of identification to coloureds and to which many, especially the young, responded. Black consciousness rejected the categorisation *coloured*, drawing all *blacks* together around the fact of their political oppression. A distinction which the Black Consciousness movement was never able to spell out clearly, was that between the movement as one based on a cultural identification, and the movement as a political methodology to counter the divide-and-rule principle. This gave rise to a lot of confusion amongst coloured youth with their built-in identity problem … . Their dilemma was that if Black Consciousness was 'merely' a political movement it could not provide the psychological iden-

tity they sought; as a cultural movement they were inclined to interpret it as demanding a shedding of all coloured, that is White, Western or European values and customs. The former would not solve their identity problem, and in the case of the latter they would, ultimately, still be aware of being converts, of being 'reformed coloureds'.

   This dilemma seems to have been partly resolved by some through interpreting Black Consciousness as a consciousness of Africa and an awareness of their being African within their own right.[43]

This prescient passage indicates the inherent structural tension involved in the attempt to prioritise a black identity in South African resistance discourse, even when those who are interpellated by it reject an already existing system of racist classification, which they believe to be imposed and oppressive. To become 'black' for Coloureds in South Africa meant the renunciation of an ethnic, cultural or even national identity, and a consequent experience of loss and dislocation not compensated for by the new discourse. Gerwel's comments also point to the difficulties of embodying blackness in a context marked by the absence of traditions and practices which make such an identity possible.

A similar problem was evident in the case of certain Indian positions during the period. While key leaders of SASO and the BCM were ethnically Indian, and the movement made strong efforts to prevent an essentialist conception of Africanness to predominate, attempts were made in 1971 to reactivate the dormant Natal Indian Congress (NIC), a movement which had aligned itself with the Congress Alliance in the 1950s and which catered specifically for ethnic Indians. The formation of the movement was strongly opposed by the BCM, which claimed that the resuscitation of an ethnically based form of organisation represented a regressive step cancelling out the achievements of the BCM in transcending ethnic forms of identification. The hostile exchanges which ensued in the early 1970s were testimony to the continued salience of ethnic identification, as well as the difficulties of erasing particularistic forms of identification, and replacing them with new forms of 'universality'.[44]

Another persistent dilemma for Black Consciousness intellectuals concerned the character of blackness itself. Did it refer to something given or substantial, or was it a changing social and symbolic construction? Here there was a constant, and perhaps necessary, slippage. At times, blackness did refer to physical and natural characteristics such as skin colour. However, for the most part the concept took on a symbolic dimension operating at the level of social meaning. In this way, Black Consciousness activists avoided the accusation that the new discourse represented an 'inverse racism'. But even this invocation of a hermeneutics of racial identification was grounded on the exclusion of a naturalistic conception of race, and this exclusion indicated the tensions surrounding its demarcation.[45]

Moreover, there were clear ideological and strategic conflicts about the

meaning of black identity in the South African situation, as well as its implications for the conduct of resistance politics. The ideological disputes registered at the Black Renaissance Convention in 1974, for example, suggest a
divergent series of political positions and interests that were articulated in
the name of Black Consciousness. More particularly, it became evident that
a homogenising conception of blackness covered over class differences
between blacks. Thus, some members of an aspirant black middle class began
to formulate demands for 'black capitalism' and 'black entrepreneurship'
based on the mobilisation of black consumer power, whereas other factions
stressed the priority of the black working classes in the struggle for black
emancipation.[46] Furthermore, as the category of blackness became more
widely available for the various sectors of the black community in South
Africa, so it led to some participants in the Bantustan system itself using the
language of Black Consciousness to pursue their interests, even though SASO
and the BCM had opposed the Bantustan leaders as collaborators within the
apartheid system.[47] What these two erasures suggest is the growing availability of the category of blackness as a point of identification, and its emergence
as a 'quasi-transcendental' signifier, that is to say, a signifier that could effectively interpellate and mobilise a wide variety of constituencies and communities. While this did mean a dissemination of its effects, it also led to a
weakening of the radical impetus of Black Consciousness itself and an incapacity to stabilise the political meaning of blackness in the South African context. This resulted in the need to create divisions amongst blacks themselves.
Hence Biko, for instance, echoing the ideas of Black Power writers in the
USA such as Malcolm X, was forced to make a distinction between 'authentic blacks', and those whose political persuasions and positions rendered
them not black.[48]

   A final complication induced by the category of blackness in the South
African context concerned the position and role of whites in the struggle for
liberation. While it was the ambiguous role of white liberals that had been
important in motivating the production of blackness in the first place, an
absolute exclusion of whites both organisationally and in a future 'non-racial'
South Africa caused complications for the BCM. These difficulties were
strategic and ethical. In strategic terms, certain whites had been, and were
potentially, useful in bringing about an end to the apartheid regime. Moreover, many whites had participated in the Congress Alliance and the South
African Communist Party, both of which had retained and, during the latter
part of the 1970s, regained a strong degree of symbolic presence amongst
blacks inside and outside the country. In ethical terms, the BCM's exclusion
of whites, if absolutised, made it vulnerable to the charge of inverse racism,
a charge which many white (and some black) liberals had made when the
movement first emerged, and which many Black Consciousness activists
acknowledged themselves in the post-Soweto ideological realignments.[49]

The material context of domination

The second major constraint on the stabilisation of blackness as an empty sig-nifier, and its transformation from what George Rude has called a 'derived' or 'artificial' notion into an 'inherent belief' with powerful popular reso-nance, is explained by the particular conjuncture in which the BCM found itself, and which it had, in part, helped to define.[50] In brief, the effects of a conjuncture dominated by the extensive implementation of apartheid by a powerful regime intent on eradicating any radical resistance to its programme strongly restricted the constitution and circulation of any oppo-sitional discourse. So even though the message and style of Black Conscious-ness has been widely perceived as elitist, this is in part a result of the material context in which the movement had to operate. Hence, for structural rea-sons, the movement faced a restricted economy of antagonistic relations and floating signifiers available for hegemonisation, as well as a limited con-stituency to address in the period leading up to the Soweto events. It was thus unable to fuse or graft its more 'artificial' system of ideas on to a deeper set of beliefs and sentiments, which animated popular and mass culture amongst blacks in South Africa.

This failure was particularly evident during and after the Soweto events, the one key moment when a fusion of Black Consciousness's more abstract ideas with popular discourses might have been realised. Why was this the case? As I have already intimated, one response to this question concentrates on the subjective interpretations put forward by many former Black Con-sciousness activists in the post-Soweto conjuncture.[51] For the most part, these activists present the shift from Black Consciousness to Charterism as a dialec-tical progression of ideas, in which members of the BCM came to 'recognise' the inherent ideological limitations of Black Consciousness discourse and then sought alternative, more progressive forms of identification. For instance, the UDF leader Popo Molefe explains the shift in the following terms:

> We saw the [BC's] strategy as parochial and hemming the expansion of the anti-apartheid movement. At another level, the approach became morally indefen-sible in the sense that if we had condemned the racism of whites, we could not posit what is immediately perceived as the reverse of that racism as an alterna-tive. We had to posit a kind of alternative capable of uniting the largest section of South Africans committed to a peaceful and just future – an alternative that could lay a foundation for racial conciliation.[52]

However, from a discourse-theory perspective, some words of caution are needed before we accept at face value these subjective accounts of the shift from Black Consciousness to Charterism. While not relegating these accounts to a realm of false consciousness, one difficulty in basing an inter-pretation on these *post factum* rationalisations resides in the fact that most of the interviews were conducted (necessarily) after the transitions themselves occurred, and in a politico-historical conjuncture in which many of the issues that were being contested and debated had already been decided. Speaking from an enunciative position in which the enigmatic process of subjectivisation has already taken place could well explain the desire on the part of the subject to construct a biographical narrative of events in which a teleological consistency and ethical high ground is stressed. This 'presentist' and 'subjectivist' reading of the past tends, therefore, to confer a *post hoc* rationality and continuity to events and processes which were in reality much more historically contingent and accidental.[53] Accounts of this sort still beg the difficult question concerning how it was that the discourse of non-racialism and democracy was able to replace Black Consciousness. Where did this language of resistance come from? How, and in what form, was it reactivated and made available? How did it manage to interpellate the new set of intellectuals who were taking the struggle forward? Why was it successful in making possible renewed and sustained mass resistance to the state?

The emergence and formation of Charterist hegemony

In order to address these questions, we need to consider another set of discursive practices that emerged during the 1970s, which were better able to connect with the already existing popular sentiments and traditions of resistance ideology. There were three major strands of oppositional discourse in the years between 1977 and 1986, each structured around its own originating myth. These were the independent trade union movement, those movements that continued the Black Consciousness tradition of resistance, and the hotchpotch of community organisations, student networks, trade unions and political parties that were unified by a common commitment to the ANC's Freedom Charter, and which were eventually to form the UDF in 1983.

The independent trade union movement embraced a number of currents of progressive, anti-apartheid worker organisations with divergent political and ideological affiliations. Emerging in the repressive conditions of the 1970s, the ideology and strategy of the union movement, especially the dominant non-racial and democratic Federation of South African Trade Unions (FOSATU), focused heavily on the creation of factory- and industry-based unions with strong democratic accountability and 'worker leadership'.[54] As against the more explicitly socialist and working-class orientation of the trade unions, the two other political discourses are both usually described as popular or populist.[55] Those Black Consciousness activists and supporters inside the country who sought to retain their former principles established the Azanian People's Organisation (AZAPO) in 1978. In June 1983, they were instrumental in forming the National Forum (NF), a series of former Black Consciousness and Unity Movement organisations, so as to co-ordinate protest against the state's reform programme.[56] The third and most important strand of opposition politics can be gathered around those groups that came to identify with the Freedom Charter. The so-called 'turn to community', which followed the state repression of the Soweto uprisings, spawned a series of localised associations and organisations, each pursuing their own particular objectives. However, in 1983 this disparate set of groups were brought together in the umbrella organisation known as the UDF in order to oppose the NP's proposed constitutional reforms.[57]

As the dialectic of resistance and repression accelerated into 'the township rebellion' of 1984 and 1985, the UDF sought not only to hegemonise other popular forces such as AZAPO and the NF, but it also sought to establish alliances with the different sections of the independent union movement. One of the main criticisms of the UDF during its emergence and formation had been the absence of working-class content in its campaigns and discourse, coupled with the poor representation of members of the working class in its leadership positions.[58] These sentiments were registered in the intense theoretical, strategic and ideological contests that occurred in the post-Soweto period, especially during the early and mid-1980s. Articles and statements in popular journals and community newspapers such as *Grassroots*, *SASPU National*, *South African Labour Bulletin*, *Social Review*, *Transformation* and *Work in Progress* voiced considerable unease at the failure to incorporate working-class elements in the popular democratic discourse which was being articulated, and about the overall objectives of such struggle.[59]

By the end of 1985 these hegemonic contests were effectively resolved. Occurring just two and a half years after the formation of the UDF in the midst of the spiralling township rebellion, the key event that symbolised its resolution was the launch of the Congress of South African Trade Unions (COSATU). Not only did the new trade union federation unify large sectors of the once fractious independent trade union movement, but on a symbolic level the formation of the biggest trade union organisation in South Africa strengthened immeasurably the political and ideological positions enunciated by the UDF and the broad Congress movement.

This realignment was evident in COSATU's adoption of the Freedom Charter as the leading document of political protest, and the changed set of political practices engaged in by unions involved in the federation. In February 1987, at its fifth national congress, the National Union of Mineworkers (NUM), which represented the largest number of workers in any affiliated union, resolved to adopt the Freedom Charter as its 'guiding document'. In a carefully worded policy statement, noting their overall objective of 'a democratic socialist society controlled by the working classes', the former affiliate of the Black Consciousness-aligned union movement known as Confederation of Unions of South Africa (CUSA), and the largest trade union organisation in South Africa, claimed apartheid and capitalism to be 'two inseparable evils to be smashed', and stated the necessity to 'join hands with other progressive unions', as long as certain conditions were satisfied.[60] In an interview explaining and justifying the NUM's shift, its leader Cyril

Ramaphosa argued that the 'Freedom Charter contains the minimum demands that have been put forward by the oppressed people in this country ... . It does not lay down a socialist programme and at the same time it is not pro-capitalist.'[61] In seeking to clarify further the political position of COSATU, the NUM campaigned for the adoption of the Freedom Charter for all affiliated unions of the federation. Despite fierce opposition from some sectors, especially the National Union of Metalworkers of South Africa, who argued for the immediate and overriding centrality of socialist demands, COSATU adopted the Freedom Charter as the 'guiding thread for political action'.[62]

Subsequent to these ideological and programmatic endorsements, COSATU played a far greater and central role in the direction of opposition politics. In the context of intense state repression following the imposition of 'states of emergency' in 1985 and 1986, and the massive killings, detentions and bannings of political activists, the organised working classes began to contest state power in a more direct fashion. The constitution of the Mass Democratic Movement (MDM) in 1989 to challenge segregated facilities in Carltonville and Boksburg, a campaign which foreshadowed a more general 'defiance campaign' of racially segregated institutions designed to coincide with the 1989 'general election', was the product of a joint UDF and COSATU initiative.[63] This reassertion of mass politics was largely possible because of the continued existence and functioning of the trade unions, which had embarked upon a series of economically and politically oriented strike actions in the phase of heightened repression.[64] In short, these interactions were to lay the basis for the alliance of COSATU, the ANC and the South African Communist Party in the transition period leading up to the first non-racial election in April 1994.

The character of Charterist discourse

How are we to understand the nature of Charterist discourse? Its distinctiveness can be plotted along three axes. These are its specific discursive form, the strategies and tactics through which it operated, and the particular organisational forms that it took. In this chapter, I will restrict my analysis to the first aspect. The identity of this new discursive articulation can be glimpsed if we examine those elements to which it was opposed and thus excluded, and those moments which were included in its constitution. The UDF's primary *raison d'être* was its opposition to apartheid domination and its proposed reform in the post-Soweto conjuncture. In his explosive speech to the inaugural meeting of the UDF in 1983, Allan Boesak spelled out the reasons for its opposition:

> The most immediate reason for our coming together here today is the continuation of the government's apartheid policies as seen in the constitutional

proposals ... In order that there should be no misunderstanding, let me as clearly and briefly as possible repeat the reasons why we reject these proposals.

- Racism, so embedded in South African society, is once again written into the constitution ...
- All the basic laws ... which are the very pillars of apartheid ... remain untouched and unchanged.
- The homelands policy, which is surely the most immoral and objection-able aspect of the apartheid policies of the government, forms the basis for the wilful exclusion of 80 per cent of our nation from the new polit-ical deal ...
- Not only is the present system of apartheid given more elasticity, making fundamental change even harder than before, but in the new proposals the dream of democracy to which we strive is still further eroded.
- So, while the proposals may mean something for those middle-class blacks who think that the improvement of their own economic position is the highest good, it will not bring any significant changes to the lives of those who have no rights at all, who must languish in the poverty and utter destitution of the homelands, and who are forbidden by law to live together as families in what is called 'white South Africa'.[65]

Labelling the government's proposals as 'divisive', 'undemocratic' and 'racist', the UDF endeavoured to mobilise and organise mass popular support in favour of a united, non-racial and democratic South Africa. Hence in the 'Declaration of the UDF' adopted at its launch the UDF leadership empha-sised common citizenship rights and the necessity for an unfragmented South Africa free from racial, ethnic and sexual divisions, as well as from economic exploitation.[66]

Though the UDF sought to embrace the widest possible layer of 'anti-apartheid' opposition to the reform programme and all it symbolised, its lowest common denominator for participation was active political resistance against the apartheid system and support for 'non-participation' or 'non-col-laboration' in 'the system itself'.[67] In this way, the UDF drew a clear bound-ary with political forces and organisations such as the Labour Party, Inkatha, or any Bantustan 'governments' and 'administrations'. Within these parame-ters, initially at least, the UDF eschewed any narrow, oppositional exclu-sivism, whether this was the perceived 'workerism' of the trade union movement, the Africanist sentiments of those sympathetic to the PAC and its allies, or the racial exclusivism of those organisations associated with the ex-BCM. As the first edition of the nationally distributed *UDF News* put it: 'Peo-ple with different approaches to the struggle have a place in the United Democratic Front.'[68]

However, as the movement developed it became clear that it differed from the former Black Consciousness organisations because of its commitment to the discourse of 'non-racialism', as well as from the mainstream FOSATU unions, in that its appeal was pitched explicitly at level of 'the people', 'the masses' or 'the nation'. This drawing of boundaries – though at this stage not absolute – was reciprocated in the numerous criticisms to which the UDF was subjected. For so-called 'workerists', the UDF's strategy of putting together an alliance of social classes meant the subordination of working-class interests and representations to middle-class and petit-bourgeois elements. Thus for Fine, de Clerq and Innes, for instance, 'populist' forms such as the UDF constituted a threat to working-class politics because they 'are afraid of a movement of black workers', hence 'they wish either to restrict it within a narrow terrain, or more usually to dissolve it in a mass political movement dominated not by the workers, but by the petit bourgeoisie'.[69] For 'non-collaborationist', 'anti-racist' forces such as those represented by the National Forum, the UDF was nothing more than an '*ad hoc* organisation consisting of many *ad hoc* committees and organisations reacting to one thing and another',[70] whose desire to build a 'non-racial South Africa' was made equivalent to liberal demands for a 'multi racial country composed of four "races"'.[71]

More positively, the new political discourse was constructed in almost classically national popular-democratic terms.[72] Hence the central agent of political struggle was to be 'the people', the demands elaborated by the new movement were for 'national democracy', and all other sectors and identities (whether they be class, gender, youth, and so on) were constructed along these lines. Central to the basic grammar of the new discursive formation, moreover, was the category of 'non-racialism', which had lain dormant for much of the post-Sharpeville period. While Black Consciousness intellectuals had assimilated the more radical Congress definition of non-racialism with the liberal idea of 'multiracialism', arguing instead for a generalised 'anti-racism', the UDF revived the older ANC principle, and placed it centre stage.[73] And despite criticisms about its practicality and theoretical coherence, it became a central plank of UDF discourse and strategy.[74]

In the South African context, the agency of 'the people', regardless of colour, class or ethnicity, when combined with demands for a united democratic state, were explosive in that they negated – almost element for element – the basic characteristics of the apartheid system as it had been instituted since 1948. All of these elements of the new discursive configuration, as well as the concrete demands and strategy of struggle, were given programmatic expression in the reactivation of the Freedom Charter as the binding and leading force of the new movement.[75]

Conclusion: explaining the emergence of Charterism and the democratic imaginary

To conclude this chapter, how did Charterist discourse come to replace Black Consciousness, and why was it successful in becoming hegemonic? At the outset, there are a number of conjunctural factors to consider. The first centres on the immediate impact of the Soweto uprisings. The detention of large numbers of radicalised youth and schoolchildren, and their subsequent incarceration with a previous generation of largely ANC-supporting resistance leaders, contributed to an inevitable 'fusion of horizons' among different resistance traditions.[76] This process of mutual learning was also assisted by the release of key political prisoners, who were able to reactivate Charterist language in the period. Moreover, it also became evident to activists and leaders that a more dispersed type of political activity was desirable in order to avoid the decimation of resistance organisations following the large-scale detentions and bannings arrests of its high-profile leadership.[77] In this context, the various disaggregated demands articulated in the Freedom Charter became important rallying-points for a proliferation of dispersed struggles against different aspects of apartheid rule. This availability was given greater weight by the increased military presence of the ANC and the growing visibility of the ANC as a political force, evident in the growing prominence of ANC symbols and slogans in the discourse of resistance, as well as the increasing interest amongst political activists and militants in seeking to understand the previous history and traditions of black resistance to white domination.[78] Finally, the high-profile campaigns for the release of jailed leaders, such as Nelson Mandela, coupled with the release of ANC and SACP stalwarts such as Billy Nair, Curnick Ndlovu, Dorothy Nyembe and Steve Tshwete in the late 1970s and early 1980s, also contributed to a growing awareness of the ANC both inside and outside the country.

Nevertheless, while these conjunctural factors account for the availability of Charterist discourse, they still beg the question as to why Charterist discourse came to hegemonise the discursive field in the post-Soweto period. In this regard, we need to look more closely at its discursive configuration. One leading interpretation suggests that the key reason for the shift concerns the main objectives of the different movements. In *Lessons of Struggle*, Anthony Marx argues that the BCM failed because it was concerned with questions of identity and subjective self-assertion, rather than the material interests of its supporters. By contrast, the UDF and the trade unions did endeavour to improve the material circumstances of the different groups they represented, and were thus more successful in winning their support. At one level, Marx is clearly right to detect problems in the BCM's leadership. The movement was dominated by radicalised students concerned to elaborate an alternative political, social and ethical consciousness centred on the formation of an authentic black identity. Moreover, while strategies were developed to transcend the imperative of consciousness-raising, and there were often vague undercurrents concerning the necessity of violence and 'the armed struggle' to achieve the aims of the movement in the South African context, very few concrete strategies were elaborated and executed in the pursuit of these goals. This meant that the style and ethos of the movement fixated on an inward logic of self-assertion, predicated on the forging of a distinctive philosophical outlook, rather than on a struggle to advance the needs and interests of the broader communities and constituencies it wished to reach. In short, while the BCM did not eschew the tasks of organising and mobilising mass constituencies such as the working classes at the point of production and in the townships, it never managed to produce the appropriate strategies and tactics for doing so.[79] It was left to the more radical and militant post-Soweto generation to put into practice many of the BCM's aspirations.

However, while Marx clearly touches on important factors in evaluating the different movements, there are three difficulties with his account. On a conceptual level, his account draws a too stark distinction between questions of identity and interests. As I have argued elsewhere, the construction and pursuit of interests logically presupposes subjective identifications.[80] More substantively, Marx underestimates the different material contexts of domination in which Black Consciousness and Charterism functioned. An important reason why Black Consciousness was unable to hegemonise different forces and the overall field of discursivity in the post-Sharpeville period was the relative sedimentation and stabilisation of social identities during the period. The period following Soweto, by contrast, was marked by a proliferation of antagonisms and the consequent existence of floating signifiers, such as 'democracy' and 'apartheid', that could be articulated by the new discourse.

Finally, Marx underestimates the intrinsic characteristics of Black Consciousness and Charterist discourses respectively. Not only was Charterism clearly available to those struggling against apartheid in the post-Soweto period, it was also a viable and credible discourse to signify and embody the various demands that were being made against the system. Moreover, although both discourses can be characterised as populist, the clear limitations on Black Consciousness becoming a collective imaginary did not pertain to Charterism. Whereas Black Consciousness stressed racial exclusivity, Charterism was avowedly non-racial; while Black Consciousness was ambiguous about who constituted the South African nation and people, the UDF stressed that *all* South Africans who were against apartheid could be part of the South African nation, and they drew a set of equivalences along these lines. Moreover, while Black Consciousness was unclear about its overall political programme, the signifier 'democracy' in Charterist discourse was able to include all social classes, and was able to accommodate numerous concrete interpretations of the nature of democracy itself.

A final set of questions concerns the relationship between these two different discourses. Does this interpretation not imply a complete discontinuity between Black Consciousness and Charterism? While in my account Charterism does represent a significantly novel discursive articulation in the post-Sharpeville period, this does not mean that it represented a complete break with the past. Rather, the constructors of Charterist discourse reactivated and rearticulated existing discourses in a new configuration. In this respect, Charterism not only drew upon the Congress tradition of the 1950s, but it also articulated elements from Black Consciousness and the trade unions. This is evident in the three defining elements of the new configuration: non-racialism, populism and democracy.

While Charterism was predicated on a direct rejection of the Black Consciousness idea of 'anti-racism' and racially separate forms of organisation, drawing instead on the ANC's much vaunted non-racialism, this does not mean that Charterism was unaffected by the appearance of Black Consciousness. Rather, the idea of non-racialism in Charterist discourse was transformed and deepened by the experience of Black Consciousness in that whites and blacks were organised and co-operated on a much more equal footing, and great efforts were made to institutionalise non-racialist practices in the organisational forms themselves. Similarly, while the UDF's populism included all South Africans opposed to apartheid, the BCM's endeavour to construct an assertive black subjectivity and political agency contributed immensely to the growing opposition to the apartheid's project endeavour to create and sediment ethnic and national differences amongst the black population. Thirdly, while the language of democracy did not strongly resonate in the discourse of Black Consciousness, it was not absent from the practices and organisational forms of the movement. The movement's stress on a humanist ethos, coupled with its commitment to foster student and popular participation in its relatively pluralistic and open organisational structures, helped to inculcate and transmit an egalitarian, communal and critical dimension into the post-Soweto context. Sometimes in close collaboration with activists and sympathisers of the Black Consciousness Movement (BCM), the progressive wings of the mainstream churches were also significant in elaborating and transmitting the concept and practice of democracy.

Lastly, the so-called 'turn to the community', evident in the emergence and flourishing of mass community organisations, also resulted in the dissemination and consolidation of democracy as a central principle of political opposition. The strategy of community politics emerged in the 1970s under the auspices of the Black Consciousness Movement (BCM). The various projects of the Black Communities Programmes (BCP) endeavoured to empower local communities and weaken the hold of specialists and experts in the administration and organisation of development. For Black Consciousness activists, the community organisation approach represented an ideal way of actualising their ideals of self-reliance and black communalism, without becoming reliant upon and ensnared in the system of white domination.[81] The destruction of the BCM, and the ideological realignment that ensued, meant that forces not associated with the BCM took up the next phase of community politics.

Notes

1 J. Brewer, *After Soweto: An Unfinished Journey* (Oxford, Clarendon Press, 1986), pp. 229–91.

2 Clearly I cannot describe the uprising in any great detail. Suffice it to refer to Molteno's summary of the events as they unfolded during 1976 and 1977. He notes that 'Soweto' involved '[t]ens of thousands of men, women and children, students, parents and workers, in some 200 Black communities throughout the country including the Bantustans [who] actively participated in the uprising. With popular militancy unprecedented in depth and scale, they clashed with police; they used fire to damage or destroy Bantu Affairs Administration Board, and other official, buildings and vehicles; they burned buses as well as commercial vehicles of White-owned businesses; they burned down beerhalls, liquor stores and post offices; two white officials were beaten to death; the homes of policemen and others considered to be collaborating with the system were attacked; they used stay-away strikes, mass demonstrations, marches, and sabotage; they organised campaigns on local and national issues; they boycotted the schools; they closed down government institutions such as the Soweto Urban Bantu Council.' See F. Molteno, 'The uprising of 16th June: a review of the literature on events in South Africa 1976', *Social Dynamics*, 5: 1 (1979), 54. For a comprehensive picture, see A. Brooks and J. Brickhill, *Whirlwind Before the Storm: The Origins and Development of the Uprising in Soweto and the Rest of South Africa from June to December 1976* (London, IDAF, 1980); A. Callinicos and J. Rogers, *Southern Africa after Soweto* (London, Pluto Press, 1977), pp. 157–73 ; South Africa Institute of Race Relations, *South Africa in Travail: The Disturbances of 1976/77* (Johannesburg, SA Institute of Race Relations, 1978); Republic of South Africa, *Report of the Commission of Inquiry into the Riots at Soweto and Elsewhere* (Cillie Commission Report), Government Printer, Pretoria, RP 55/1980, Vol. 1 (1980); B. Hirson, *Year of Fire, Year of Ash. The Soweto Revolt: Roots of a Revolution?* (London, Zed Press, 1979); J. Kane-Berman, *Soweto: Black Revolt, White Reaction* (Johannesburg, Ravan Press, 1978); T. Lodge, *Black Politics in South Africa Since 1945* (Johannesburg, Ravan Press 1983), pp. 321–62.

3 Making 'Soweto' equal to an 'event of the social' must be qualified. For the initiators and participants of the student revolt, the dislocatory effects of Soweto were a product of social antagonism. In other words, at least for the marching students there had already been a 'positivisation of the ontological lack' which is, as Žižek has suggested, constitutive of subjectivity and political acts. The black schoolchildren involved in the march had already externalised an enemy responsible for its own subjective blockage. This is clear from a cursory examination of the placards and slogans deployed by the students, which identified the objects of imposition: 'Down with Afrikaans', 'Afrikaans is oppressor's language!', 'Blacks are not dustbins – Afrikaans stinks!', 'We are not Boers!', 'If we must do Afrikaans, Vorster must do Zulu!', and so forth. However, the event still functioned as a dislocation in that it shattered the white imaginary, and in its later role galvanised an alternative liberatory imaginary for blacks generally. If we are to locate an originary dislocatory moment it would be the imposition of Afrikaans as the medium of instruction – an apparently marginal issue in itself,

but in the context of the deteriorating system of Bantu education, it provided the rupture which unleashed all of the subsequent events. See S. Žižek, *The Sublime Object of Ideology* (London, Verso, 1989), pp. 178–82.

4   M. Murray, *South Africa: Time of Agony, Time of Destiny* (London, Verso, 1987), p. 17; J. Saul and S. Gelb, *The Crisis in South Africa* (London, Zed Books, 1986), pp. 63–98; A. Norval, 'Social ambiguity and the crisis of apartheid', in E. Laclau (ed.), *The Making of Political Identities* (London, Verso, 1994), pp. 115–37; H. Wolpe, 'Apartheid's deepening crisis', *Marxism Today*, January (1983), 7–11.

5   A. Gramsci, *Selections from the Prison Notebooks of Antonio Gramsci* (London, Lawrence & Wishart, 1971), pp. 177–8.

6   See J. Hanlon, *Apartheid's Second Front: South Africa's War Against Its Neighbours* (Harmondsworth, Penguin Books, 1986).

7   S. Gelb, 'South Africa's economic crisis: an overview', in S. Gelb (ed.), *South Africa's Economic Crisis* (Cape Town, David Philip, 1991), pp. 13–23.

8   M. Morris, 'State, capital and growth: the political economy of the national question', in S. Gelb (ed.), *South Africa's Economic Crisis* (Cape Town, David Philip, 1991).

9   G. Bloch, 'Room at the top?: the development of manufacturing 1939–1969', *Social Dynamics*, 7:2 (1981), 10–21; G. Bloch, 'Sounds in the silence: painting a picture of the 1960s', *Africa Perspective*, 25 (1984), 3–23.

10 S. Greenberg, *Legitimating the Illegitimate: State, Markets and Resistance in South Africa* (Berkeley, University of California Press, 1987); D. Hindson, 'Alternative urbanisation strategies in South Africa: a critical evaluation', *Third World Quarterly*, 9:2 (1987), 583–600; M. O. Sutcliffe, 'The crisis in South Africa: material conditions and the reformist response', paper presented to *The Southern African Economy after Apartheid Conference* (University of York, 1986).

11 K. Grundy, *The Militarization of South African Politics* (Oxford, Oxford University Press, 1988), pp. 58–71; P. Frankel, *Pretoria's Praetorians: Civil–Military Relations in South Africa* (Cambridge, Cambridge University Press, 1984).

12 S. Greenberg, *Race and State in Capitalist Development* (Johannesburg, Ravan Press, 1980); S. Greenberg, 'Economic growth and political change: the South African case', *Journal of Modern African Studies*, 19:4 (1980), 667–704.

13 S. Friedman, 'The struggle within the struggle: South African resistance strategies', *Transformation*, 3 (1987), 58–70; D. Hemson, 'Trade unions and the struggle for liberation in South Africa', *Capital and Class*, 6 (1978), 1–41; B. Pogrund, 'The Durban strikes', *Africa Report*, March–April (1973), 25–6.

14 Murray, *South Africa*, p. 17.

15 R. Davies and D. O'Meara, 'The state of analysis of the Southern African region: issues raised by South African strategy', *Review of African Political Economy*, 29 (1984), 69; R. Davies and D. O'Meara, 'Total strategy in Southern Africa: an analysis of South African regional policy since 1978', *Journal of Southern African Studies*, 11: 2 (1985), 183–211.

16 D. O'Meara, ' "Muldergate": the politics of Afrikaner nationalism', *Work in Progress*, 22 (1982), 15–21.

17 Republic of South Africa, *Report of the Commission of Inquiry into Legislation Affecting the Utilisation of Manpower* (Pretoria, South African Government Printer, 1978).

18 S. B. Bekker and R. Humphries, *From Control to Confusion: The Changing Role of Administration Boards in South Africa, 1971–1983* (Pietermaritzburg, Shuter & Shooter, 1985).

19 R. Cohen, *Endgame in South Africa: The Changing Structures and Ideology of Apartheid* (London, James Curry, 1986), pp. 48–59; Saul and Gelb, *The Crisis in South Africa*, pp. 63–4.

20 H. Wolpe, *Race, Class and the Apartheid State* (London, James Curry, 1988), p. 91.

21 J. Baskin, *Striking Back: A History of COSATU* (London, Verso, 1991).

22 Murray, *South Africa*, p. 148.

23 D. Hauck, *Black Trade Unions in South Africa* (Washington, Orbis Books, 1982), p. 10; K. Luckhardt and B. Wall, *Working for Freedom: Black Trade Union Development in South Africa throughout the 1970s* (Geneva, World Council of Churches,1981), pp. 41–2.

24 S. C. Nolutshungu, *Changing South Africa* (Cape Town and Manchester, David Philip and Manchester University Press, 1982), p. 78.

25 F. Cachalia, 'The state, crisis and restructuring, 1970–1980', *Africa Perspective*, 23 (1983), 30–5.

26 Wolpe, *Race, Class and the Apartheid State*, pp. 92–3.

27 See R. Fatton, *Black Consciousness in South Africa: The Dialectics of Ideological Resistance to White Supremacy* (New York, State University of New York Press, 1986); Hirson, *Year of Fire, Year of Ash*, pp. 308–30; A. Callinicos and J. Rogers, *Southern Africa after Soweto* (London, Pluto Press, 1977).

28 See J. Frederikse, *The Unbreakable Thread: Non-Racialism in South Africa* (London: Zed Books, 1990), pp. 166–83; T. G. Karis and G. M. Gerhart, *From Protest to Challenge, Volume 5: Nadir and Resurgence, 1964–1979* (Bloomington and Indianapolis, Indiana University Press, 1997), pp. 310–43; A. Marx, *Lessons of Struggle: South African Internal Opposition, 1960–1990* (Oxford, Oxford University Press, 1992), pp. 32–105.

29 H. Barrell, 'Conscripts to their Age: African National Congress Operational Strategy, 1976–1986' (D. Phil. Thesis, University of Oxford, 1993); S. Ellis and T. Sechaba, *Comrades Against Apartheid; The ANC and the South African Communist Party in Exile* (London, James Curry, 1992), pp. 80–5; R. Kasrils, *Armed and Dangerous: My Underground Struggle Against Apartheid* (London, Heinemann, 1993), pp. 122–4.

30 E. Laclau and C. Mouffe, *Hegemony and Socialist Strategy* (London, Verso, 1985), p. 189.

31 See Fatton, *Black Consciousness in South Africa*, pp. 123–5; Hirson, *Year of Fire, Year of Ash*, pp. 282–307; Lodge, *Black Politics in South Africa*, pp. 335–6; Marx, *Lessons of Struggle*, pp. 59–60.

32 See Brookes and Brickhill, *Whirlwind Before the Storm*, pp. 198–228; Karis and Gerhart, *Protest to Challenge*, pp. 169–70, 183–4 ; Kane-Berman, *Soweto*, pp. 103–24.

33 For a discussion of the concept of a 'surface of inscription', itself borrowed from Michel Foucault's account of discursive formations in *The Archaeology of Knowledge* (London, Tavistock, 1972, see E. Laclau, *New Reflections on the Revolution of Our Time* (London, Verso, 1990), pp. 60–8.

34 As we know from historical scholarship, Biko's picture of pre-colonial African

societies as egalitarian, non-exploitative and communal is fictive; that is, it functions as a myth which conceals divisions in order to portray a utopian vision which is antithetical to apartheid domination. For a discussion of the necessity to deconstruct myths in African history, see for example B. Davidson, *The Search for Africa: A History in the Making* (London, James Curry, 1994).

35 See D. Howarth, 'Complexities of identity/difference: Black Consciousness ideology in South Africa', *Journal of Political Ideologies*, 2:1 (1995), 51–78; D. Howarth, 'Constructing and representing blackness: Black Consciousness discourse and its media', in L. Switzer (ed.), *The Oppositional Press in South Africa* (Cambridge, Cambridge University Press, forthcoming).

36 S. Biko, 'Some African cultural concepts', in S. Biko, *I Write What I Like* (Harmondsworth, Penguin Books, 1978), p. 55.

37 *Ibid.*, pp. 55–6.

38 *Ibid.*, pp. 60–1.

39 Even those leaders and figures in the black community, such as Chief Gatsha Buthelezi, who were generally suspicious of the BCM's radicalism, began to stress the concept of blackness as a key mobilising mechanism. See G. Buthelezi, 'Black Solidarity and self-help', in H. van der Merwe *et al.* (eds), *African Perspectives on South Africa: A Collection of Speeches, Articles and Documents* (Cape Town, David Philip, 1978). See also G. Mare and G. Hamilton, *An Appetite for Power: Buthelezi's Inkatha and the Politics of 'Loyal Resistance'* (Johannesburg, Ravan Press, 1987), pp. 149–52.

40 See F. Meer, 'Black nationalism – homeland nationalism', in T. Sundermeier (ed.), *Church and Nationalism in South Africa* (Johannesburg, Ravan Press, 1975), p. 130.

41 See Biko, *I Write What I Like*.

42 See Nolutshungu, *Changing South Africa*, pp. 153.

43 J. Gerwel, 'Coloured nationalism?', in Sundermeier (ed.), *Church and Nationalism in South Africa*, pp. 71–2.

44 F. Meer, 'The Natal Indian Congress, 1972', *Reality*, March (1972), 5; South African Students' Organisation, 'Letter from Barney Pityana to all SRC's and local committees. Re: SASO vs NIC Controversy, 1972', William Cullen Library Collection, University of Witwatersrand.

45 For an interesting discussion of this tension from within the ranks of Black Consciousness, see N. C. Manganyi, *Being-Black-In-The-World* (Johannesburg, SPRO-CAS/Ravan Press, 1973), p. 18. See also L. Kuper, *Race, Class, and Power: Ideology and Revolutionary Change in Plural Societies* (London, Duckworth Co., 1974), p. 97.

46 S. Motsuenyane, 'Black entrepreneurship', in van der Merwe *et al.* (eds), *African Perspectives on South Africa*, pp. 171–6; S. Motsuenyane, 'The beginnings of a black bank', in van der Merwe *et al.* (eds), *African Perspectives on South Africa*, pp. 165–71; H. Nxasana and F. Fisher, 'The labour situation in South Africa', in T. Thoahlane (ed.), *Black Renaissance: Papers from the Black Renaissance Convention, December 1974* (Johannesburg, Ravan Press, 1976), pp. 53–8.

47 G. Buthelezi, 'Report back', in van der Merwe *et al.* (eds), *African Perspectives on South Africa*, pp. 569–86; G. Buthelezi, 'My role within separate development politics', in van der Merwe et al. (eds), *African Perspectives on South Africa*, pp. 454–60.

48 Biko, *I Write What I Like*, pp. 62–3.
49 F. Chikane, *No Life of My Own: An Autobiography* (London, Catholic Institute of Race Relations, 1988), pp. 85–105; Frederikse, *The Unbreakable Thread*, pp. 166–83; P. Lekota, 'Lekota on the UDF', *Work in Progress*, 30 (1984), 4–8.
50 G. Rude, *Ideology and Popular Protest* (London: Lawrence & Wishart, 1980), pp. 28, 35–6.
51 The reliance on retroactive interpretations of historical change is evident in Julie Frederikse's and Anthony Marx's acconts of the failure of Black Consciousness and the rise of democratic non-racialism. See Frederikse, *The Unbreakable Thread*, pp. 166–83; Marx, *Lessons of Struggle*, pp. 91–105.
52 Popo Molefe cited in Marx, *Lessons of Struggle*, p. 103.
53 D. Howarth, 'The ideologies and strategies of resistance in post-Sharpeville South Africa: thoughts on Anthony Marx's *Lessons of Struggle*', *Africa Today*, 41:1 (1994), 33–4.
54 J. Foster, 'The workers' struggle: where does FOSATU stand?', *South African Labour Bulletin*, 7:8 (1982), 68–79.
55 R. M. Levine, 'Class struggle, popular democratic struggle and the South African state', *Review of African Political Economy*, 40 (1987), 7–31.
56 T. Lodge, 'Rebellion: the turning of the tide', in T. Lodge and B. Nasson (eds), *All, Here and Now! Black Politics in South Africa in the 1980s* (London, Hurst & Co., 1991), pp. 142–4.
57 *Ibid.*, p. 47.
58 A. Callinicos, *South Africa between Reform and Revolution* (London, Bookmarks, 1988), pp. 60–5, 93–103, 106–9; M. Francis, 'The past is theirs, the future is ours' (BA Honours Dissertation, University of the Western Cape, 1984); Marx, *Lessons of Struggle*, pp. 128–30, passim; Murray, *South Africa*, pp. 229–38; Saul and Gelb, *The Crisis in South Africa*, p. 21.
59 See Saul and Gelb, *The Crisis in South Africa*, pp. 16–26; 229–42; D. Howarth and A. Norval, 'Strategy and subjectivity in South African resistance politics: prospects for a new imaginary', *Essex Papers in Politics and Government*, 85 (1990).
60 Baskin, *Striking Back*, p. 214.
61 C. Ramaphosa, 'An interview with Cyril Ramaphosa', *South African Labour Bulletin*, 12:3 (1987), 23; see also C. Ramaphosa, 'The Freedom Charter and the economy: fundamental workers' rights', in J. Polley (ed.), *The Freedom Charter and the Future* (Johannesburg, A. D. Donker, 1988).
62 D. Niddrie, 'Building on the Freedom Charter', *Work in Progress*, 53 (1988), 8–12.
63 Lodge, 'Rebellion', pp. 111–12.
64 Marx, *Lessons of Struggle*, pp. 189–234.
65 A. Boesak, *If This is Treason, I Am Guilty* (London, Collins, 1988), p. 60, 61, 62–3.
66 United Democratic Front, 'United Democratic Front Launch Document', 20 August 1983, William Curren Library Collection, University of Witwatersrand.
67 See Boesak, *If This is Treason, I Am Guilty*, p. 63.
68 *UDF News*, 1 (1983), 3; Lekota, 'Lekota on the UDF', 4–8.
69 B. Fine, F. de Clerq and D. Innes, 'Trade unions and the state: the question of legality', *South African Labour Bulletin*, 7:1/2 (1981), 41.

70 Lybon Mabasa, cited in *Work In Progress*, 30 (1983), 10–11.
71 N. Alexander, 'Nation and ethnicity', *Work in Progress*, 28 (1983), 6–13.
72 Levine, 'Class struggle, popular democratic struggle and the South African State', 7–31; Saul and Gelb, *The Crisis in South Africa*, pp. 21–6; J. Saul, 'South Africa: the question of strategy', *New Left Review*, 160 (1986), 1–30.
73 Frederikse, *The Unbreakable Thread*, pp. 166–83.
74 See D. Innes, 'Unity and the Freedom Charter: worker politics and the popular movement', *Work in Progress*, 41 (1986), 11–16; D. Innes, 'The case for a worker's programme', *Work in Progress*, 50, (1987), 23–32; K. Jochelson, G. Moss and I. Obery, 'Defining working-class politics', *Work in Progress*, 41, (1986), 17–20.
75 M. Matiwane and S. Walters, *The Struggle for Democracy: A Study of Community Organisations in Greater Cape Town from the 1960s to 1985* (Cape Town, UCT Press, 1986); T. Lodge, 'Remembering the Freedom Charter', *South African Labour Bulletin*, 11:7 (1986), 112–17; R. Suttner and J. Cronin, *Thirty Years of the Freedom Charter* (Johannesburg, Ravan Press, 1986).
76 Marx, *Lessons of Struggle*, pp. 96–8. See also I. Naidoo and A. Sachs, *Island in Chains: Ten Years on Robben Island by Prisoner 885/63* (Harmondsworth, Penguin Books, 1982), pp. 271–8.
77 See Matiwane and Walters, *Struggle for Democracy*.
78 S. Davis, *Apartheid's Rebels: Inside South Africa's Hidden War* (New Haven, Yale University Press, 1987), pp. 117–19.
79 See Fatton, *Black Consciousness in South Africa*, pp. 63–80.
80 See Howarth, 'The ideologies and strategies of resistance in post-Sharpeville South Africa', pp. 33–7. See also Ch. 4 of this volume.
81 M. Ramphele, 'Empowerment and symbols of hope: Black Consciousness and community development', in B. Pityana *et al.* (eds), *Bounds of Possibility: The Legacy of Steve Biko and Black Consciousness* (London: Zed Books, 1991), pp. 214–27.

The constitution and dissolution of the Kemalist imaginary

Indeterminacy would be the most appropriate term to describe the political situation of Turkey in the 1990s. The three military interventions that Turkey witnessed between 1960 and 1980 occurred as a result of the state's struggle to keep disorder and ambiguity at bay. Ironically, all attempts to (re)create order resulted in a deepening of this ambiguity and incoherence. They also failed to (re)construct order on the basis of the Kemalist principles, which formed the foundations of the Turkish secular state. The Gramscian concepts of an 'organic crisis' or 'crisis of hegemony'[1] capture this deepening of political indeterminacy in Turkey and indicate a shift that has occurred in Kemalist hegemony.[2] Kemalism is the reformist discourse often described as the founding and official ideology of the Turkish Republic. Even in the 1990s the major official documents, such as the Constitution, recognise Kemalism as the founding and regulating idea of any state and political practice. However, the 1990s also witnessed a subversion of Kemalist hegemony. The increasingly ambiguous and unstable political and social frontiers are indicative of the fact that Kemalism has lost its ability to mediate among floating elements in order to produce political consensus. In other words, despite its desire to fix totally the meaning of all social and political activities and its past success in hegemonising the social, Kemalism has been unable to hegemonise the whole field of meaning and prevent the proliferation of new nodal points that remain unintegrated into the Kemalist discursive system, posing a threat to its unity. In this chapter, I focus on the initially expanding and then receding limits of Kemalist hegemony. My analysis proceeds by tracing this transformation in the forms of political struggle between the 1960s and the 1990s.

The historiography of modern Turkey has long been dominated by the nationalist, secularist and modernist views, which treat the Turkish Revolution as a decisive break with the past. According to these views, the past represents obscuratism and darkness while the Turkish Revolution is identified with the Enlightenment. In the 1970s, Marxist scholars attempted to break with this official 'history-writing'. They understood the Turkish Revolution as a bourgeois revolution realised by the intelligentsia and the capitalist class.[3] Another attempt to break with the official history-writing opposed itself to both the modernist and the Marxist discontinuity theses. This view suggested a continuity between the Ottoman bureaucratic tradition and the Turkish Republic. 'Revolution', therefore, could not be the appropriate term to describe the formation of the new Turkish state, since no actual transformation was observed in cultural, social and economic structures. The continuity thesis finds its defenders amongst the 'leftist liberals' and a variety of scholars from various disciplines including history, sociology and political theory.[4]

In contrast to these dominant views, I want to articulate a genealogical approach that opposes any search for 'origins' and attempts to construct 'a history of the present', rather than revealing an 'objective' history of Turkey. This genealogical approach is a pluralist one in the Foucauldian sense of pluralism: it situates Kemalism within 'a play of special transformations, each one different from the next (with its own conditions, rules and level of impact), linked together', moving along a series of dependencies.[5] In so doing, it frees Kemalism from analyses treating it either as the culmination of the past, a mere resemblance, a continuous form, or as a radical rupture, an unintelligible split between events, that makes any notion of gradual change unthinkable. This approach focuses around the complex procedures which led to the emergence and influenced the development and changing hegemonic appeal of Kemalism.

Using Laclau and Mouffe's theory of discourse, this chapter treats Kemalism as a *discourse*, that is, a horizon of 'multifarious practices, meanings and conventions' 'through which a certain sense of reality and understanding of society were constituted'.[6] In so doing, the chapter focuses on Kemalism's articulatory character. Articulation is a practice which works through the construction of *nodal points* – or 'privileged condensations of meaning'[7] – which partially fix meaning in the plurality of floating elements circulating in the political and social arena. Stressing the 'partial' character of any discursive fixation also implies a recognition of the impossibility of a final closure of signification.[8] Treating Kemalism as a discourse, therefore, provides a ground for an understanding of its hegemonic constitution. It also enables the analyst to situate Kemalism's failure to totally hegemonise the multifarious meanings of the discursive field in Turkey, a failure which has become more discernible in the organic crisis of the 1990s.

Two more concepts of the conceptual apparatus of discourse theory will be essential to the approach developed here. These are the categories of *myth* and *imaginary*. The mythical dimension will be understood as providing the core of any political discourse struggling for hegemony insofar as the function of myth is to put forward a new representational structure in order to suture a dislocated social field. In other words, when a society comes face to face with the collapse of its hegemonic political order – such an event was the collapse of the Ottoman Empire – then this structural dislocation has to be administered through the formation of a new myth if social coherence is to be restored. In this sense, 'the effectiveness of myth is essentially hegemonic: it involves forming a new objectivity by means of a rearticulation of the dislocated elements'.[9] My argument will be that Kemalism was clearly marked by such a mythical dimension. Furthermore, Kemalism initially proved so successful in dominating the discursive field that it was transformed into a collective imaginary that could structure the discursive field making possible Turkish identity. Insofar as collective imaginaries exhibit precise, albeit contingent, patterns of constitution and dissolution, my analysis should be primarily viewed as a genealogy of the discursive constitution of the Kemalist myth, its expansion into an imaginary horizon for the absolute representation of Turkish identity and, most importantly, of the various dislocations of this hegemonic project and of the attempts to reconstitute repeatedly its imaginary dimension.

The chapter is divided into four sections. The first section deals with the constitution of Kemalist hegemony following the transformation of the Kemalist mythical space into an imaginary, while the second and third sections attempt to unravel the conditions of possibility for the dissolution of Kemalist imaginary in the 1980s and the 1990s. The concluding part examines the possibilities of Turkey becoming a more democratic society after the dissolution of the Kemalist hegemonic core in the 1990s.

Kemalism and democracy: from myth to imaginary

Chronologically, the formulation of Kemalism as an ideology coincides with the establishment of the one-party regime between 1923 and 1931.[10] The *Cumhuriyet Halk Firkasi's* (Republican People's Party, RPP) programme of 1931 is the first official document which ennumerates the six major principles of Kemalism. These are republicanism, nationalism, populism, statism, secularism and revolutionism. Briefly, republicanism underlies the Kemalist elite's faith in the Republic as 'a polity that represents and applies the ideal of national sovereignty in the best and most reliable manner'.[11] Nationalism suggests a new form of identification, Turkishness as against a fragmented Ottoman identity, which displaces religion and tradition as sources of social and political unity and legitimation. Populism, as an earliest philosophical attachment of the Turkish intelligentsia, expresses the idea of people-as-sovereign and underlies the Kemalist myth of a homogeneous, united and harmonious society. In this framework, statism refers to the core of revolutionism: the mobilisation of the people from above for the construction of a secular modern rational society. The principle of secularism entails the secularisation of state administration and the orientation of social life around the principles and forms that science and technology have provided for modern civilisation. Kemalism gives priority to secularisation, modernisation and the rationalisation of society.

The years between 1930 and 1945 witnessed the emergence of Kemalism as a mythical space that represented a new perception of order promising to administer effectively the dislocations marking the collapse of the Ottoman Empire. The proposed order relied upon the creation of a new secular, modern and Western Turkish identity, and the representation of the Turkish nation as an undivided, homogeneous and harmonious totality. In this respect, the myth of homogeneous society here had a dual function. On the one hand, it functioned as a metaphor of fullness in order to legitimise the one-party regime. On the other, it constituted a surface on which a set of structural dislocations were inscribed. By assuming a symmetry between what is represented and the space of representation, the myth eliminated any distance between its concrete content, that is, the particular pillars of the actual Kemalist order, and the universal need for order in general. This myth established a set of equivalences, first, between the Republic and the 'nature' of the Turkish nation; secondly, between the modern West and Turkishness; and, finally, between the classless 'nature' of Turkish society and one-party rule.

As a result of the political decisions taken by the then President Ismet Inönü, 1 November 1945 was an historic moment in Turkish politics in which one-party rule ended and a change of direction towards a more democratic regime began. The multi-party experiment, which is often identified with the *Demokrat Parti* (Democratic Party, DP) administration, heralded the emergence of a right-wing populism that has since assumed the role of articulating the demands of excluded groups who, despite the Kemalist reforms, continued to identify themselves with Islam, and with the forgotten history of Muslim Turks. Using the signifiers of popular culture in communicating with the masses, or the 'periphery', in Mardin's words, 'the DP legitimised Islam and the rural values'.[12] The DP 'emphasised populism and popular sovereignty and demanded that political initiative emanate from below, from the people, and not from above, from the party'.[13] The Democrat's slogan 'Enough! The word belongs to the Nation' was a good echo of the popular hostility against the Republican's claim to be acting 'for the people ... in spite of them'. The rise of populist democracy showed that the subordinated 'social-cultural heterogeneity of the periphery, now subsumed under the overarching belief in Islam', not only continued to resist the 'orthodoxy of progressivism, anchored in a secular, positivist ideology', but also advanced in its struggle for recognition.[14]

'Myth', as Laclau suggests, has a metaphorical nature since 'its concrete or literal content represents something different from itself: the very principle of a fully achieved literality'.[15] In this sense, the rising popular hostility against the one-party rule that dominated the political scene in the 1940s and the 1950s made visible the incomplete and metaphorical nature of the Kemalist mythical space. Although the legitimacy of the Kemalist modernist project was unquestionable, the frustrations that it created in the popular sectors could not be compensated for by the myth of a homogeneous and undivided society. This structural inability became the very condition for the emergence of 'democracy' as a new political myth in the general discursive field. In fact, it was presented as an alternative to the dominant Kemalist discourse; 'democracy' emerged as a nodal point antagonistic to the Kemalist discourse. In this framework, the myth of 'democracy' was to rearticulate the dislocated elements which Kemalism seemed unable to articulate in its mythical chain, through the constitution of a new space for the representation of popular grievances.

However, this development eventually resulted in the expansion of the Kemalist mythical space. Kemalism managed to hegemonise the signifier 'democracy' and to incorporate it into its own discursive chain. In 1960, the 'statist intelligentsia' 'did decide to act' against the DP rule, 'proclaiming ... that the takeover represented the desire of the entire military establishment and that they were safeguarding democracy and the state, and protecting the legacy of Atatürk'.[16] The military takeover made clear that Kemalism was without doubt 'the definitive source of public policies'[17] and that the Kemalist elite was there to consolidate democracy. Thus, the Kemalist discourse integrated 'democracy' into its hegemonic field. This integration became evident in the discursive strategies that the Republican elite implemented to legitimise the military regime and the expansion of their role. For example, the 1961 Constitution was a manifesto that emphasised the irreversibility of the identification between Kemalist modernisation and democratisation. It aimed at the decentralisation of power and the diffusion of functions.[18] For this purpose, a mechanism of checks and controls was established against the centralisation of political power in the parties. The Constitution attempted to regulate almost every aspect of social and political life. It expanded individual rights, civil liberties and associative freedoms, and provided guarantees of their performance.[19] The Constitution of 1961 was also 'an attempt to maintain Atatürkian thought as a political manifesto'.[20] Article 153 stated that 'no provision of the Constitution was to be interpreted to nullify certain specific laws which were passed during the Atatürk era' and called 'the laws of revolution'.[21] The article in question provided a guarantee for the unquestionable position and supremacy of Kemalist reforms within the framework of the political regime. Although the article did not enumerate the six principles of Kemalism, its emphasis on the continuity between the Constitution and the laws of revolution implied that these principles still constituted the core of the Turkish polity. This dual function of the Constitution clearly indicated that the transformation of the Kemalist *myth* of modernised, westernised, secularised and rationalised society into an *imaginary* began. The absorption by the Kemalist myth of the signifier 'democracy', which initially emerged as an antagonistic force threatening its hegemony, is clearly one of those cases in which 'the moment of representation of the very form of fullness dominates to such an extent that ... myth is transformed into an imaginary'.[22]

In the relatively liberal environment of the 1960s and 1970s, separated identities were allocated to differential positions in the discursive field by a discursive logic based on a clear set of oppositions: rightist versus leftist, traditionalist versus modernist, obscurantism versus progressive ideals, and ultra-nationalist versus Marxist. However, it is important to see the role that the imaginary of 'democratic Kemalism' played within this framework. The discursive logic of Kemalism constituted a set of equivalences between the Kemalist modernisation project and democratic ideals. Democratic and modernist Kemalism became an imaginary, which was 'the condition of possibility for the emergence of any object'.[23] For instance, Turkism shared with Kemalism 'a desire for a safe, prosperous, happy and modernized Turkey'.[24] It suggested nationalism as a 'third way' to modernise Turkey without necessarily sacrificing traditional values or national specificity. The left, claiming that the Turkish revolution was an anti-imperialist bourgeois revolution, saw in Kemalist modernisation the potential to overcome 'the ills of the feudal or semi-feudal structure of Turkey'.[25] The *Türkiye Komünist Partisi* (Turkish Communist Party), for instance, constructed its socialist discourse along the developmentalist and relatively anti-imperialist perspective of Kemalism.[26] Similarly, since the 1940s, Islam had identified with the republican state by reconciling itself with modernity. Although expressed through different discursive strategies, it prioritised a tacit, yet no doubt reluctant, consent to the Kemalist modernisation project. Mardin states that the *Millî Selamet Partisi* (National Salvation Party, NSP), namely, the Islamist party which was founded in 1972 and represented in parliament between 1973 and 1980, was unusual in Turkish history for successfully reaching a synthesis with modernism.[27] It was Kemalism's hegemonising action that opened the possibility for a multitude of subject-positions (not necessarily Islamic or secular in form) to emerge and articulate themselves with the central subject-position of a 'secular-modern' Turkishness.

However, one must also note that Kemalism ultimately failed to reconstitute the plurality of the social-religious sphere in a manipulable-universal whole. Kemalism's failure led to a proliferation of disparate ways in which Islam could be articulated and its attempt to displace Islam from the public domain by articulating it in this ideological chain of equivalences opened the very possibility of the politicisation of Islam.[28] Kemalism was the signifier of 'recognition' in the political sphere, and of a non-Western way of modernisation. It acted as a horizon in which all political struggles could recognise their condition of possibility. The proliferation of articulations around a so-called Kemalist subject position eventually erased the dividing line between a possible Kemalist identity and its others. Kemalism was transformed into an empty signifier, as 'the chain of equivalences which [were] unified around this signifier tend[ed] to empty it, and blur[red] its connection with the actual content with which it was originally associated'.[29] In other words, as it began to signify its own absence, its position became ambiguous and indeterminate.

Nevertheless, the centre, which had expressed its wish to regulate politics in the Constitution of 1961, still failed to incorporate fully and determine the social and political spheres, that is, to control a field of discursivity exceeding its hegemonic grasp. The failure is evident in the emergence of minor parties with radical views, inspired by ideological trends such as Islamic fundamentalism, ultra-nationalism and revolutionary Marxism. By the end of the 1960s, as a result of the growth in political radicalism, the political sphere was divided around two poles – the Marxist left and the extremist right – with the mediating and unifying powers of the Kemalist imaginary being severely weakened. Violence became the main element not only of the confrontations between purist Marxist and ultra-nationalist identities, but also of nearly all forms of political relation, paving the way for the two further military interventions in 1971 and in 1980. The multiple forms of antagonism, undermining the hegemony of the centre, creating an erosion of the centre's self-certainty, annihilating its totalising effects, showed the radical contingeny of the centre and, thus, the radical impossibility of suturing the gap between ordering and order.

The rediscovery of Kemalism by the military

The military takeover of 1980 declared as its ultimate goal the re-establishment of civilian parliamentary rule as soon as the army had brought peace to the streets and order to the government. This motive was similar to those who carried out the 1960 coup, namely, to 'regulate democracy' through constitutions which, as Heper states, served to 'carve an arena for the state against "politics"'.[30] Differing slightly from the 1960 takeover, the military regime of 1980 placed a stronger emphasis on the state's divorce from politics.

The 1980 military regime adopted a position strongly emphasising national unity and the existence of the Turkish Republic at the expense of democracy. In a sense, this was the reincarnation of Kemalism's original totalitarian inclinations. Although parliamentary rule was restored quickly, this quasi-totalitarian dimension continued to shape politics through the introduction of constitutional restrictions on political participation.

Identification with Atatürkism was a result of the military's determination to replace 'alien' ideologies with something more Turkish, an attitude firmly rooted in the historical alliances between Kemalists and the military elite. A new ethos affecting all aspects of social and political life was developed around the image of an harmonious society. The military also emphasised the significance of religion in maintaining the nation in unity and integrity, and in creating a 'non-ideological and "consensual" society'.[31] Through the reconciliation with Islam, conceived as a part of Turkishness, the military regime rearticulated the Kemalist definition of community as secular, rational and modern. The intention was to prove the rationality of Islam, and to make its rational aspects the guiding principles of a peaceful, harmonious community life. In that sense, orthodox Islam became an ideological means in the hands of the state to regain mass support for the Kemalist regime, and to contain the rising tide of Islamism. This led to the introduction of a Turkish–Islam synthesis within an ideological articulation sustaining an authoritarian political regime and a social structure resistant to any alteration. However, the articulation of Islam into official Kemalism also meant a recognition of the power of Islam. Saylan explains that, despite the recognition of secular principles by the Turkish–Islam synthesis, Islam was regarded as the core of culture.[32] The flirtation of the military regime with the Turkish–Islam synthesis eventually resulted in the hegemonic articulation of the latter into the state discourse.

Dissolution of the Kemalist imaginary in the post-military era

The authoritarianism of the post-1980 era, fostered by an emphasis on harmony and unity and a fear of politics, and guaranteed by the military with a carefully drafted constitution, was suggested as a Kemalist answer to the fragmentation and polarisation of the pre-1980 political system. Ironically, it triggered the pluralisation and diversification of extra-parliamentary forms of political activity by blocking the channels for attaining parliamentary representation by ordinary citizens. Simultaneously, it became evident that the crackdown on non-official political activities, instead of reinforcing the hegemonic appeal of Kemalism, in fact led to a proliferation of new sites of identification for popular struggles and for the rearticulation of their popular demands on the national political level.

What is encountered here is a kind of 'return of the repressed' that surfaced through 'unsual' forms of representation. This new trend, fostered also by the effects of global developments, is evident in the rise of particular anti-state discourses with no claim to state power. Among these, special attention ought to be paid to the rise of gender issues in the women's rights movement in particular, to the Green movement, to issues of ethnic and cultural recognition that arose around the Kurdish question, and, finally, to some forms of Islamism.

All these events also signalled the beginning of the end of the Kemalist imaginary. From this point of view, the most significant development of the post-1983 period has been the divorce of democracy from Kemalism. The authoritarian outlook of the new regime, which drew its logic from Kemalist principles, gave a renewed impetus to discussions over the compatibility between Kemalism and democracy. Anti-statist discourses contributed to this phenomenon by breaking with the main principles of Kemalism. In doing so, they discredited the idea of 'social engineering' that had been a constant element of populist discourses from the Young Turk movement to Kemalism.

The rise of Islamism also had its part in the dissolution of the Kemalist hegemony, reviving the possibility to reconceptualise democracy. It is not always true that the Islamist projects wished to democratise society. Most of them were, and are, unable to conceptualise what type of community they want to achieve.[33] Therefore, their endorsement of democracy should rather be seen within the context of their emergence as a pole antagonistic to the dominant political order: by putting forward the demand for a democratisation of the political system they managed to show and challenge the limits of the Kemalist hegemony.

The growing diversity of Islamist, as well as anti-Islamist, subjectivities, undermined the polarisation of the social sphere between the modern and the traditional. The Islamist attempts to bring the modern closer to the traditional blurred the boundaries between modern and traditional identities. Their success in identifying themselves with modernist ideals – democracy being one of them – broke the Kemalist monopoly on modernisation. Instead of Islam being hegemonised by Kemalist modernisation, modernisation was hegemonised by Islam. The transformation of modernisation into being 'everybody's project' became one of the most prominent indicators of the shift of Kemalism from a powerfully hegemonic discourse into one identity among others contending for hegemony. The Kemalist imaginary was reduced to a limited mythical space, as even modernisation, which in the past could only be conceived in Kemalist lines, was now given a multitude of different mythical representations – the Kemalist being only one of them.

In sum, the proliferation of counter-identities, particularly Islamic and traditionalist ones, and the increasing visibility of the limits of the hegemonic discourse in an immensely antagonistic and politicised community, has shaped the political domain in Turkey since the 1980s and marked the dissolution of the Kemalist imaginary. The political struggle, in opposition to that of the 1960s and 1970s, was no longer expressed via a chain of equivalences clustered around Kemalism. A variety of new identities constitute themselves in opposition to Kemalism. A dual process is thus in operation. On the one hand, Kemalism has lost its metaphorical power and its imaginary dimension. In other words, it becomes less and less able to express a metaphorical fullness, and to absorb social demands and dislocations. This dissolution of the Kemalist imaginary indicates a shift in its hegemonic position.[34] On the other hand, this does not indicate an absolute dissolution of the Kemalist forces. The revival of Islam as a hegemonic discourse in post-1980 Turkey, for instance, showed that Kemalism's 'secular' and 'modern–western' subject-position increasingly became less able to create and sustain popular consensus. Nevertheless, while Kemalism lost its claim to constitute the quasi-universal core of national identity, it reappeared in the chain of identifications as a particular political project, which stated its vigorous antagonism to 'religion'. In question, thus, is the transformation of a hegemonic discourse that managed to function as an imaginary horizon, into a discourse struggling for hegemony; a mythical space that strives to survive in the political arena.

Conclusion: democracy and the loss of a hegemonic centre

Within this context it becomes more difficult to answer a lingering question, namely, what are the chances of Turkey becoming a democracy? Despite the political ambiguity, the conditions of possibility for a more democratic politics are present in Turkey, as we approach the next century. The challenge that the counter-hegemonic discourses pose to Kemalism evokes in people a strong opposition towards totalitarian projects. Thus, democracy arises as a strong possibility insofar as the simultaneous emergence of new forms of identities, along with the dissolution of old ones, leads to a proliferation of forms of representation, imposes a language of civil society and rights, and makes possible a politics of recognition, breaking with the long-standing identification of democracy with the national will, that was sustained by the Kemalist imaginary.

Despite this shift, which fosters hopes for a more democratic Turkey, there are also signs of an anti-democratic backlash. Kemalism's totalitarian tendency can still be traced back to its claim to be hegemonic in articulating antagonistic subject positions around secularism and national unity. Given that the rise of Islam is an irrefutable fact, its anti-Islamism can only appeal to certain groups of intellectuals and civil–military bureaucrats. But the years between the Islamist Party's – that is, the *Refah Partisi* (Welfare Party) – success in the local elections of 1993 and its closing-down by the *Anayasa Mahkemesi* (Constitutional Court) in the spring of 1998 have shown that Kemalist anti-Islamism is still capable of mobilising certain political groups around the ideal of a secular state. The ongoing tension between Islam and Kemalism, given that the fundamentals of the Turkish state are constitutionally Kemalist, and that the military is determined not to compromise its mission of safeguarding those fundamentals at the expense of democracy, polarises the social space and jeopardises the democratisation of society.

A similar danger lies in the nationalist answer to the Kurdish question. Kemalist nationalism underlies the state's position against the Kurdish struggle. Interestingly, in a recent development, Kemalist nationalism has started to form alliances with the extreme right, which now intensively uses the Kemalist myths and symbols, in order to stop the rise of Kurdish nationalism. As Tanil Bora points out, the state's 'national reflex' thesis, first used in post-1980 trials of the *Milliyetçi Hareket Partisi* (Nationalist Action Party), legitimises the rise of an extremist Turkish nationalism versus Kurdish nationalism, and is adopted to justify the violent attacks carried out by the extremist nationalists against the Kurds, or the supporters of a non-military solution to the problem.[35] Thus, the creation of a polarised social space around the Kurdish question bears the danger of the normalisation of coercion and violence.

Kozanoglu defines the chaotic state of Turkish politics and society with reference to a 'pop age.' He says 'Turkey is burning with the fire of the pop age'. Nothing escapes the culture of this pop age: 'westernisation, Westernism, locality, Orientalism, fanatic laicism, extreme religiousness, excessive sentimentalism, excessive cruelty, frivolity, conservatism, "free"ness, modernism, nationalism, cries of war, wishes for peace'.[36] Thus, whether or not Turkey will be transformed into a more democratic society is rather ambivalent and remains an open question. The conditions of possibility for either development are definitely present. However, ambivalence lingers as the question remains unanswered. Democracy will ensue only when this instability and ambivalence is accepted and institutionalised, and not represented as an evil that has to be eliminated.

Notes

1 A. Gramsci, *Selection from Prison Notebooks*, Q. Hoare and G. N. Smith ed. (London, Lawrence & Wishart, 1991), p. 210.
2 For a similar argument see F. Keyman, 'Kemalizm, modernlik ve gelenek: Türkiye'de demokratik açilim olasiligi', *Toplum ve Bilim*, 72 (1997), 84–5.
3 For discussions on the Turkish Revolution as a 'bourgeois revolution' see Sungur Savran, 'Osmanli'dan Cumhuriyet'e: Türkiye'de burjuva devrimi sorunu', *11. Tez*, 1 (1985), 172–214; D. Perinçek, *Kemalist Devrim* (Istanbul, Aydinlik, 1979). For the scholary work produced from a Marxist perspective see T. Timur, *Türk Devrimi ve Sonrasi, 1919–1946* (Ankara, Dogan, 1971) and S. Aksin (ed.), *Türkiye Tarihi 4: Çagdas Türkiye 1908–1980* (Istanbul, Cem, 1989).
4 The most notable examples are the two historical encyclopaedias edited by Murat Belge: *Tanzimat'tan Cumhuriyet'e Türkiye Ansiklopedisi* (Istanbul, Iletisim, 1986, 6 vols) and *Cumhuriyet Dönemi Türkiye Ansiklopedisi*, (Istanbul, Iletisim, 1983, 10 vols). See also M. Tunçay, *T.C.'nde Tek Parti Yönetimi'nin Kurulmasi (1923–1931)* (Ankara, Yurt, 1981).
5 M. Foucault, 'Politics and the study of discourse', in G. Burchell, C. Gordon and P. Miller (eds) *The Foucault Effect: Studies in Governmentality*, (London, Harvester Wheatsheaf, 1991), pp. 58–9.
6 A. J. Norval, *Deconstructing Apartheid Discourse* (London, Verso, 1995), p. 2.
7 D. Howarth, 'Reconstructing Laclau and Mouffe's Approach to Political Analysis', *Staffordshire Papers in Politics and International Relations* 30 (Stoke-on-Trent, Staffordshire University, 1996), p. 13.
8 E. Laclau and C. Mouffe, *Hegemony and Socialist Strategy, Towards a Radical Democratic Politics*, (London and New York, Verso, [1985] 1990), p. 113.
9 E. Laclau, *New Reflections on the Revolution of our Time* (London, Verso, 1990), p. 61.
10 The most representative sources that the chapter deals with to construct a 'history of present' vary from government and official documents such as constitutions, laws, decrees and minutes of parliament to party programmes and speeches of political leaders. Much of the discussion of the Kemalist discourse is based on the speeches of the Kemalist leaders, particularly those given by Mustafa Kemal Atatürk himself, and a textbook of 'civic education' for

secondary schools, *Vatandas için Medenî Bilgiler*, dictated by Atatürk. In the scope of this chapter, I make bibliographical reference to these documents and scholarly work only where a direct reference is needed.

11 The Republican People's Party, 1931 programme. For a detailed analysis of this programme see T. Parla, *Türkiy'de Siyasal Kültürün Resmî Kaynaklari: Kemalist Tek-Parti Ideolojisi ve CHP'nin Altioku* (Istanbul, Iletisim, 1992), p. 35 onwards.

12 S. Mardin, 'Center–periphery relations: a key to Turkish politics', *Daedalus* (Winter 1973), 184.

13 F. Ahmad, *The Making of Modern Turkey* (London, Routledge, 1993), p. 105.

14 I. Sunar and I. Sayari, 'Democracy in Turkey: problems and prospects', in G. O'Donnell, P. C. Schmitter and L. Whitehead (eds), *Transition from Authoritarian Rule: Southern Europe*, (Baltimore and London, Johns Hopkins University Press, 1986), p. 170.

15 E. Laclau, 'New reflections on the revolution of our time', in Laclau (ed.), *New Reflections on the Revolution of Our Time*, p. 63.

16 K. Karpat, 'Military interventions: army–civilian relations in Turkey before and after 1980', in M. Heper and A. Evin (eds), *State, Democracy and the Military: Turkey in the 1980s* (Berlin and New York, Walter de Gruyter, 1988), p. 141.

17 M. Heper, 'State, party and society in post-1983 Turkey', *Government and Opposition*, 25 (1990), 324.

18 Sunar and Sayari, 'Democracy in Turkey: problems and prospects', pp. 174–5.

19 *Ibid.*

20 M. Heper, 'State and society in Turkish experience', in Heper Evin (eds), *State, Democracy and the Military*, p. 7.

21 *Ibid.*

22 Laclau (ed.), *New Reflections*, p. 64.

23 *Ibid.*

24 J. M. Landau, 'Nationalist Action Party in Turkey', *Journal of Contemporary History*, 17 (1982), 601–2.

25 E. Kürkçü, 'Iyi iste, modernlestik, basimza gelecek var!', in L. Cinemre and R. Çakir (interview), *Sol Kemalizme Bakiyor* (Istanbul, Metis, 1991), p. 133.

26 *Ibid.*

27 S. Mardin, 'Religion in modern Turkey', *International Social Science Journal*, 29:2 (1977), 279–99.

28 B. Sayyid, 'Sign o'times: kaffirs and infides fighting the ninth crusade', in E. Laclau (ed.), *The Making of Political Identities* (London, Verso, 1994),p. 271.

29 E. Laclau, 'Why do empty signifiers matter to politics?', in E. Laclau, *Emancipation(s)* (London, Verso, 1996), pp. 40–4.

30 Heper, 'State and society', p. 5.

31 Ü. Cizre-Sakallioglu, 'Kemalism, hyper-nationalism and Islam in Turkey', *History of European Ideas*, 18:2 (1994), 262.

32 G. Saylan, *Islamiyet ve Siyaset: Türkiye Örnegi* (Ankara, V, 1987), pp. 68–9.

33 R. Çakir, 'Refah'i elestirmenin yollari', *Birikim*, 59 (1994), 15–20.

34 Laclau (ed.), *New Reflections*, p. 65.

35 See T. Bora, 'Almanya'da dazlaklar Türkiye'de yobazlar! Neo-fasizan potansiyel ve ilgilileri', *Birikim*, 51 (1993).

36 C. Kozanoglu, *Pop Çagi Atesi* (Istanbul, Iletisim, 1995), back cover.

13 *Jason Glynos*

Sex and the limits of discourse

Sex –*n*. 1 either of the main divisions (male and female) into which living things are placed on the basis of their reproductive functions. 2 the fact of belonging to one of these. 3 males or females collectively. 4 sexual instincts, desires, etc., or their manifestation. 5 *colloq*. sexual intercourse. –*adj*. 1 of or relating to sex (*sex education*). 2 arising from a difference or consciousness of sex (*sex antagonism*; *sex urge*). –*v.tr*. 1 determine the sex of. 2 (as sexed *adj*.) a having a sexual appetitie (*highly sexed*). b having sexual characteristics.

Concise Oxford Dictionary[1]

In this chapter I show how, in the context of sex and, in particular, the *sexed subject*, the French psychoanalyst Jacques Lacan can be seen to break with a biology versus social construction dichotomy. In other words, his contribution should definitely *not* be seen as just another recipe in which the ingredients remain the same (biology, culture) but whose respective doses change. I approach Lacan's conception of the sexed subject by distinguishing it from both the biological subject (whether cast in terms of anatomy, hormones, genes, and so on) and the cultural subject (socially determined, overdetermined, evolving) – a clarification which may bring with it important consequences for the way we think about political analysis from a discourse-theoretic point of view. For instance, this account can be seen to provide the elements with which to combat various types of exclusionary logics that is a staple concern of many feminist postmodernists. The fear here is that conceiving men and women in terms of positive features always carries the risk of unfairly excluding others from the provision of basic primary goods. Thus, benefits linked to the definition of people's status as married heterosexual couples will have an unequal impact upon those couples who do not possess the positive properties described in the definition. Lesbian and gay couples, for example, may be excluded on this basis, suffering discriminatory treatment as a result.

The claim I would like to make in this chapter is that Lacan offers us a way of conceiving sexual difference which does not rely on defining the sexed subject in terms of positive properties. And in order to do so I explore the specificity of a psychoanalytic alternative to the reduction of the sexuation process to either biological determinants on the one hand, or social determinants, whether fixed or shifting, on the other. If references to biological determinants and meanings signal the *discourse* of biological foundationalism; if references to cultural ideals and meanings signal the *discourse* of social constructionism; and if references to performatively constituted identities signal what I shall call a *discourse* of a 'disseminating' postmodernism; Lacan's conception of sexual difference takes its reference point to be the *limits* of discourse. The aim of this chapter, then, is twofold. First, to reframe standard contemporary theoretical discourses on sexual identity; and second, to suggest an alternative way of formulating sexual difference.

Toward the limits of discourse: a first articulation

Dictionary entries are there to occasionally remind us that the relationship between a word and its meaning is not as simple as we might first expect. It has, for instance, very little to do with '*it*', namely, its non-linguistic referent. Take sex, for example. In response to the string of words 'What does sex mean?', we are not too surprised when we are offered another string of words; and another if need be; and so on. We do not usually expect to find ourselves engulfed in some paradigmatic experience of sex. Indeed, it is misleading to think that this experience would in any way help us understand what sex *means*. And here is the proof: someone emerging from such an experience can still demand, perhaps with even greater urgency, to know what it means! Indeed, one could say that relying on some extra-discursive referent for *meaning* is a way to avoid the somewhat troubling idea that sex has more to do with speech and its *limits* than with, for example, some sort of activity. This, at least, is what psychoanalysis teaches.

In this view, then, what do we do when faced with the enigma of sex? We talk about it a gread deal – indeed, endlessly; and this because there is no 'natural' word, no final resting place, that could finally put an end to the search for its ultimate meaning, its essence. Indeed, sex, according to psychoanalysis, is very much related to this missing final word, this necessary failure to say it all. From which it is only a short step away to Lacan's infamous declaration that 'there's no such thing as a sexual relation'![2] For it is not simply a matter of having an Ideal Relation which is progressively approached but which ultimately fails in its empirical realisation (that is, conceiving it in terms of a *regulative* ideal). Instead, the very place that such an Ideal Relation *would* have occupied is *itself* missing. These ideas will be further clarified in the main body of the chapter. For now, however, I would like to suggest why a psychoanalytic conception of the process of sexuation might be worth investigating.

The sex/gender debate surrounding sexual identity is often characterised

as oscillating between two poles. On the one side, we usually find a conception of sexual identity that is rooted in biological meanings (for example,
reproductive capacity, anatomy, genes, hormones, and so on) – one that participates in a discourse of biological foundationalism; on the other side, we
find sexual identity to be a product of cultural meanings (for example, what
it means in a particular society to be a father, a wife, and so on) and cultural
ideals – one that participates in a discourse of social constructionism. Perhaps
we could say that the 1980s and early 1990s were characterised by a swing
toward the latter pole. Scholars were keen to point out how one's sexual
identity, as defined in politics and law for example, carried with it very material consequences. Academics, especially feminist and critical race academics,
became increasingly sensitive to the way identities were constructed, thereby
highlighting them as condensations of a whole set of institutionalised power
relations. Thus, a new realm of political contestation opened up. It was not
only a matter of fighting for equal treatment at the level of power relations
(sexual difference should not, it is argued here, operate as an admissible reason for making a professional decision); there was also an effort to make
identity construction itself a political battleground. Indeed, there is an
attempt to free sexual identity not only from a strong hetero-normativity (in
which sexual difference is conceived in terms of a rigid binary, man/woman),
but also from *any* form of sexual normativity (such that sexual difference was
conceived in terms of a potentially infinite multiplicity). But the term 'social
construction' is no longer restricted to academia. It has become common-
place among practising politicians, journalists and academic administrators,
in whose realms it is regularly invoked in order to acknowledge it, to pay lip
service to it, to berate it, to misunderstand it, and sometimes, especially
within university villages, to legislate it.

Nevertheless, as we enter the twenty-first century, we seem to be witnessing the beginning of a swing back to the opposite pole. It is becoming more
and more acceptable in public discourse to talk about biological determinants
and sexual identity in the same breath (as in, for example, the notorious gay
gene). And I am sure many reasons could be offered by way of explanation.
However, I would like here to make the following speculation: that the very
proliferation of sexual identities spurred on by the postmodern, social-con-
structionist impetus has brought to the fore an invariant form which is
reducible neither to a list of positive meanings, nor to cultural ideals. Perhaps
it is the simultaneous invisibility of, and sensitivity to, this invariant form,
that has prompted a kind of 'biological backlash'. What I would like to suggest is that psychoanalysis provides us with a way of articulating this real
invariance that avoids a biological relapse without, however, falling into a
kind of discursive idealism. This is because Lacan locates this invariance not
in some 'external reality' or 'extra-discursive referent'; nor in cultural ideals
or meanings; instead, this real invariance finds its proper place at the *limits*
of discourse. The astonishing thing is that the effects exerted by *this* real (*qua*

limits of discourse) can be just as momentous as any effects exerted by external reality or by trenchant cultural norms! It is at the level of this invariance
– the limits of discourse – that Lacan locates the psychoanalytic conception
of sexual difference. As paradoxical as it may sound, a Lacanian perspective
suggests that a more nuanced conception of the *limits* of discourse provides
the most promising way forward in the development of a discourse-theoretic
approach to political analysis.

   Now, for purposes of clarity, the remainder of the chapter will follow, in
broad outline, the sequence I articulated in the introduction. In other words,
there will be a gradual passage in the focus of my analysis from the discourse
of biological foundationalism to the discourse of social constructionism to
the discourse of postmodern 'dissemination' to the *limits* of discourse. But
this passage can also be put in Lacanian terms. And it is worth pausing here
for a moment in order to understand precisely the nature of the Lacanian
grid, since it will serve to frame the bulk of the chapter. In a first approach,
then, we could say that the above sequence corresponds to a movement from
the imaginary order to the symbolic order to the real order.

   For present purposes the orders can be understood as follows. The imaginary order will be identified with the order of *meaning* (which I will take to
be equivalent to identity or the signified); the symbolic order will refer to the
order of the ideal (or pure signifier) which structures meaning; and the real
order aims at that which inhabits the symbolic order but which is reducible
neither to ideals nor to symbolically structured meanings. In this view, the
discourse of biological foundationalism is a discourse of biological meanings.
Here it is the dimension of the imaginary that dominates. The discourse of
social constructionism, however, straddles the imaginary and symbolic
orders. It is a discourse in which the imaginary-symbolic dimension dominates. This is because social constructionism highlights both cultural *meanings* on the one hand, *and* cultural *ideals* or pure signifiers on the other.
Finally, the related discourse of postmodern 'dissemination' can be said to
give priority to the symbolic order, the order of the pure signifier. It is the
performative dimension of adopting and playing with signifiers that is
emphasised here, a play that celebrates the contingent relation between signifier and signified and the consequence of a potentially infinite fluidity of
identity. Finally, the Lacanian conception of sexual difference aims at that
which remains invariant even within the context of a potentially infinite
range of identities. This invariance is of the order of the real.

Sexual difference: from imaginary meanings to symbolic ideals

True to the postmodern, poststructuralist ethos, there have been many sustained and virtuosic expositions detailing the trouble with gender and its
relation to sex, expositions which have helped clarify, modify and develop
the terms and theory of the sex debate in the context of feminist, gay and

lesbian studies. Judith Butler, for example, shows how culture haunts even the most scientific of investigations into sex. Indeed, it is there that she finds its most insidious presence, for it is there that it feigns the absence of cultural contamination most forcefully. In one of her classic deconstructive moves, she shows how cell biologists manage to prove what was already implicitly assumed at the outset.[3]

According to Butler, cell biologists show that the *essence* of sexual differ-ence (what it ultimately *means* to be a man or woman) resides not simply in the well-known Y chromosome but in the 'master gene' that inhabits it. For it was the Y chromosome which had been seen until then as ultimately responsible for our sexual differentiation. The beauty of this further refine-ment lies in the fact that we can now explain why some ten per cent of the population do not fit neatly on either side of the XX-female and XY-male divide (where male and female refer to anatomically distinct beings). More specifically, it explains the odd occurrence of an XY-*female*. But what we dis-cover behind this genetic pizzazz, Butler suggests, is an argument found wanting.

To make explicit the circularity of the argument Butler wishes to expose, we may cast the proposed scientific inquiry in the form of a question: what is the biological-genetic cause of a particular anatomical difference? This, however, is almost immediately substituted, and thus made effectively syn-onymous with, the question: what is responsible for the determination of one's sexuality as either feminine or masculine? Answer: a particular DNA sequence within the Y chromosome. And how can we confirm this? By *look-ing* to *see* if the subject is a man or a woman (!). In other words, we have a slippage (that we might say is of the order of a *landslide*) in which the isola-tion of a biological cause whose effect is a particular bodily configuration, instead of effecting a displacement in our conception of sexual identity, actu-ally functions as evidential *support* for an entrenched convention. In attempting to redefine biological sexual difference in terms of chromosomes and/or genes, cell biologists, in the very same gesture, reinstate the culturally sedimented conception of sexual identity, conceived in terms of the presence or absence of the penis. In this case, then, scientific knowledge is at the *ser-vice* of cultural meanings, it does not interrogate them – it effectively takes on a *conservative* role.

In addition, it illustrates why there are no such things as 'pure' facts. A pure fact is simply something that is taken for granted and not put into ques-tion. By itself, of course, this observation is neither astonishing nor offensive. What Butler is objecting to, however, is the idea that a biological fact can come to be seen as *fixing* one's sexual identity, one's gender, in a way that passes responsibility for sexual identity, and the sexual behaviour this engen-ders, from the subject to the genes. She shows how easy it is for a biological fact (presence or absence of a master gene) to insist upon its factual status, its 'neutrality', so as to reassert, with even greater authority, a still prevalent cultural convention. She shows how the very split sex/gender is culturally conditioned and tries to pass itself off as natural, a kind of biological reductionism in which gender is seen to be determined by biology.

Another interesting dimension that Butler highlights, and which showcases the above-mentioned slippage more spectacularly, is the way in which individuals whose anatomy is irreducibly ambiguous are declared male or female. She suggests that it is here that the cultural convention of identifying the male with the penis and the female with the absence of the penis is most clearly propagated through the simultaneous privileging of the former over the latter. There is a clear default mode in which any protruding body part in the groin area effectively constitutes a male trump card over the copresence of an orificial cavity.

In these ways, therefore, a culturally naturalised and differentially privileged phenotypic biology becomes central to one's sexual identity. Sexual identity is determined by *anatomical* sexual difference. In other words, we find the most deeply ingrained cultural convention being played out within the very sanctity of the laboratory, namely, that anatomy (sex) is sexual destiny-identity (gender). In setting out to determine what the essence of sexual difference is, cell biologists (at least those under Butler's scrutiny) simply reinforce what it always-already was, and not without throwing in a few biogenetic fireworks for good measure.

Let us take a step back now and examine a little more precisely the nature of the gender/sex opposition that is implied in Butler's analysis. Clearly the type of dialectic Butler envisages is not a crude one. A crude conception of the gender/sex relation would be one in which 'gender' gains its specificity through its opposition to sex, conceived as a biological *factum brutum*. In this view, gender is strictly identified with culture, with the cultural meanings differentiating men from women: active/passive, breadwinner/housecarer, public/private, culture/nature, reasonable/emotional, competitive/caring, and so on. Gender is viewed as a social construction and thus subject to change. In contrast, the differences inhering in the bodies of men and women are assumed to be pre-given and unchangeable, a fact of nature. Everything would then depend on the 'reach' of the biological body, on its ability to dictate behaviour. The more information harboured by it, the less room for political manoeuvre. And given the Bible's fall from grace as a source of natural and thus justified differential treatment, the concomitant rise in the seventeenth century of a materialist view of the body, and the later addition of Darwinism, the scope of biological determinism has not been insignificant.

But with the dissemination of poststructuralist ideas in the late 1960s and early 1970s (often associated with the proper names of Foucault and Derrida) came a sustained onslaught on what were termed binary oppositions. As the deconstructionist net widened, many such oppositions came to be regarded as responsible for the insidious propagation of power differentials. And, of course, the oppositions gender/sex and culture/nature were not unexpected casualties. The culture/nature opposition meant that, in practice, too many political differences were being naturalised. As long as one could link differences in social roles and behaviour to differences in biology (whether anatomical, hormonal, or genetic), politicising social roles in sexual politics was rendered virtually impossible.

The way out of this impasse involved extending the notion of gender (or culture), transforming it so as to subsume as an *effect* the very opposition gender/sex (or culture/nature). In other words, it involved recognising how discourse was itself responsible for the very distinction discursive/extra-discursive; that gender and biological sex, in order to acquire their oppositional value, relied on each other. This is how Butler understands the gender/sex dialectic. The point, of course, is not to deny physical differences between men and women *qua* biological animals. The point, rather, is to highlight how sociocultural discourse actually conditions *whether and how we see* differences, and consequently how those differences become politically significant.

In order to make this last point clear, I will refer to another empirical example, an example discussed by Linda Nicholson.[4] Nicholson refers to Thomas Laqueur's study of medical literature, specifically that deriving from eighteenth-century Western societies.[5] According to Laqueur, the eighteenth century marked a period of transition from a 'one-sex' view of the body to a 'two-sex' view. Instead of today's common perception of female and male sexual organs as clearly distinct (hence justifying the number 'two'), the view then was rather different. For a start, there was no distinct word for vagina; nor was there a distinct word for ovaries. The vagina and cervix were viewed collectively as a less developed penis; and testicles, as a term, included what today we see as distinct: testicles *and* ovaries. In this earlier, 'one-sex' view, then, 'the female body was seen as a lesser version of the male body "along a vertical axis of infinite gradations"'.[6] Thus, during the eighteenth-century transition to the 'two-sex' view, it was culture itself that mediated the move to a new culture/biology configuration. It was the modification of discourse through the introduction of new signifiers that opened up the possibility of a different *construction* of biological differences, allowing subjects to literally 'see' themselves in a totally different way – a way, moreover, which with the passage of time did not escape the very strong tendency to 'naturalise' such differences. From a 'two-sex' perspective, the female body was seen as 'an altogether different creature along a horizontal axis whose middle ground was largely empty'.[7]

Foucault also points to this transition by highlighting how the category hermaphroditism was delegitimised.[8] Hermaphroditism gradually gave way to *pseudo*-hermaphroditism: since there were 'actually' *two* sexes, not gradations of a single sex, one had to uncover the 'truth' underlying the misleading and confusing surface appearances. And while the second view (founded on biological science) may appear less hierarchical and thus less prone to subordination arguments than the first view (founded on Aristotle or the Bible), this did not prevent these newly conceived biological differences from having unwelcome political implications. They were simply different. How the new biological 'facts' were spurred on and caught up with social forces, such as industrialisation, urbanisation and a growing differentiation between domestic and public life, determined the scope of political struggle.

Variations on a foundationalist theme

I want now to locate the foregoing discussion on sexual difference in a broader feminist-theoretic context. More specifically, I want to show how the distinction between a discourse of biological foundationalism and a discourse of social constructionism is not always very clear-cut. This, in turn, will allow me to shift my focus on to, thereby putting into question, the logic of foundationalism itself.

I begin by invoking Linda Nicholson's conceptualisation of the feminist-theoretic landscape. For she has very usefully constructed an analytical tool with which to make sense of a whole range of positions adopted by feminist theorists in relation to the social construction/biology debate. This tool takes the form of a continuum, a biological foundationalist continuum. At one extreme we find strict biological essentialism.[9] At the other extreme, with which Nicholson aligns herself, biology shrinks to the point where it 'cannot be used to ground claims about "women" or "men" transculturally'.[10] Nicholson finds this spectrum approach useful precisely because while most feminist theorists today *explicitly* declare themselves to be social constructionists, they in their analysis and practice end up reintroducing a measure of biological foundationalism through the back door.[11] Thus, the range of cross-cultural gendered attributes (explicitly or implicitly) linked to biological attributes, coupled with the strength of those links, determines the feminist theorist's position on the spectrum. Nicholson suggests that this type of inadvertent and tempting 'relapse' into biology has consequences which are proportional to the degree of relapse. The problem is 'its tendency to generate faulty generalisations that represent projections from the theorist's own cultural context'.[12] And the only way to avoid this problem is to renounce biological foundationalism absolutely.

In addition, Nicholson suggests that biological foundationalism is not only responsible for problematic cross-cultural projections, it is also responsible for the impasses generated by *intra*cultural difference feminisms – feminisms that subscribe to a clear-cut distinction between men and women on the basis of sets of positive properties. For example, despite the obvious attempt to be culturally and historically sensitive, Carol Gilligan's *In a Different Voice*[13] and Nancy Chodorow's *The Reproduction of Mothering*[14] were soon shown to possess a multitude of blind spots. These blind spots, Nicholson argues, were a direct result of the implicit biological foundationalism they relied upon in differentiating men and women, blind spots which were readily picked up by lesbians, women of colour, working-class women, and so on. In their effort to distinguish women and men, differences among women had clearly been erased.

Thus, Nicholson's overview allows us to specify the impasse facing many varieties of identity politics. Each variety, according to Nicholson, lies somewhere along the biological foundationalism continuum. Her point is that cultural differences should not be seen to *supplement* biological constants; instead the latter should be seen as themselves an *effect* of culture. This involves a shift in perspective. 'It means coming to see [cultural] differences as that which "go all the way down" affecting the very criteria of what it means to be a man or a woman in diverse societies.'[15]

Now, if a discourse of *biological* meanings cannot serve as a legitimate foundation upon which to ground differences between men and women, we might be tempted to opt for a foundation grounded in a discourse of *cultural* meanings. Nicholson, however, declines this option. This is because deconstruction demonstrates to us how *any* appeal to foundational *meanings* (of the order of the *imaginary*) is suspect: biological givenness would simply be replaced by cultural givenness, leaving the logic of foundationalism intact.

Sexual difference: from the symbolic to the real

What we see unfolding in arguments such as those offered by Butler and Nicholson is, in Lacanian terms, a passage from the imaginary order to the symbolic order; we shift from the positivity of our 'scientific' and cultural *meanings* to the *ideals* that structure them; from a discourse of biological foundationalism to a discourse of social constructionism proper; from an automatic and unthinking assumption of a cultural hetero-biological norm to its visibility as such. And coupled with this movement comes the possibility of interrogating this cultural ideal.

Now, if Butler and Nicholson show us how the very distinction gender/sex is socially constructed and thus prone to the constant displacement ('dissemination') postmodernists highlight, Lacan shows us how this constant displacement itself, the symbolic order, is always-already traversed by a fundamental and solid deadlock.[16] In a move which has not ceased to raise suspicions of essentialism, Lacan argues that one can *still* speak of two sexes, two sexed subjects. But he claims to do this without regressing into a crude biologism or fixed normativity, and without advocating a forever fluid and open cultural normativity. He argues that sex *is* this deadlock and that the two sexes constitute two ways of coping with it. In other words, sex is, at one and the same time, the condition of the impossibility of the sexual relation and of the possibility of making up for it by *discoursing* about this impossibility. So, if we define the sex of the subject according to how it positions itself with respect to this impossibility, we are, according to Lacan, presented with two logical possibilities. The speaking being may take up a position either *at* the limit of the symbolic (pure *signifier*) or *as* the limit (that is, partaking of the *real* order). Thus, the interesting complex we call sexuality arises from the purely contingent grafting of this *logical* bipolarity arising out of the real deadlock of the symbolic order on to the *culturally* conditioned (and ultimately fluid) *biological* bipolarity.[17]

Perhaps we can clarify this point further by noting that even relatively new sexual identities, as in the case of 'lesbian' or 'gay' subject positions (understood as signifiers accompanied by imaginary effects), often do not escape the bi-polar genito-anatomical referent. Anatomy almost always presents itself as a constitutive factor in the determination of their identities. It would seem, however, that we can think up new identities which would interrogate this apparent necessity. Some fetishistic practices may engender identities which seem to move in this direction. Now Lacan would accept this potentially infinite play in the realm of *substantive* (that is, imaginary-symbolic) sexual identity. However, in his theory of sexuation, he aims at a totally different level. The idea is that there is a certain *substanceless* structure whose contours, in the domain of sexuality, can be discerned irrespective of the particular positive configuration. (By substance, here, I mean the dimension of experience that is exhausted by imaginary meanings and symbolic signifiers.)

We can approach the issue of the subject's sex in terms of discourse and its limits in yet another way. If the speaking subject is inextricably linked to the order of the signifier, if the speaking being is *inhabited* by language, it does not follow that it can be *reduced* to it, an observation that is strictly correlated with the failure to achieve a successful objective identity, to close the gap between the symbolic and the real. And the sex of the subject emerges on the basis of its relation to this failure. In other words, the subject's sex is conceived as one of two ways in which it fails to grasp the Whole, to achieve a fully sutured objective identity. Man and woman constitute two logical modalities of the failure to achieve an imaginary-symbolic identity; which implies that, between them, they are also logically *incommensurable*.[18] And this, in turn, implies it is not possible to formalise the sexual relation. Lacan's infamous phrase 'there is no such thing as a sexual relation' indicates that it is not possible to even *write* the Ideal Relation, let alone aspire to achieve it! 'There is no sexual relation' indexes the limit to any kind of formalisation.

We can also approach the sex of the subject from a sociopolitical perspective. The Lacanian subject is not the discursively constructed *substantive* subject of liberalism (individual, atomic, autonomous, free), nor of communitarianism (social, structured, determined), nor of a certain strand of post-structuralism (multiple, diffuse, overdetermined, evolving). All these remain framed by a subject/predicate dichotomy that operates on the single plane of predicative (that is, imaginary-symbolic) substance, even if this substance is perforated by contingency. Rather, whether one is man or woman depends on how one situates oneself in relation to the impossibility of saying every-thing, of saying it all. Thus, in Lacan, 'man' and 'woman' do not function on the level of predicates, on the level of substance. As Žižek writes: '*"mascu-line" or "feminine" is not a predicate providing positive information about the subject* ... . [Instead, it is] *a specific modality of how the subject failed in his or her bid for identity which would constitute him or her as an object within phenomenal reality.*'[19] Man and woman are not predicative-substan-tive for the very reason that they pertain to the *failure* of predicative sub-stance. In other words, it is not sufficient to say, as it might be tempting to do, that, since the subject is tied to the signifier, its identity can be modified by substitution, by the adoption of a new signifier. Lacan is arguing that there is a structure which, though inscribed in the symbolic, is incommensurable with it. It is not simply a question of bearing witness to the contingency of a signifier's hegemonic sway in order to conclude that *any* signifier will do. It is more the case that *no* signifier will *ever* do.

The point is that without the proper support of the symbolic and/or bio-logical in terms of a bipolarity, the taking up of the logical impasse into a knot will not occur so smoothly or inevitably. It is only insofar as the imag-inary-symbolic furnishes us with a bipolar support on to which the logical impasse can be grafted that this impossibility has the chance to present itself as a 'natural' possibility, one that promises the Ideal of a sexual relation. What I am suggesting, then, is that there is absolutely no guarantee that *biological* sexual difference (absence/presence of body part or other physio-logical characteristic) should align itself with *cultural* sexual difference (active/passive, public/private, and so on) or with the *logical* sexual differ-ence (pure signifier/real) under the banner male/female (or man/woman, masculine/feminine). This lack of guarantee also goes by the name of cas-tration. For castration names this constitutive openness, this dehiscence, of the symbolic order. In the absence of a real limit in discourse, we would indeed have the possibility of a perfect relation, of a perfect overlap between the imaginary and the symbolic. The paradox, of course, is that we would be completely unaware of this perfect relation. For it is precisely this *deadlock* that opens up the self-reflective distance that permits us to con-ceive the possibility of the sexual relation in the first place. In other words, *the sexual relation emerges as a fantasmatic possibility only against the back-ground of a real impossibility*. Or, to put it another way: the possibility of discursive identity formations emerges against the background of the *limits* of discourse.

Conclusion

In this chapter, I have suggested that if there is an invariance that charac-terises sexual difference, it is most properly approached in terms of its impos-sibility – an impossibility which emerges not out of any biological misfitting, nor out of any lack of our ability to modify culture's content, but out of a basic deadlock proper to the symbolic order that we are, on this occasion, calling sex. The sexed subject, therefore, becomes conceivable in terms of the *mode* with which the subject copes with the *limits* of discourse.

This has methodological consequences. It means, for instance, that a psychoanalytically informed discourse-theorist looks out not only for evidence of discursive limits, of discursive failure, but he or she also tries to establish the *modality* of this failure: can we characterise this modality as either feminine or masculine? But this is not all. For a Lacanian approach suggests that the logical modalities of the sexual impasse, precisely because they are logical, can be clearly severed from their substantive substrate and rendered in formal, quasi-transcendental terms;[20] which means that we should expect to find such modal bifurcations in the context of other discursive formations.[21] In other words, though my discussion in this chapter focused upon debates in the domain of sexuality, its insights are generalisable: insofar as we find the foundationalist versus social constructionist debate being played out within the domains of Marxism, anti-racism, environmentalism, nationalism, and so on, the Lacanian perspective I have elaborated retains its relevance.

I have argued that a shift of focus from biological meanings to cultural meanings remains foundationalist in spirit. It marks a transition from a discourse of biological reductionism to a discourse of a certain kind of social constructionism that does not escape foundationalism conceived as an appeal to a transcendental signified, even if this turns out to be cultural in content rather than biological. Thus, the further shift in focus from *meanings* (whether biological or cultural) to (cultural) *ideals* is a productive one. It is productive insofar as it allows us to interrogate the ideals that structure our meanings, thereby helping to make the latter more fluid. How? By highlighting the contingency with which the cultural ideals are linked to meanings, especially sex-related meanings that carry social and political consequences. This shift of focus tracks a move from the discourse of a nonfoundationalist social constructionism to a discourse of postmodern 'dissemination'. However, again from a Lacanian perspective, this marks a shift *within* the realm of discourse. It involves a shift from the imaginary to the symbolic dimensions of discourse.

The Lacanian contribution involves emphasising the real *limits* of discourse and how this opens up a novel way of approaching sexual difference in which the subject, far from being effaced, is considered critical. Of course, it is extremely important to be able to properly theorise the constitutive inadequacy of a cultural ideal to fulfil its role. For it is incorrect to assume that, subject to contextual constraints, *any* ideal can hegemonise the field of meaning. And one of the most sophisticated accounts of this process is presented to us in the work of Ernesto Laclau. From a discourse theoretic point of view the impossibility of closure implies that all attempts to hegemonise ideals by concrete contents fail. In other words, identity is always qualified as partially fixed. According to this view, the tension between an impossible-to-fulfil ideal and its various possible contents is constitutive.

We immediately see how the Lacanian intervention contributes to the further development of discourse theory. It deepens discourse theory by highlighting how this very tension itself can have one of two modalities. It involves pointing out that this constitutive tension, this failure, has *two* logical modalities which are independent of the particularity of the ideals at stake. In this view, each sexed subject has a specific relation to the *limits* of discourse, to the *failure* of ideals to fully institute themselves, *not* in relation to another living being or thing. And what we call sexuality is nothing but the particular manner in which this *logical impasse* gets caught up in the culturally-mediated biological difference, along with all the tragicomical consequences, including political consequences, to which this gives rise.

Notes

I would like to thank Yannis Stavrakakis, Aletta Norval and David Howarth for providing me with very useful feedback on earlier drafts of this chapter.

1 *The Concise Oxford Dictionary* (Oxford, Clarendon Press, 1990).
2 See, for example, J. Lacan, *The Seminar of Jacques Lacan, Book XX: Encore (1972–3)*, ed. J-A. Miller, trans. B. Fink (New York, W. W. Norton, 1998), p. 59.
3 J. Butler, *Gender Trouble* (New York, Routledge, 1990), pp. 106–11.
4 L. Nicholson, 'Interpreting gender' in L. Nicholson and S. Seidman (eds), *Social Postmodernism: Beyond Identity Politics* (Cambridge, Cambridge University Press, 1995), p. 47. For similar analyses, see E. Martin, 'The egg and the sperm: how science has constructed a romance based on stereotypical male–female roles', *Signs,* 16:3 (1991), 485. See also H. Moore, 'DIVIDED WE STAND: sex, gender, and sexual difference', *Feminist Review* (1994), 47–78.
5 T. Lacqueur , *Making Sex* (Cambridge, Mass., Harvard University Press, 1990).
6 Nicholson, 'Interpreting gender', p. 46, quoting Lacqueur, *Making Sex*, p. 148.
7 Lacqueur, *Making Sex*, p. 148, as cited by L. Nicholson, 'Interpreting gender', p. 46.
8 See, for example, M. Foucault (ed.), *Herculine Barbin, Being the Recently Discovered Memoirs of a Nineteenth Century Hermaphrodite*, trans. R. McDougall (New York, Colophon, 1980).
9 See, for example, the work of Andrea Dworkin. The vast majority of evolutionary psychologists fall within this category too.
10 Nicholson, 'Interpreting gender', p. 49.
11 For an analysis of this type, see for example C. Mouffe, 'Feminism, citizenship, and radical democratic politics', in J. Butler and J. W. Scott (eds), *Feminists Theorize the Political* (New York, Routledge, 1992), p. 369, especially her examination of Carole Pateman's work at pp. 373–7.
12 Nicholson, 'Interpreting gender', p. 49.
13 C. Gilligan, *In a Different Voice: Psychological Theory and Women's Development* (Cambridge, Mass., Harvard University Press, 1983).

14 N. Chodorow, *The Reproduction of Mothering* (Berkeley, University of California Press, 1978).
15 Nicholson and Seidman, *Social Postmodernism*, p. 11.
16 Here I should point out that my analysis of Judith Butler is restricted to her book *Gender Trouble*.
17 S. Žižek, *Metastases of Enjoyment* (London, Verso, 1994), p. 155.
18 By logically incommensurable I mean that man and woman 'have no common measure' with which they may be compared (or paired) with each other. Why? First, because they are characterised not by their relation to each other but to a Third, to the limits of discourse. And secondly because they each relate to the limits of discourse differently.
19 Žižek, *Metastases of Enjoyment*, p. 159 (emphasis added).
20 By invoking the term quasi-transcendental I mean to highlight how this logical form simultaneously aspires to articulate itself (thereby also submitting itself to a kind of testing) to new contexts as they present themselves, one by one, and has precise historical conditions of possibility. In this view, the status of the universal human right can also be characterised as quasi-transcendental. Though it has precise historical conditions of possibility (that is, social, philosophical and poitical events leading up to the French Revolution), it aspires to articulate itself to ever-new demands and circumstances, going beyond the particular context which gave rise to it. In short, it harbours universal aspirations. But this aspiration is cast not positively (in the style of 'All x are submitted to the logical form' on account of a specified set of positive features), but negatively (in the style of 'There is no x that can be said, in advance, to be excluded by the logical form'). This understanding of quasi-transcendentalism draws upon Jacques Lacan's formulae of sexuation, as elaborated in Lacan, *The Seminar of Jacques Lacan, Book XX*, p. 73.
21 In fairly broad terms, one could cite the work of Slavoj Žižek as evidence of an attempt to do just that, always emphasising the ethical implications of such analyses. A similar attempt at a quasi-transcendental typologisation, this time in relation to Derrida's *oeuvre*, can be discerned in the work of Rodolphe Gasché. See, for example, his *The Tain of the Mirror* (Cambridge, Mass., Harvard University Press, 1986), especially Part Two. In *The Tain of the Mirror*, Gasché describes such modalities in terms of infrastructures – infrastructures of the arché-trace, of *différance*, of supplementarity, of iterability, of re-mark. What most distinguishes these two approaches is perhaps the capital importance ascribed to the subject in Lacanian-informed discourse analyses.

Trajectories of future research in discourse theory

In this chapter I will draw out some of the key themes that cut across the different contributions to this volume and reflect upon their significance within the discourse-theory research paradigm. I shall also open up new avenues of research by drawing on previously under-explored idioms of analysis. However, in so doing I shall not aim to develop new arguments in full. Rather, I focus on four main themes. I shall begin by examining the concept of political frontiers and its relation to the organisation of political space on the one hand, and the individuation or delineation of identity on the other. I will argue that it is necessary to distinguish between the general logic of individuation of identity and the formation of political frontiers. This distinction, I propose, unlocks new possibilities of research the most important of which is the exploration of different modalities of political subjectivity. This is discussed in the second section of this chapter, where I argue for the need to explore systematically a wide range of modalities of subject formation in addition to those traditionally emphasised in discourse theory. To supplement this argument, I discuss ways in which some of the contributions to this book may advance the development of a typology of relations between kinds of frontier formation and political subjectivity. The third section analyses the distinction between myth and imaginary, and its relation to pertinent categories in the Gramscian tradition. My focus here is on the requirements for a clear delineation of both myths and imaginaries and their relation to particular social formations. Finally, I discuss the category of hegemony and its relation to specific forms of political regime. I distinguish between different uses of the concept hegemony, and argue for the further development of the ethical dimensions of hegemony, specifically in the case of a democratic hegemonic formation.

Political frontiers

The need to develop the category of political frontiers in discourse theory stems from its post-Marxist framework of analysis. Laclau and Mouffe's starting-point opposes determinism and any principle of an *a priori* societal logic underlying the construction of social and political identities. In brief, their argument is that if any identity, and by extension society, is no longer a given and immutable datum, if its character cannot be determined in a naturalistic fashion, then it can no longer be individuated on the grounds of *positively* attributed characteristics.[1] Consequently, some other way of delimiting identity has to be found. Laclau and Mouffe locate this mechanism in the drawing of frontiers. It is through the consolidation or dissolution of political frontiers that discursive formations in general, and social and political identities more specifically, are constructed or fragmented.[2] Having briefly summarised the general conditions that may delimit an identity or discursive formation, it is now necessary to turn to the political articulation of these insights.

Discourse theory argues that political frontiers are inherent in the political as such: 'there is only politics where there are frontiers'.[3] Bennington gives a similar centrality to the relation between frontiers and politics, arguing that it is impossible to clarify the conceptual status of the frontier without working through its political status.[4] These intuitions are confirmed in the contributions to this volume. As many chapters show, the drawing of boundaries and the construction of frontiers are indeed central to the activities of politics, and they are central in a specific manner. At the outset, they are always symbolic in character.[5] The symbolic character of political frontiers, and of the identities that are fashioned through the drawing of political frontiers, is not of a secondary character. It is not a symbolism that overlays a natural, real identity. Rather, as recent developments in political theory have shown, especially those drawing on post-structuralist insights, it is constitutive.[6]

Moreover, political frontiers serve not only to individuate identity, but also to organise political space through the simultaneous operation of the logics of equivalence and difference.[7] The operation of these logics in the construction of political frontiers may be elucidated with reference to the Gramscian idea of transformism. According to Gramsci, transformism is a process that involves a gradual but continuous absorption and domestication of 'the active elements produced by allied groups – and even of those which came from antagonistic groups and seemed irreconcilably hostile'.[8] Expressed in terms of the operation of the logics of equivalence and difference, a transformist project consists of efforts to expand the systems of difference defining a dominant bloc. If such a project is successful, it will result in a lessening of the antagonistic potential of the remaining excluded elements and a broadening of the hegemonic bloc. A failure of transformism, on the other hand, may lead to the expansion of the logic of equivalence, the construction of clear-cut political frontiers and a proliferation and deepening, rather than a limitation, of antagonistic relations. Thus, these are two basic logics, standing in a relation of reciprocal delimitation to one another.

Moreover, depending on which of these are dominant, social space is divided in different ways.[9] Where the logic of equivalence predominates, social division tends towards a dichotomisation of political space, a paratactical division of the social into two opposing camps. Where the logic of difference is deployed as a dominant strategy, a more complex articulation of elements, militating against such dichotomisation, is facilitated. However, a set of questions with respect to these logics arises. For instance, does the predominance of one of these logics have further consequences for the types of politics prevalent in a particular society? Does the predominance of either logic lead to the construction of different types of political identity and relation amongst political groups? Is a politics of strong frontiers more likely to be found in authoritarian, non-liberal, rather than democratic societies? Does a successful hegemonic project depend upon the institution of strong, clear-cut frontiers?

As a first response, let us start with the first two questions concerning the relation between frontier construction and political subjectivity. In *Hegemony and Socialist Strategy*, Laclau and Mouffe argue that there is a coincidence between the presence of frontiers and the construction of 'an enemy'. In other words, where clear-cut relations of equivalence are prevalent, relations between competing groups tend to take a 'friend–enemy' form.[10] Following Carl Schmitt, Mouffe argues that political discourse 'attempts to create specific forms of unity among different interests by relating them to a common project and by establishing a frontier to define the forces to be opposed, the "enemy"'.[11] In contrast to this, where the logic of difference predominates, they hold that the multiplicity of articulations between subject positions makes it more difficult to construct such 'an enemy'. Two examples of popular struggles, that of British Chartism and the French Revolution, in which the logics of equivalence and difference function in two opposing ways, may serve to clarify this rather abstract argument.

As Gareth Stedman Jones's analysis of Chartist discourse shows, Chartist ideologues drew an equivalence among different elements of the nation or people against the monopolisers of political representation and power, so that there was a division between those who were represented and those who were not.[12] However, through gradual parliamentary reforms, representation was extended to ever wider sections of society. By the 1840s 'the nation' was broken up; there was no longer a 'nation' or 'people' unified against an enemy. Rather, the nation now was dissolved in a number of different subject positions. This dissolution of the chain of equivalences that constituted the people into different subject-positions served to stabilise the social formation, and prevented antagonistic relations from developing. The opposite situation is also possible. Instead of an expansion of the logic of difference, a dissolution of differences and a strengthening of frontiers can take place, as was the case during the French Revolution.

Following Furet, one can argue that the history of the Revolutionary period can be seen as the history of the unfolding of the logic of equivalence inherent in the idea of 'the people', created in opposition to the people's enemies.[13] The system of equivalences defining 'the people' was based on the Jacobinist logic that established equivalences between the values of liberty and equality, the nation that embodied those values, and the individuals that had to implement them. This chain of equivalences transformed isolated individuals into a collective entity, the people, making them the supreme source of legitimacy and the Revolution's sole agent. However, the idea of the people on its own could not produce revolutionary energy; an enemy was needed, and here the notion of an 'aristocratic plot' was introduced. The 'aristocratic plot' was expandable and included not only the aristocracy, but also Royal authority and the old society. Moreover, the introduction of an 'aristocratic *plot*' made it unnecessary to define the enemy, since it was a secret. In this way, an exclusionary logic could function that defined, on the one hand, the people, the general will as representing good and, on the other, the people's enemy, the aristocratic plot, as embodying evil. Thus, a political frontier was created, constructing the enemy as the negative reverse of 'the people'. By means of the expansion of the logic of equivalence and subversion of differential positions a political frontier was created that divided the political space into two antagonistic camps.

Generalising from these examples, it is clear that any society has to be able to forge an image of its unity in order to institute itself as a society.[14] This is precisely the role and function of political frontiers. Moreover, as we have seen, an important part of the formation of any identity is that it is opposed to something else, to 'an other'. Thus, frontier formation is a *sine qua non* of identity formation. This concludes our first response to the questions set out above: the logics of equivalence and that of difference, standing in a relation of tension to one another, are both necessary to the individuation of an identity. In some cases, paratactical frontier formations may predominate, while in others complexifying formations may dominate, and in each case different relations amongst political groups will be produced. However, it is crucial to bear in mind that even though one or the other logic may predominate, both are necessary for the formation of political identities. The example of the campaign against Manchester's second runway is a case in point. As Griggs and Howarth point out, while the groups leading the campaign forged a frontier against the proponents of the runway, differential identities continued to exist. Manchester Friends of the Earth, Earth First!, KAMJAG, MAJAG, and so forth, worked together, but they retained a degree of autonomy and distinctness. Neglecting either of these dimensions would impoverish political analysis and understanding.

Identities and subjectivity

If the argument presented above is correct, then the differential and equiv-alential dimensions of identity should carry equal weight. In other words, if any identity can be constituted only through a combination of differential and equivalential logics, neither one nor the other can be privileged theoret-ically. To return to Griggs and Howarth's example. The differences between Manchester Friends of the Earth, Earth First!, KAMJAG and MAJAG are as important *theoretically*[15] as the fact that these groups were articulated together into a chain of equivalence that placed them in opposition to those who were in favour of the construction of the second runway.

Nevertheless, things are not quite that straightforward. There is in dis-course theory a tendency to privilege the moment of negativity, of frontier construction and of the development of antagonisms. Nowhere is this clearer than in the fact that the 'friend/enemy' relation is treated as constitutive of politics as such. If indeed there are politics only where there are frontiers, and if frontiers consist in the construction of antagonistic 'friend/enemy' relations, then the moment of frontier formation is unequivocally privileged over the differential dimensions of identity. This privileging is not only pre-sent in the political arguments developed by Laclau and Mouffe, but also in the manner in which the intellectual resources upon which they draw in the course of the elaboration of their argument are developed.[16]

Is it possible that one may provide a non-essentialist account of identity formation that does not privilege the antagonistic over the differential dimension of identity?[17] Indeed, as I will argue, this reformulation is possi-ble from within the account of identity formation offered by Laclau and Mouffe in works after *Hegemony and Socialist Strategy*. Refining several of their arguments in later writings, they distinguish implicitly between the indi-viduation of identity and the construction of antagonistic relations.[18] How-ever, these suggestions are not explicitly developed in their work. In this regard, there are two refinements in particular that are crucial. First, in *New Reflections on the Revolution of Our Time*, Laclau distinguishes between antagonism and dislocation. Secondly, in her most recent writings, Mouffe suggests that a distinction needs to be made between 'enemies' and 'adver-saries'. With respect to the former, in *New Reflections on the Revolution of Our Time* the concept of dislocation[19] takes on the role of indicator of the 'limits of the social' reserved earlier for antagonism, with the consequence that antagonism no longer simply coincides with the moment of individua-tion of identity. Rather, it becomes one possible articulation amongst many. On this reading, the site of identity formation can be regarded as one of *inde-terminacy*. In other words, it is an open space for considering a variety of ways in which the relation between self and other may be conceived. *From this site, it becomes possible to think of social division in terms other than the 'friend/foe' relationship.*

Contemporary political theory is replete with historical cases that outline different ways of thinking and systematising different relations to 'the other'. Bauman's work on the figure of the stranger,[20] Dillon's work on that of the refugee,[21] Balibar's work on racism,[22] Tully's writing on intercultural relations and constitutional development[23] and Connolly's writings on relations of agonistic respect[24] all develop different modalities of relations between self and other. Moreover, Mouffe's most recent writings distinguish relations between enemies and adversaries, and also move in this direction. For Mouffe, as for Laclau, politics is essentially concerned with the formation of an 'us' as opposed to a 'them'. However, it is crucial that Mouffe now distinguishes the 'us/them' relation from that of the 'friend/enemy'. Even more importantly, this is done in the context of a discussion of democratic politics. This separation of relations opens up a whole terrain of investigation in which the *complexities of different modalities of subject formation* may be explored.[25]

Any exploration of these modalities and their conditions of existence, which aim to capture the complexity of processes of subject formation, should take place within the horizon of the deconstruction of binary relations. Derrida's work on binary hierarchies at the core of the metaphysics of presence – essence/accident, mind/body, speech/writing, and so forth – shows that the identity of each of the terms is essentially reliant on that of its other, and that the frontier separating the two is essentially impure. Derrida's argument about philosophical texts hold *mutatis mutandis* for identity in general, since the non-closure he describes is the non-closure of any discursive form. Thus deconstruction not only exposes the essential violence by which dualisms are established, it also brings into view – and this is the crucial insight offered by deconstructive analysis – the essential subversion of the 'separate identities' upon which dualistic thought relies. In this reading, it must be clear that the relation between 'the self' and 'the other' is infinitely more complex than any dichotomous distinction allows. As Derrida argues, the outside infects the inside, and *vice versa*, making any simplistic dualism and either/or thought suspect.[26] In Lacanian psychoanalytic discourse, a similar point is expressed by the term *extimité*, which problematises the opposition between inside and outside by showing, for instance, that although the Other is at the heart of me, it is also something strange to me.[27] Thus, both deconstruction and psychoanalysis offer detailed treatments of 'inside/outside' relations that may be deployed to come to a more adequate understanding of the complexities of relations between self and other. For instance, the logics of supplementarity, remark, and iterability[28] all provide different accounts of the 'inside/outside' relation which may throw light on the nature of relations between subjects, as well as the role of the other in the construction of the identity of the self.[29] Similarly, the psychoanalytic conceptions of introjection and projection offer mechanisms that may provide insights into self/other relations. Following from this, it is clear that an adequate account of political frontiers has to show the impurity of all forms of relational identity, while making visible the irreducible multiplicity of the site in which those violent dualisms are produced, as well as the complexity of the nature of self/other relations.

In sum, drawing upon the later writings of Laclau and Mouffe, the core of my argument so far has been that the *general logic of individuation can and ought to be distinguished from the formation of political frontiers, and the constitution of antagonistic forms of identity*. One of the consequences of this refocusing is that it becomes necessary to investigate the specificity of the political logic of frontiers, and the conditions under which different frontier formations are constituted. Several of the contributions to this volume address this question. It is to some of these contributions that I now turn.

The role of substantive research

I have already referred to a set of examples in contemporary political theory in which there are attempts to develop characterisations of different modalities of subjectivity. The chapters in this volume also contribute to this task. In what follows I will attempt to provide a provisional characterisation of the kind of typology of modalities of subject formation that stands in need of further research and development.

In their analysis of Argentinian politics from 1955 until 1973, Barros and Castagnola show how the ordering of political space instituted by Peronism forged a dichotomous division of society around the nodal point of 'social justice'. This sharp division not only shaped the nature of Peronism itself, but also delimited the field of political action for non-Peronists. Moreover, the fixity of identity that this division brought about, has had a lasting effect on Argentinian politics during the second half of the twentieth century. For instance, even after the 'Liberating Revolution' that brought Peron to a fall, political space remained divided between a Peronist and anti-Peronist pole. This condition of fixity also had further far-reaching consequences, the most important of which was the inability of political forces to effect a rearticulation of political frontiers that would, potentially, be able to subvert the dichotomous division of society into two opposing camps. As Barros and Castagnola point out, in this situation it was impossible to stabilise the political formation through the construction of a hegemonic project that cut across societal divisions, since that would only have been possible on condition that there was a presence of floating signifiers and a mobility of frontiers.[30] Both these conditions were absent, resulting in a social stalemate. A not dissimilar political stalemate has characterised the Northern Ireland situation over the past few decades. In the case of Provisionalism, political frontiers were articulated around an article of faith, namely, that justice and democracy could only be realised in a united state, and this divided the social into two opposing camps. Nevertheless, and in contrast to the Argentinian

case, the 'hardness' of their original position has been subverted by a continuous rearticulation of frontiers that, over time, increasingly put into question
the idea that justice could only be reached in a unitary state. However, as
Clohesy shows, despite this greater mobility of frontiers and the gradualist
expansion of the systems of difference that defined it, the discourse of Provisionalism has not succeeded in forging a fully-fledged political imaginary.
Instead, Provisionalism has remained a myth rather than becoming a structuring principle of society, unable to articulate its vision as the vision for society as a whole. In the case of Kemalism the opposite process has occurred. As
a result of agitation from different forces in Turkish society, Kemalism is losing its status as a fully-fledged political imaginary, and is under pressure from
competing myths. The clearcut frontiers of Kemalism, articulated around the
nodal points of republicanism, nationalism, populism, statism, secularism
and revolutionism which gave modern Turkey its identity as a secular, modern and Western nation-state, has become increasingly blurred during the
1990s. As Çelik argues, Islamist and Kurdish subjectivities, amongst others,
are contributing to the dissolution of the Kemalist frontiers, inaugurating a
political situation of 'indeterminacy' in which Kemalism is unable to mediate between competing sectors of society, thus facilitating the development
and entry of novel modalities of subjectivity on the political scene.

   It is worth reflecting further upon the logics at work in the first three cases
cited above. It is not by accident that all of them are concerned with the construction of *nationalist identities*. National identity is the form, *par excellence*, of identification that is characterised by the drawing of rigid, if
complex, boundaries to distinguish the collective self, and its the other.[31] As
Linda Colley argues, once confronted with an alien 'them', an otherwise
diverse community can become a reassuring 'us', as was the case with the
British after 1707 when they came to define themselves as a single people,
'not because of any political or cultural consensus at home, but rather in reaction to the Other beyond their shores'.[32] The political frontiers associated
with the construction of national identities tend, more often than not, to be
paratactical in nature, dividing 'us' from 'them', the 'self' from the 'other',
through the drawing of relatively clear-cut frontiers. These examples highlight the importance of frontiers for national identity formation. Far from
being given only through 'positive' characteristics, identities coagulate, or are
given their unity, in and through that which distinguishes them from others.

   However, the paratactic nature of these frontiers, and the force with
which they are usually asserted and maintained, should not be allowed to
mislead us into believing that they are immutable, unchangeable and simple.
The former misconception, namely that they are unalterable, is quickly dispelled by focusing on the reversible movement from myths to imaginaries.
Imaginaries that at one point appear to be deeply rooted may be challenged
and subverted with surprising ease at another. The subversion of the Marxist–Leninist conception of economic democracy by neoliberal discourse is a

case in point, as Adamson shows in his discussion of contemporary Romania. Equally, the idea that they are 'simple' is easily problematised. While paratactical frontiers may simplify political space by instituting clear-cut boundaries, this should not be assumed to be the result of simple, non-complex forms of identity constitution. For instance, the construction of a homogenous conception of the nation under Kemalism entailed a set of extremely complex discursive manoeuvres, including an articulation of the relation between Turkishness and Islam, which in turn began to break down in the 1980s. Similarly, the forging of Provisionalist unity was a complex matter, evidenced in the need to renegotiate continuously that unity in the face of forces, which threatened to lead to the dissolution of its appeal.

However, the complexities involved in the forging of identities are illustrated much more clearly in the set of examples dealing with *extra-institutional political and social movements*. The proliferation of gay forms of identification in Hong Kong during the 1980s and 1990s is a case in point. In contrast to the common perception that such identities are constituted primarily by reference to a heterosexual/ homosexual axis, Ho's and Tsang's analysis demonstrates the inability of such binary divisions to capture the intricate and multiple sites of identification and contestation within the gay communities of Hong Kong. Far from singular divisions, lesbigay individuals and organisations are constituted through complex articulations of overlapping subject positions, some of which stand in a relation of tension to one another. Similarly, Harvey's and Halverson's discussion of women's struggles in Chiapas contests forms of analysis that deploy binary oppositions – ranging from the dichotomy between experience and epistemology to that between universalism and particularism – to make sense of political struggles. They draw out the deconstructive subversion of these binaries through an account that focuses on a radical conception of difference, and conclude that the significance of Zapatista discourse at the local level is precisely its shunning of an exclusive anti-government rhetoric in favour of an emphasis on a variety of struggles contesting exclusionary practices, both within the movement and in the wider society. It is noteworthy that in both the cases of gay struggles in Hong Kong and of women in the Chiapas much of what has been achieved has been gained by engaging in contestation outside the traditional, formal political arena. Further research into the formalisation of the relation between the division of political space and the presence or absence of specific modalities of subject formation is needed. Such systematisation is not unrelated to the question of the relation between, and the delineation of, myths and imaginaries.

Myths and imaginaries

The distinction between myth and imaginary is a productive one, allowing one to understand and analyse hegemony construction as a *process*. Rather than being bound to a static analysis, involving what may amount to simplistic judgements as to whether or not a specific discourse is hegemonic at a given point in time, the introduction of these concepts shifts the analytical focus to the *movement* from myth to imaginary and *vice versa*.[33] However, this distinction stands in need of further refinement. In particular, further theoretical clarification is needed in the identification and delineation of collective social imaginaries. While a particular social order may be characterised by the presence of many competing myths, it is less clear whether the same may be true of imaginaries. For instance, in thinking of post-war Britain, it is clear that welfarism acted as an imaginary horizon through which most societal demands could be articulated. What however is the status of the Thatcherite project, or of the discourse of New Labour in relation to this imaginary? Could it be argued that Thatcherism succeeded in becoming a collective imaginary on a par with that of welfarism? If so, did this entail the displacement of the welfarist imaginary?

While there is an empirical dimension to these questions, they cannot be settled solely by substantive investigation. What is needed is further conceptual clarification. Attempting to solve this problem by reference to 'society' will not do, since discourse theory explicitly problematises 'society' as a referent. However, there is no problem with an analysis based upon a discursive formation identified in and through its political frontiers. Given this, one may argue that the identification of a particular imaginary depends upon the *actual formation* identified. This would make it possible to argue for the existence of more than one collective social imaginary at any specific point in time. To return to the example above. An analysis of Thatcherism as a social imaginary will not preclude analysing welfarism as an imaginary. This approach to the identification of social imaginaries would remove the problem of the apparent contradiction in specifying that there may be more than one political imaginary structuring social relations in a particular society. This is so for two reasons. On the one hand, since 'society' is not a valid object of analysis, reference to a particular society only creates an artificial objection. On the other, just as there may be more than one hegemonic nodal point structuring any particular discursive formation, there may be more than one operative imaginary. As Laclau and Mouffe argue, 'insofar as the social is an infinitude not reducible to any underlying unitary principle, the mere idea of a centre of the social has no meaning at all'.[34] This is not to deny that just as some nodal points may be more highly overdetermined than others, one imaginary may play a more politically significant role than another at any given point in time. These are matters for empirical determination. However, it does direct research away from the misleading assumption that any given 'society' may have one and only one imaginary horizon structuring social and political demands. Nevertheless, there is a further conceptual issue that needs to be addressed. It concerns the fleshing-out of the categories of myth and imaginary in terms of types of hegemonic relations.

Types of hegemony

How do the categories of myth and imaginary map on to the more traditional forms of hegemony discussed by Gramsci? Before addressing this question, it is necessary to distinguish the way the term 'hegemony' is being used here. In Gramsci, hegemony denotes both a type of political relation, and a substantive achievement. In the former case, one is concerned with a *type of articulatory relation* where persuasion predominates over the use of force, while in the latter, one is concerned with whether or not a particular force has managed to achieve supremacy by imposing its will on to the rest of society through the creation of consent and the incorporation of interests of rival forces.[35] In talking about myth and imaginary and their relation to hegemony I am concerned with the latter, that is, with the types of *substantive* hegemony that may be achieved in any given social order. In this respect, it is useful to recall Gramsci's important distinction between economic–corporate and national–popular struggles.

In his early works, Gramsci argues that the working class can only become hegemonic if it takes into account the interests of other social classes and finds ways of combining them with its own interests. It therefore has to go beyond economic–corporate struggles in order to become a national force.[36] Breaking with the last redoubt of class determinism in Gramsci, Laclau reformulates Gramsci's distinction between economic–corporate and hegemonic forms of organisation into that between myths and imaginaries.[37] Just as in the case of economic–corporate consciousness, myths operate at the level of the interests of a particular group. And, like the Gramscian use of hegemony, the term 'imaginary' is reserved for those cases where a particular group succeeds in moving beyond its particular interests onto a universal terrain.[38] Hegemony here consists of a universalisation of particularistic demands, a process that can never be fully achieved.

Even with these clarifications there remain further questions to be addressed. Most pressing is that of the relation between the logic of hegemonic practice and particular forms of political regime. For instance, in what ways do democratic and authoritarian forms of hegemony differ? In *Hegemony and Socialist Strategy* Laclau and Mouffe discuss the distinction between democratic and authoritarian hegemonic practice with respect to Lenin's legacy.[39] The roots of authoritarian practice, they argue, are to be found in the interweaving of science and politics, and the consequent epistemological privileging of a vanguard party. By contrast, the democratic practice of hegemony calls into question the transparency of relations of representation and recognises that the identity and interests of social agents are the result of contingent articulatory practices. The logic of this discussion is further elaborated upon in their conception of 'radical democracy'.[40] Insofar as the identity and interests of social agents cannot be led back to a positive and founding unitary principle, a radical pluralism can emerge, and

this pluralism is to be considered democratic insofar as 'the autoconstitutiv-
ity of each one of its terms is the result of displacements of the egalitarian
imaginary'.[41]

The question remains whether these preconditions are sufficient to
account for the practice of *democratic* hegemony? To put it differently, what
is the *differentia specifica* of a democratic hegemony? In answer to this question, Mouffe argues that modern democracy's specificity lies in the recognition and legitimation of conflict, and in the refusal to suppress it by imposing
an authoritarian order. Here it is necessary to quote her at length, for she
clearly articulates how democracy is to be understood in relation to our earlier discussion of the friend/enemy distinction:

> Breaking with the symbolic representation of society as an organic body … a
> democratic society makes room for the 'adversary', i.e. the opponent who is no
> longer considered an enemy to be destroyed but somebody whose existence is
> legitimate and whose rights will not be put into question. The category of the
> 'adversary' serves here to designate the status of those who disagree concern-
> ing the ranking and interpretation of the values. Adversaries will fight about the
> interpretation and the ranking of values, but their common allegiance to the
> values which constitute the liberal democratic form of life creates a bond of sol-
> idarity which expresses their belonging to a common 'we'. It must be stressed,
> however, that the category of the enemy does not disappear; it now refers to
> those who do not accept the set of values constitutive of the democratic forms
> of life. … There is no way for their demands to be considered legitimate within
> the 'we' of democratic citizens, since their disagreement is not merely about
> ranking but of a much more fundamental type.[42]

Thus, Mouffe holds that democratic politics is not concerned with overcom-
ing the 'us/them' distinction. It is concerned, however, with a different way
of establishing that distinction. A pluralist democratic order, she argues, 'sup-
poses that the opponent is not considered as an enemy to be destroyed but
as an adversary whose existence is legitimate and must be tolerated'.[43] The
'adversary' is thus a category, or an articulation, to be more precise, that is
particularly appropriate to democratic politics.

This account of democracy is developed against the intellectual tradition
that attempts to provide a rationalistic justification of democracy. Rather
than such a justification, a defence of democracy, she argues, requires the
construction of democratic life forms and practices. Were we to reduce politics to a realm inhabited by rational individuals, the antagonistic dimension
would be erased, and the possibility of apprehending what constitutes the
specificity of a pluralist democratic answer to the political problem – that is,
the legitimation of conflict and the creation of institutions whose aim is to
transform antagonism into agonism' – would be foreclosed.[44]

Having said this, what is needed here is a further theorisation of the
movement from enemy to adversary, of the *transformation* of antagonism
into agonism, and of the *different logics* pertaining to each. If deliberative

models of democracy, in the positing of an ideal situation, eliminate the very place of the enemy, a conception of democracy which starts from the political logic of the 'friend/enemy' distinction, needs to provide an account for the transformation of the enemy into an adversary, and of the specificity of the logic of the adversary in a democratic context.[45] While discourse theory provides us with a sophisticated conceptualisation of the decision inaugurating politics, further reflection is needed on the bridging of the gap between the moment of hegemonic institution *tout court,* and the institution of a particular regime, such as a democracy. There are two aspects of this problem that need further conceptual clarification. They concern, first, the relation between the undecidability of the structure and the moment of hegemony which attempts to institute a 'decision' in one direction or another[46] and, second, that of the conception of political subjectivity entailed by the first.

These two aspects are intimately related. It is clear that the conceptualisation of hegemony offered here – as a practice of an imposition of a decision on an undecidable terrain – is neutral with respect to the *type* of hegemony instituted. However, Derrida's account of undecidability displays no such neutrality. On the contrary, it entails a specific conception of the relation between self and other, namely, an *ethical* relation in which there is an openness of the self to the other.[47] This ethical dimension is absent from the treatment of hegemony as a type of political relation. Thus, there is clearly a tension here which needs to be resolved. One way in which this may be done is to reintroduce the Gramscian discussion of hegemony as a practice of ethico-political leadership and with it the normative aspect of the concept.[48] While retaining the important distinction between the conception of hegemony as a political practice of articulation and the construction of a specific type of hegemony, it becomes possible to think of the *differencia specifica* of the democratic practice of hegemony. This would be found in the constitution of a very specific relation between self and other as part and parcel of the very institution of a democratic order. From here it is possible to re-emphasise the importance of the Gramscian emphasis on consent, and to look towards certain trends in contemporary political theory that aim to reconstruct accounts of the normative dimensions of politics without falling back onto a sterile foundationalism.

A multitude of exciting new avenues of research thus awaits further exploration. In summary, these include a systematic exploration of different modalities of political subjectivity; the conditions under which they are likely to appear, and their relation to specific kinds of frontier formation; the movement from myth to imaginary and *vice versa,* and its relation to hegemony; the different dimensions of hegemony, with specific emphasis on the need to flesh out its ethical implications; and, finally, the need to bring all of these insights to bear on developments in contemporary political theory.

With its sophisticated theoretical grounding and breadth of intellectual resources, discourse theory is eminently situated to take on these challenges, as this book has begun to demonstrate.

Notes

I would like to thank David Howarth and Yannis Stavrakakis for their constructive comments on earlier drafts of this chapter.

1 Laclau and Mouffe argue in *Hegemony and Socialist Strategy*, and Laclau in *New Reflections on the Revolution of Our Time*, that to affirm the essence of something consists in affirming its *positive* identity. See E. Laclau and C. Mouffe, *Hegemony and Socialist Strategy: Towards a Radical Democratic Politics* (London, Verso, 1985); and E. Laclau, *New Reflections on the Revolution of Our Time* (London, Verso, 1990), p. 187.

2 Laclau, *New Reflections on the Revolution of Our Time*, p. 160.

3 *Ibid.*

4 G. Bennington, *Legislations. The Politics of Deconstruction* (London, Verso, 1994), p. 262.

5 Every social community produced and reproduced by the construction of frontiers is imaginary. The distinction between real and imaginary communities is therefore a fallacious one. See E. Balibar, 'The nation form: history and ideology', in E. Balibar and I. Wallerstein, *Race, Nation, Class. Ambiguous Identities* (London, Verso, 1991), p. 93.

6 The perceived naturalness of political identities is not primary, but is secondary, a result of the sedimentation of these constitutive symbolic processes. However, it is not enough to emphasise the symbolic character of political and social identities. Such an emphasis all too often leads to a simplistic assertion of the constructed nature of all identity, as if, once it has been asserted, one could move on and start the real political analysis which, more often than not, proceeds in a perfectly empiricist fashion by simpl treating what is the result of political intervention as given. That is to say, mere acknowledgement of the symbolic character of political processes is clearly not sufficient to overcome the empiricist naturalism that blights much political analysis. Moreover, such superficial acknowledgement often also leads to an extreme form of voluntarism: if political identities are 'constructed', they must be infinitely malleable, and we must be able to pick and choose amongst a range of available identities.

7 Elsewhere I have discussed the manner in which the account offered by Laclau and Mouffe of the operation of political logics coincides with the First/Third-World distinction. See Aletta J. Norval, 'Frontiers in question', *Acta Philosophica*, 2 (1997), 51–76.

8 A. Gramsci, *Selections from the Prison Notebooks* (London, Lawrence & Wishart, 1980), pp. 58–9. It should be noted that for Gramsci, transformism is one of two methods by which a class may be come hegemonic. Given that the consent upon which it is built is passive in nature, transformism is a 'bastard' form of hegemony which should be contrasted with expansive hegemony. The latter consists in the creation of an active and direct consensus, giving rise to a genuine national popular will. See C. Mouffe, 'Hegemony and ideology in

Gramsci', in C. Mouffe (ed.), *Gramsci and Marxist Theory* (London, Routledge & Kegan Paul, 1979), pp. 182–3.

9 Consequently, neither the conditions of total equivalence, nor that of total difference, ever fully obtain. Following Derrida, I would add that they are always found in *hierarchical* combination, where one takes precedence over another in the ordering of political space. On this reading, the moment of frontiers would not be privileged a priori. Rather, which dimension takes precedence would depend entirely on the political context under discussion.

10 Žižek points out in this regard that Laclau and Mouffe must be understood as anti-Schmittian Schmittians, for they acknowledge the fundamental status of antagonism, yet, instead of fetishising it in a 'heroic warfare conflict', they inscribe it into the symbolic as the political logic of the struggle for hegemony. S. Žižek, *The Ticklish Subject. The Absent Centre of Political Ontology* (London, Verso, 1999), p. 172.

11 C. Mouffe, *The Return of the Political* (London, Verso, 1993), p. 50. See also C. Mouffe (ed.), *The Challenge of Carl Schmitt* (London, Verso, 1999).

12 For this discussion I draw on G. Stedman Jones, *The Language of Class* (Cambridge, Cambridge University Press, 1983).

13 F. Furet, *Interpreting the French Revolution* (Cambridge, Cambridge University Press, 1981).

14 C. Lefort, *The Political Forms of Modern Society* (Cambridge, Polity, 1986), p. 191.

15 This is not to say that *politically* these two dimensions are always of equal importance.

16 Take, for instance, their use of Saussure in the theorisation of relations of equivalence and difference. Laclau and Mouffe transposes Saussure's account of syntagmatic and paradigmatic relations to the political terrain, arguing that identity is constituted, and socio-political space ordered through the operation of both systems of difference (syntagmatic relations) and systems of equivalence (paradigmatic relations). It is important to note, however, that unlike in their political application, the linguistic argument on the relation between paradigms and syntagms at no point privileges the moment of the paradigmatic over the syntagmatic. In fact, it could be argued that for Saussure the syntagmatic is privileged over the paradigmatic since he states that, from the point of view of the organisation of language, syntagmatic solidarities are the most striking. F. de Saussure, *Course in General Linguistics* (Bungay, Suffolk, Fontana/Collins, 1974), pp. 123–4, p. 127.

17 I will not discuss the detail of this argument here. Suffice it to say that it is possible from a Wittgensteinian perspective.

18 Elsewhere I have developed this distinction from a Wittgenstinian perspective. See Norval, 'Frontiers in question'.

19 Laclau, *New Reflections on the Revolution of Our Time*, pp. 39–41.

20 Z. Bauman, 'The making and unmaking of strangers', in P. Werbner and T. Modood (eds), *Debating Cultural Hybridity* (London, Zed Press, 1997).

21 M. Dillon, 'The sovereign and the stranger', in J. Edkins, N. Persram and V. Pin-Fat (eds), *Sovereignty and Subjectivity*, Critical Perspectives on World Politics (Boulder, Lynne Rienner, 1999), pp. 117–40.

22 Nevertheless, as is clear from the work of, for example, Balibar, it may be

possible to map something of the complexity of models of racism, and the forms of exclusion which it fosters and sustains: the distinctions between auto-referential (those in which the bearers of prejudice, exercising physical or symbolic violence, designate themselves as representatives of a superior race) and hetero-referential racism (in which it is, by contrast, the victims of racism who are assigned to an inferior or evil race); between a racism of extermination/ elimination (an 'exclusive' racism; for example, Nazism) and racism of oppression or exploitation ('inclusive' racism; for example, colonial racisms) all give one important insights into the manner in which contemporary exclusions may function. What is particularly striking in Balibar's work is his sensitivity to the fact that these categorisations are not ideally pure structures, but they identify historical trajectories which disallows talk of a single invariant racism, or a single form of exclusion. Indeed, what is crucial in his analysis is the emphasis on the intermixing and *impurity* of these forms of categorisation in our contemporary world. E. Balibar, 'Racism and nationalism', in Balibar and Wallerstein, *Race, Nation, Class*, pp. 38–9.

23 J. Tully, *Strange Multiplicity. Constitutionalism in an Age of Diversity* (Cambridge, Cambridge University Press, 1995).

24 W. E. Connolly, *Identity\Difference* (Ithaca, Cornell University Press, 1991); and W. E. Connolly, *The Ethos of Pluralization*, Borderlines, vol. 1 (Minneapolis, University of Minnesota Press, 1995).

25 For a discussion of some of the concrete modalities this may take see, for instance, C. Mouffe, 'For a politics of nomadic identity', in G. Robertson, M. Mash, L. Tickner, J. Bird, B. Curtis and T. Putnam, *Traveller's Tales. Narratives of Home and Displacement* (London, Routledge, 1994), pp. 105–13; A. J. Norval, 'Hybridization: the im/purity of the political', in J. Edkins *et al.* (eds), *Sovereignty and Subjectivity*, pp. 99–114; A. J. Norval, 'Rethinking ethnicity: identification, hybridity and democracy', in P. Yeros (ed.), *Ethnicity and Nationalism in Africa: Constructivist Reflections and Contemporary Politics* (London, Macmillan, 1999).

26 This does not, however, mean that identity is so open that it becomes contradictory to speak of identity at all. Quite the contrary. For Derrida the theme of identity and therefore of stability is always crucial to the treatment of identity, that is, if one understands by that stability not something in the order of absolute solidity, but rather as standing in the order of historicity, a stability which can always once again be destabilised. However, the question remains as to how identity can be characterised as stable, such that it remains recognisable as the same across many different occurrences. Here the crucial notion of *iterability*, which designates both repetition and alteration, provides a tool with which to account for identity without assuming an eternal essence to be grounding such identity. For Derrida, iterability presumes a minimal remainder that is not reducible to a singular essence, is repeatable in principle and allows for such stabilisation to occur. Yet, this element is always impure, its meaning never quite sutured, allowing for it to be altered when grafted on to new contexts. This allows a further deepening of our understanding of the essentially contextual dimension of the formation of identity that, nevertheless, always involves an element of decontextualisation. Moreover, it facilitates an understanding of the interplay of both continuities and discontinuities in historical articulation of

identity. For a discussion of iterability, see J. Derrida, 'Limited Inc.', *Glyph* 2, (1977), 192–254.

27 D. Evans, *An Introductory Dictionary of Lacanian Psychoanalysis* (London, Routledge, 1996), pp. 58–9.

28 For a discussion of these infrastructures as they are analysed in Derrida's writings, see R. Gasché, *The Tain of the Mirror. Derrida and the Philosophy of Reflection* (Cambridge, Mass., Harvard University Press, 1986), esp. chs 8 and 9.

29 See, for instance, Howarth's deployment of 'iterability' in his account of the constitution of 'blackness' in Black Consciousness discourse in South Africa. D. Howarth, 'Complexities of identity/difference', *Journal of Political Ideologies*, 2:1 (1996), 51–78.

30 Laclau and Mouffe, *Hegemony and Socialist Strategy*, pp. 135–6.

31 I have explored this logic of nation-building in some depth in Aletta J. Norval, *Deconstructing Apartheid Discourse* (London, Verso, 1996).

32 L. Colley, *The Britons. Forging the Nation 1707–1837* (London, Vintage, 1996), p. 6.

33 For a further discussion of the movement from myth to imaginary, see, D. Howarth, 'Reflections on Ernesto Laclau's *New Reflections on the Revolution of Our Time*', *Politikon: South African Journal of Political Studies*, 19:1 (1991), 120–34. For an analysis of this movement in apartheid discourse, see Norval, *Deconstructing Apartheid Discourse*, pp. 101–73.

34 Laclau and Mouffe, *Hegemony and Socialist Strategy*, p. 139.

35 For an in-depth discussion of the concept of hegemony in Laclau and Mouffe's work, see D. Howarth, 'Ideology, hegemony and political subjectivity', in I. Hampsher-Monk and J. Stanyer (eds), *Contemporary Political Studies 1996*, vol. 2, pp. 944–56.

36 Mouffe, 'Hegemony and ideology in Gramsci', p. 180.

37 This distinction is first introduced in *New Reflections on the Revolution of Our Time*. See, Laclau, *New Reflections on the Revolution of Our Time*, pp. 60–8.

38 In Laclau's most recent work there is an extended discussion of the relation between the universal and the particular. See, especially, E. Laclau, *Emancipation(s)* (London, Verso, 1996), Ch. 2.

39 Laclau and Mouffe, *Hegemony and Socialist Strategy*, pp. 55–8.

40 The main arguments for radical democracy are developed in Laclau and Mouffe, *Hegemony and Socialist Strategy*, Ch. 4; and in Mouffe, *The Return of the Political*.

41 Laclau and Mouffe, *Hegemony and Socialist Strategy*, p. 167

42 C. Mouffe, 'Politics, democratic action, and solidarity', *Inquiry*, 38:1–2 (1995), 107.

43 C. Mouffe, 'The radical centre. A politics without adversary', *Soundings*, 9 (1998), 16.

44 Mouffe, 'Politics, democratic action, and solidarity', p. 108.

45 I first developed this argument in A. J. Norval, 'Aporetic logics and democratic politics', Conference on 'Politics, Friendship and Democracy to Come', Institute of Contemporary Art, London, 29–30 November 1997, mimeo.

46 See E. Laclau, 'Deconstruction, pragmatism, hegemony', in C. Mouffe (ed.), *Deconstruction and Pragmatism* (London, Verso, 1996), pp. 47–67.

47   See Norval, 'Aporetic logics and democratic politics'; Howarth, 'Ideology, hegemony', p. 951.
48   Howarth, 'Ideology, hegemony', p. 954.

Index

Please note that references to footnotes contain an 'n' following the page number.

Breinigsville, PA USA
10 June 2010

239540BV00002B/10/P